AF361309

# CONVERSION AND CATASTROPHE IN GERMAN-JEWISH ÉMIGRÉ AUTOBIOGRAPHY

*Conversion and Catastrophe in German-Jewish Émigré Autobiography* is a collective biography of four German-Jewish converts to Christianity, recounting their spiritual and confessional journeys against the backdrop of the Holocaust and its aftermath. Focusing on personal testimonies that fuse historical trauma and spiritual illumination into one narrative, the book explores how Jewish emigrants interpreted their experiences of persecution and displacement through the hermeneutics of Christian conversion. It draws on autobiographies, novels, religious writings, and newspaper articles as well as unpublished archival materials such as diaries, lecture notes, and private correspondence.

The book explores how chosen genres of writing both enabled and hindered self-understanding. It also assesses whether the literary paradigm of Christian conversion, highlighting an individual's separation from a past sinful self, is suitable for expressing a collective catastrophe. Applying psychoanalysis, disability studies, and autobiographical theory to the life writing of converted Jews, the book offers new avenues for conceptualizing the Jewishness of historical subjects who disavowed their ties to Judaism.

(German and European Studies)

ABRAHAM RUBIN is an assistant professor in the Department of Religious Studies at the University of Dayton.

# GERMAN AND EUROPEAN STUDIES

General Editor: James Retallack

# Conversion and Catastrophe in German-Jewish Émigré Autobiography

ABRAHAM RUBIN

UNIVERSITY OF TORONTO PRESS
Toronto Buffalo London

PUBLISHED IN ASSOCIATION WITH THE
UNITED STATES HOLOCAUST MEMORIAL MUSEUM

© University of Toronto Press 2025
Toronto Buffalo London
utorontopress.com
Printed in the USA

ISBN 978-1-4875-5734-8 (cloth)     ISBN 978-1-4875-5736-2 (EPUB)
ISBN 978-1-4875-6109-3 (paper)     ISBN 978-1-4875-5735-5 (PDF)

German and European Studies

Publication cataloguing information is available from Library and Archives Canada.

Cover design: Val Cooke
Cover image: Karl Jakob Hirsch, *Die Vertreibung*. W3.25b. Etching. 24.8 x 19.7 cm. 1915.
Karl Jakob Hirsch Collection, Ludwig-Maximilians-Universität München.

Published in association with the United States Holocaust Memorial Museum.

The United States Holocaust Memorial Museum's Jack, Joseph, and Morton Mandel
Center's mission is to ensure the long-term growth and vitality of Holocaust Studies. To do
that, it is essential to provide opportunities for new generations of scholars. The vitality and
the integrity of Holocaust Studies requires openness, independence, and free inquiry so that
new ideas are generated and tested through peer review and public debate. The opinions
of scholars expressed before, during the course of, or after their activities with the Mandel
Center do not represent and are not endorsed by the Museum or its Mandel Center.

The German and European Studies series is funded by the DAAD with funds from the
German Federal Foreign Office.

We wish to acknowledge the land on which the University of Toronto Press
operates. This land is the traditional territory of the Wendat, the Anishnaabeg, the
Haudenosaunee, the Métis, and the Mississaugas of the Credit First Nation.

University of Toronto Press acknowledges the financial support of the Government of
Canada, the Canada Council for the Arts, and the Ontario Arts Council, an agency of
the Government of Ontario, for its publishing activities.

*Anyone who changes his religion remains somehow tainted, and it seems impossible to cleanse him. This suggests that people value constancy above all else, not least because, divided into factions as they are, they must forever be concerned with the security and permanence of their group. Neither feelings nor convictions are the issue here. We must endure where fate, rather than choice, has placed us. To remain loyal to a nation, a city, a prince, a friend, a woman, and to focus everything on that relationship, to work and sacrifice and suffer for it – that is valued. Disloyalty, on the other hand, remains odious, and fickleness is ridiculed.*

*This is a harsh, very serious view of the matter; but we can look at it from another perspective which permits a more kindly and lenient view. Certain character traits we by no means approve of, certain moral blemishes in others we find especially titillating. If we may be allowed an analogy, we would say that it is the same as with venison roast which the gourmet much prefers slightly gamy. We find a divorced woman or a renegade especially fascinating. Persons who otherwise would perhaps seem merely interesting and charming suddenly appear wondrous.*

– Johann Wolfgang von Goethe,
"Winckelmann and His Age" (1805)[1]

# Contents

# Illustrations

# Acknowledgments

I wrote the bulk of this book at the Martin Buber Society of Fellows in the Hebrew University of Jerusalem. The Buber Society provided the financial support and intellectual freedom that made this study possible. I wish to thank my colleagues, as well as the institute's directors Yigal Bronner and Raz Chen-Morris, for the four wonderful years I spent at the Buber Society. My friends Alena Witzlack-Makarevich, Ruth Wenske Stern, Oz Aloni, Dennis Halft, Dan Baras, Beatrice Baragli, and Mirjam Lücking patiently endured numerous conversations about this book and enriched my work with their generous insights. Naomi Seidman read through the manuscript and offered invaluable suggestions over a series of dinners and walks we shared in Rechavia in the summer of 2022.

I spent the fall semester of 2021 working on the manuscript as a visiting researcher at the Forschungskolleg Humanwissenschaften in Bad Homburg. I am grateful to Christian Wiese for inviting me to the FKH and for his unflagging support of my academic career since my time as a doctoral student. I also wish to thank the Johanna Quandt Young Academy and its managing director, Katharina Welling, for funding and coordinating my stay. During my time in Bad Homburg, I enjoyed the company and conversation of Andrea Gremels, Frederike Felcht, Patrick Koch, Till van Rahden, Will Levine, Nika Siegel, and the institute's director, Matthias Lutz Bachman. I put the final touches to the manuscript at the University of Hamburg as a Senior Research Fellow at the Maimonides Centre for Advanced Studies in the summer of 2023. In Hamburg, I benefited from a lively intellectual community that included Doerte Bischoff, Rachel and Chip Manekin, Jim Diamond, Alan Mittleman, Isaac Slater, Sarah Wobick-Segev, Ze'ev Strauss, and again, Patrick Koch. I wish to thank the centre's director, Giuseppe Veltri, and staff for their *Gastfreundlichkeit*. I had the pleasure of working on the proofs for this book during the summer of 2024 as a guest of the Buber-Rosenzweig-Institute at Goethe University Frankfurt through the generous support of a DAAD Research Fellowship.

At Duquesne University, I am grateful to Daniel Burston, the foremost scholar of the life and thought of Karl Stern, for sharing his expertise with me. Jeffrey McCurry, Director of the Simon Silverman Phenomenology Center, and Duquesne's university archivist, Thomas E. White, were gracious hosts during my brief work visit to the Karl Stern Collection. Irene Friedl, Sven Kuttner, and Bernd Schledermann at the Abteilung Altes Buch of the Ludwig-Maximilians-Universitätsbibliothek in Munich helped me navigate the Karl Jakob Hirsch Nachlaß. Many thanks to the Georgetown University Special Collections and to John Zarrillo for making the Heinrich Kronstein Collection available to me. Silke Schaeper at the Maimonides Centre and Chris Tangeman at the University of Dayton Libraries helped track down some of the more obscure bibliographic sources found in this study. I am grateful to Michael Simonson and Elena Butuzova at the Leo Baeck Institute and Ruby Landau-Pincus at the YIVO Institute for Jewish Research for helping me access the CJH collections from afar. I also wish to thank the librarians at the National Library of Israel, the Deutsches Exilarchiv 1933–1945 in Frankfurt am Main, the Exilbibliothek at the University of Hamburg, and the Universitätsarchiv Frankfurt am Main for their assistance.

My sister Michal Rubin read through various iterations of the manuscript and assisted in the research and editing of this book. I owe a debt of gratitude to Koby Oppenheim, friend, mentor, and intellectual sparring partner, for reading and discussing my scholarly work with me since graduate school. Paul Morrow, Joseph Flipper, Nick Rademacher, Vivian Liska, Cedric Cohen-Skalli, Arie Dubnov, Shira Merom, John Brenkman, Gilad Shenhav, Iris Idelsohn-Shein, Elliot Ratzman, Idit Alphandary, and Ayala Levin read and commented on parts of this manuscript at different stages of its evolution. I am grateful to Elisa Carandina at INALCO, Maurice Ebileeni at the University of Haifa, Galia Benziman at the Hebrew University of Jerusalem, and Yaakov Mascetti at Bar-Ilan University for inviting me to present my work on this project at their institutions. I wish to thank my colleagues in the Religious Studies Department at the University of Dayton for the Midwestern and Marianist welcome I received upon joining the faculty in the fall of 2022. I could not have wished for a more hospitable and supportive academic environment.

I am grateful to my editor at the University of Toronto Press, Stephen Shapiro, for his initial interest in this project and for patiently guiding it through the review and publication process. The feedback I received from Stephen and the manuscript's three anonymous reviewers helped refine the form and argument of the book. I had the good fortune of working with Janice Evans, managing editor at UTP, and Matthew Kudelka, the manuscript's meticulous copyeditor, during the book's production stages. At the Mandel Center for Advanced Holocaust Studies, I wish to thank Laura Foster for her support of this project and Steven Feldman for his editorial assistance with the copyedited version of the manuscript.

My parents Shimshon and Lisa Rubin, my models for *ahavat torah veda'at*, have been a constant source of support and guidance. I was regenerated by Shabbats with Sara, Yehuda, Naomi, Shuey, and Sparkle Halper. Yonah, Anabella, Sol, and Sofia Rubin were a reminder that there is a world beyond academia. This book is dedicated to my wife Estelle Madeleine Vard for her love, kindness, and patience. I could not have written this book without her presence in my life.

This book was published with the support of the United States Holocaust Memorial Museum, the Leo Baeck Institute of New York, the University of Dayton Research Council, and the Martin Buber Society of Fellows.

# CONVERSION AND CATASTROPHE IN GERMAN-JEWISH ÉMIGRÉ AUTOBIOGRAPHY

# Conversion and the Problem of Persuasion

When the celebrated Swiss actor Ernst Ginsberg (1904–1964) sat down to write his memoirs, he wrestled with the question of what place to assign his conversion to Catholicism. Raised in an assimilated Jewish home in bourgeois west Berlin, Ginsberg enjoyed a thriving stage career in Munich, Hamburg, and Darmstadt until 1933, when he was forced to flee Germany. Ginsberg ended up in Zurich, where he revived his theatrical career. Recapping thirty years at the Zürcher Schauspielhaus, Ginsberg took pride in a slew of key roles, including Tartuffe, Hamlet, and Mephisto, that cemented his reputation on the Swiss stage. A deeply religious man, Ginsberg attributed much of his success to his devout faith and considered his conversion to be one of the defining moments of his life. Yet after discussing the matter with friends, he chose to omit the story of his 1935 conversion to Catholicism from his memoirs.

The editor of the posthumously published memoir, Elisabeth Brock-Sulzer, speculates that Ginsberg felt it did not fit in with the work's theatrical themes and personal anecdotes. Brock-Sulzer overlooks another reason for Ginsberg's omission: the problematic timing of his conversion, in that he was a Jew fleeing Nazi persecution in the mid-1930s. Conversion to Christianity during the Nazi period was and remains a controversial topic among Jews that commonly invokes accusations of betrayal and disloyalty. Fortunately for the reader, Brock-Sulzer defied Ginsberg's explicit wishes and included an extended excerpt from the purged chapter in her introduction. The apologetic tenor of Ginsberg's account suggests that his hesitations about sharing the story of his turn to Catholicism were rooted in a deep discomfort concerning the motivation and timing of his decision.

Ginsberg writes that since 1930, he and his wife had wanted to convert, situating his desire to embark on this new religious path well before the Nazi takeover. He goes on to explain that

> what held us back from the decisive step was the fact that we did not want to appear to the Jews, who were undoubtedly facing a difficult time of trial, *as deserters from the Jewish fate*. But when it became clear that the persecutions were not at all directed against religion, but against descent, these inhibitions disappeared, especially since it became obvious that National Socialism also considered believing Christians, who were serious about their faith, as enemies that were to be exterminated.[1]

Ginsberg's apologia captures the fraught nature of his conversion. Confronted with the prospect of being labelled a defector, Ginsberg defended his decision by asserting the futility of conversion as a means of saving himself from the Jewish fate. In fact, the very futility of religious conversion in the face of racial persecution was what justified its timing as an act guided by pure faith. The author's ambivalence first manifests itself in his disavowal and defence and then again in his decision to purge the story of his conversion from the memoir altogether.

Another episode, this one from the memoir's final chapter, resonates with the self-censored conversion episode, pointing us to the limits of what Ginsberg could consciously address in his narrative. In 1963, Ginsberg was invited to Berlin to star in a theatre production of Romain Rolland's *Robespierre* at the newly opened Volksbühne. Ginsberg, who returned to his native city for the first time in thirty years, was scheduled to appear in sixty performances. But on the eve of his fifty-eighth show, he was involved in a near-accident that left his leg paralysed so that he was incapable of taking the stage. That evening a vehicle sped towards Ginsberg as he was crossing the street. He managed to dodge the car, but the shock of this close encounter left him permanently disabled, bringing his illustrious stage career to an unceremonious end. Doctors were incapable of diagnosing the cause of his disability, and Ginsberg himself offered no speculation.[2] Yet if the site of this accident and its symbolic significance offer any clue, the event seems to have been a traumatic repetition of Ginsberg's flight from Berlin thirty years earlier.

This narrative fails to confront the open wound left by the experiences of racial stigma, discrimination, and persecution from which Ginsberg fled through immigration and conversion – two events that occurred in quick succession. The only testimony to this repressed trauma seems to be the story Ginsberg recounts about the inexplicable physical disorder to which he succumbed after dodging the car. His body was communicating the psychic injury that Ginsberg never explicitly articulates in his memoir. In psychoanalytic terms, one might read Ginbserg's debilitating condition as a "conversion disorder" – that is, a physical expression of a truth to which the subject cannot consciously admit.[3] A close reading of Ginsberg's memoir suggests that the religious conversion and the subsequent conversion disorder were connected by virtue of a shared logic of displacement. A conversion disorder allows the subject to articulate unresolved psychic injuries that are beyond the grasp of consciousness. The disavowed, overdetermined religious conversion functioned in a similar manner, enabling Ginsberg to repress the traumas of persecution, flight, and survival. Both the conversion and the disabling psychosomatic symptoms operated as dissociative responses to a loss that Ginsberg never fully confronted in his memoir.

Ginsberg's bowdlerized memoir touches on a problem that recurs in the autobiographical writings of German-Jewish émigrés who converted from Judaism to Christianity during the years 1933 to 1945 and sought to defend their confessional choices in writing. This book tells the story of four of them. *Conversion and Catastrophe* explores the fraught relationship between religion, politics, and Holocaust memory through the autobiographical writings of German Jews who interwove the stories of their wartime survival with those of their spiritual salvation. Focusing on personal testimonies that fuse historical trauma and religious illumination within a single narrative, this study looks at how Jewish émigrés interpreted their experiences of persecution and displacement through the hermeneutics of Christian conversion. The question at the heart of this book is, what kind of self-understanding did this choice of genre enable or, alternatively, obstruct? To what degree was the literary paradigm of Christian conversion, with its emphasis on the individual's complete detachment from a former sinful self, an appropriate vehicle for articulating what was essentially a collective catastrophe that befell the very community that the convert was seeking to place at a distance?

This study looks at how its protagonists presented their new religious identity in relation to their Jewish background. It analyses the rhetorical means they used to persuade themselves and their audiences of the authenticity of their religious transformation at a time when Jewishness was perceived as an intractable racial trait and conversion from Judaism was viewed as a craven act of communal betrayal. Contrary to the idea that conversion represented a radical break with one's Jewish past, this study demonstrates the ways in which the political and cultural dilemmas of German-Jewish identity were carried over into the converts' autobiographical accounts of religious transformation. By bringing the tools of literary criticism and autobiographical theory to bear upon the life writing of converted Jews, this book offers new avenues for conceptualizing the Jewishness of historical subjects who disavowed their ties to Judaism.

Following Lisa Silverman's methodological example, my study seeks to theorize Jewishness "without making Jewish self-identification the ontological foundation of Jewish experience and Jewish history."[4] Alongside Silverman, scholars such as Scott Spector, Leora Auslander, and Samuel Moyn contest the notion that explicit self-identification should be the determining factor in theorizing the Jewishness of historical subjects or their cultural production. Limiting the purview of German-Jewish history to those figures who asserted their Jewishness, Moyn argues, "can foster blindness to the possibility of internally conflicted yet lived and sometimes tacitly affirmed identities which owe the principle and nature of their uneasy coherence to the vagaries of historical development."[5] Spector similarly urges scholars to focus on the "troubled subjectivities" of historical figures, for whom "Jewish identity was neither something intrinsic and inherited, nor was it stable and capable of being taken for granted."[6] A variation on these claims is made by Leora Auslander, who suggests that we should approach Jewishness as "a set of cultural practices ... [that] is transmitted, reproduced and transformed even when the people doing so are not consciously acting as Jews."[7] According to Auslander, limiting our understanding of "Jewishness" to the study of individuals and cultural artefacts that were categorically identified as such prevents us from tackling the "messy problem of what being a Jew is all about."[8]

The book consists of four case studies, each devoted to analysing the "messy problem" of Jewishness in convert autobiography. The chapters explore the complex cultural, political, and biographical concerns that found their expression in the converts' accounts of religious transformation. The figures include Karl Stern (1906–1975), a professor of psychiatry and erstwhile Zionist who converted to Catholicism in 1943 after immigrating with his family to Montreal during the Second World War; the Expressionist painter and novelist Karl Jakob Hirsch (1892–1952), who embraced Protestantism as an émigré in New York and sought to re-establish himself in post-war West Germany by publishing a memoir about his conversion in 1946; renowned novelist Alfred Döblin (1878–1957), who converted to Catholicism in Los Angeles during the Second World War and published a memoir about his spiritual journey in 1949, four years after resettling in West Germany; and a prominent scholar of intellectual property and antitrust law, Heinrich Kronstein (1897–1972), who converted to Catholicism shortly after arriving in the US in 1935 and played a key role in the development of German–American academic cooperation in the post-war era. To piece together the life stories of these converts, I draw on their autobiographies, novels, and religious writings, as well as unpublished archival materials.

Each chapter examines the different ways in which Jewishness shaped each convert's identity and continued to play a role in his self-understanding after conversion. The "Jewishness" I refer to does not consist of any innate qualities or hereditary characteristics, but rather of the external ascriptions of difference and the residual attachments that continued to inform each convert's self-image after conversion. Contrary to the classic Jamesian model of conversion, which posits a complete caesura between the individual's pre- and post-converted self, the protagonists in my study never managed to fully cast off their Jewish past. This lingering Jewishness was the product not only of the insurmountable barriers of societal prejudice or their continued stigmatization, but also of the ambivalent, unresolved attachments they bore to their community of origins.

Previous scholarship on conversion from Judaism in the modern era focuses primarily on the sociocultural factors leading to apostasy or on the material and psychological motivations underlying the abandonment of Judaism. While these studies draw on the converts' personal testimonies, they rarely attend to the retrospective and constructed nature of these documents. Considering this, I approach the testimonies of my protagonists not as factual records but as self-conscious literary artefacts, fictional reconstructions of a past meant to consolidate one's self-image in the present. Despite their questionable veracity, these autobiographical accounts illuminate the ways in which German-Jewish converts negotiated their religious identities in relation to the cultural expectations of their surrounding environment and the generic constraints of their chosen medium. As Thomas Kselman insightfully points out, "conversion narratives offer us privileged access to the interplay between individuals and the world they both inhabit and interpret."[9]

I will not be analysing these narratives against the hard facts of the lives they presume to recount. Rather, my interest lies in the ways these individuals rendered their experiences meaningful by converting them into literary form. We cannot presume to grasp the converts' true motives, but we can account for the symbolic and poetic frameworks they employed to narrate their experiences. Analysing the literary and religious resources they turned to in order to make sense of their stories provides us with another kind of historical understanding, one that reveals the cultural and personal meanings that converts attached to their suffering and survival. As Karl Morrison explains,

> there is, interpretatively speaking, little to distinguish a fictive reconstruction of an actual event from the fictional invention of one that never happened. The result is not to dismiss the entire literature of conversion as without historical reliability. It is to establish the study of conversion as a venture in poetics, for texts witness to processes of composition and to habits of thought at work in them more than to the dramatic events that the texts portray. Processes and habits are historical, too.[10]

Attending to the poetic form of these autobiographical narratives does not, then, stand in opposition to the historicity of the converts' experiences; rather, it offers another kind of historical understanding, illuminating the hermeneutic practices that allowed them to make sense of their realities and position themselves in the social world. These autobiographical texts reveal as much about the culture and historical context in which they were produced as they do about their individual authors.[11]

A question that arises while reading these autobiographical narratives is why the converts chose the confession they did. Why did Kronstein, Döblin, and Stern turn to Catholicism while Hirsch embraced Protestantism? The opposition between Judaism and Christianity is central to these stories, yet there is very little effort on the authors' part to account for the denomination they embraced. One explanation implied in some of these works relates to the cultural and geographical background of the authors. Karl Stern, who grew up in a traditional Catholic region of Bavaria, may have gravitated towards that denomination because of its familiarity and its associations to his childhood environment. It was also an advantageous denomination to convert to in the majority Catholic province of Quebec, where he resettled during the war. Kronstein was exposed to Catholicism in his youth. At Georgetown University, where he was a faculty member, it surely did not hurt to be Catholic. In Hirsch's case, the pastor of the Presbyterian church where he was baptized was a German-Jewish convert who drew displaced German-Jewish refugees to his congregation and offered them the moral and material support they couldn't find elsewhere. His confessional choice was primarily the result of the social and support networks available to him during his time in New York. In such cases, the social and cultural environments in which the exiles found themselves played no small role in their choice of religious denomination. This study is focused less on why the individual chose a certain confession over another and more on the way the convert marshalled the theological and symbolic resources of that confession in order to construct a coherent life story.

What determined my choice of case studies was their shared cultural, linguistic, and historical context. All four of my protagonists were German Jews who narrated their conversion to Christianity in relation to the rise of National Socialism and their experiences of persecution, exile, and survival. They witnessed the defeat of 1918 and the immediate collapse of the German Kaiserreich. They were involved in and influenced by the cultural and intellectual effervescence of the interwar years. They lived through the political unrest of the Weimar era, and some, like Hirsch and Döblin, actively aligned themselves with the revolutionary left. All four witnessed the Nazi rise to power and bore the brunt of antisemitism. Even when they did not acknowledge antisemitism's virulent and inexorable presence in their lives as a factor in their decision to convert, its traces permeate their narratives. Three of them – Döblin, Hirsch, and Kronstein – returned to West Germany after the war and sought to rebuild their lives in their homeland with varying degrees of success. Their stories contribute a new perspective to the history of German-Jewish returnees during the early years of the Federal Republic.

While researching this book I encountered the autobiographical writings of numerous other German Jews who converted in the 1930s and 1940s, such as the social worker and author Lily Pincus (1898–1981), theatre director Ernst-Josef Aufricht (1898–1971), the actor Ernst Ginsberg (1904–1964), the Catholic author Hilda Graef (1907–1970), the Canadian theologian Gregory Baum (1923–2014), art historian Alfred Neumeyer (1901–1973), the independent scholar of Christian mysticism Alfons Rosenberg (1902–1985), and the British journalist Rolland Hill (1920–2014). While their stories correspond to many of the key themes I discuss in the following chapters, these figures did not place conversion at the centre of their autobiographical narratives and thus fall outside the focus of this study. I occasionally allude to their life narratives in those places where their stories intersect with or illuminate my account of the book's main protagonists.[12]

Another fact that bears mentioning is that the figures I focus on are all men. The autobiographies of German-Jewish women who converted out of Judaism around the time of the Holocaust did not assign a central place to their religious transformation or organize their life narratives around it. A notable example, one that narrowly falls outside this book's time frame yet illustrates my point, is that of Edith Stein's unfinished autobiography *Aus dem Leben einer jüdischen Familie*, written between 1933 and 1939.[13] Stein's autobiography never presumes to offer a well-developed narrative of her spiritual path. In contrast to the works of Stern, Döblin, and Kronstein, the circumstances of Stein's turn to Catholicism remain on the margins of her posthumously published autobiography. But more significantly, Stein's autobiography differs from those of her fellow converts in the very framing of her story. In contrast to her male counterparts, who place themselves at the centre of their narratives, Stein weaves her life story into a broader family history that hearkens back to her maternal great-grandparents, and she devotes extensive parts of the text to her mother's life. This discrepancy might be attributed to the gendered expectations of the autobiographical form. As Mary G. Mason argues, women's autobiographies do not commonly draw on "the dramatic structure of conversion that we find in Augustine's *Confessions*, where the self is presented as the stage for a battle of opposing forces."[14]

Kronstein, Stern, Hirsch, and Döblin narrate their spiritual and confessional transformations against the backdrop of the Holocaust and its aftermath.[15] Their writings evince a shared effort to reconcile their Jewish past with their new religious identities and to legitimize their confessional choices in relation to the Jews' collective fate during the war. In their autobiographical writings, all four struggle to discern the providential design behind their personal destiny and narrate their turn to Christianity as a direct result of the fate of the Jews during the Nazi years. In their efforts to explain their radical religious transformation, the converts resort to the motifs and conventions of the Christian conversion narrative. They interpret their personal ordeals by drawing on biblical archetypes and typologies or by invoking traditional tropes of sin and repentance, blindness and insight.

Their stories can be interpreted through the prism of spiritual autobiography, but they can similarly be read as survivor testimonies, migrant literature, and chronicles documenting the erratic trajectories of Jewish lives in the first half of the twentieth century. This study examines the authors' attempts to endow their experiences of persecution with spiritual meaning, by asking how the literary form and religious traditions that informed their autobiographical texts shaped their understanding of the Holocaust. To borrow James Young's apt formulation, the aim of this study "is to understand the manner in which historical actuality and the forms in which it is delivered to us may be intertwined: it is to know what happened in how it is represented."[16]

A large part of my study is devoted to sketching out the political and historical context in which my protagonists converted and the responses that their religious transformations elicited. In piecing together the public responses to these conversion narratives, I show the complexities that

Figure 0.1.  Yiddish-language article by Jacob Lestschinsky in *The Forward*, reporting on the conversions of Karl Jakob Hirsch and Alfred Döblin (1948). The headline reads "The New Apostates: Sick Souls who Left the Jewish People." The National Library of Israel, The Historical Jewish Press Collection.

were involved in coming out as a Christian after the Holocaust. The life narratives in question were read by diverse audiences who understood the meaning of conversion very differently. Such conversions were perceived as highly controversial in the Jewish world and were covered in a sensational manner by certain press organs, such as the Yiddish-socialist *Forverts* and the German-émigré weekly *Aufbau*. Catholic press outlets, particularly in Germany, celebrated these personal stories and harnessed them to revise the Church's record during the Holocaust. Post-war German critics in the Western occupation zones tied the public professions of Christian faith made by prominent figures such as Döblin and Hirsch to the question of collective guilt and the Allies' policies of German re-education. Critics in the Soviet occupation zone, and what would later become the German Democratic Republic, often elided the Holocaust and the converts' Jewish background altogether, reading these texts as illustrations of their authors' false consciousness and political blindness. Probing the rich reception history of these texts reveals the social and cultural pressures that the converts negotiated when they shared their Christian identities with the world.

*Conversion and Catastrophe* makes an original contribution to the fields of Holocaust and memory studies by exploring the role of conversion in mediating the meaning that Jewish converts to Christianity found in their persecution, migration, and survival both during and after the war years. It inquires into the personal, political, and poetic implications of fashioning the narrative of one's wartime experience around the conceit of conversion. By asking how these stories were constructed, what details they included or left out, who their intended audiences were, and what claims to identity they made, I aim to understand how these survivor testimonies related to, departed from, and engaged with other contemporaneous forms of private and public Holocaust memory.

## Conversion and the Porous Boundaries of Modern Jewish Identity

In *Leaving the Jewish Fold: Conversion and Radical Assimilation in Modern Jewish History*, Todd Endelman argues that conversion and apostasy are of central importance to our understanding of the modern Jewish experience. While it would stand to reason that those who disavowed their Jewishness fall outside the orbit of Jewish history, Endelman explains that their attempts at "radical assimilation" merely represent "the most extreme form of strategies – acculturation and integration – that all Jews who entered the modern world pursued."[17] He thus proposes that we regard converts, "not as outsiders, free of all links to other Jews, but as occupants of the far end of a broad spectrum of assimilatory behavior, as actors responding to the same pressures and tensions that bedeviled other Jews. Their reaction to discrimination and stigmatization differed in degree, not in kind, from that of other acculturated Jews."[18]

Endelman's social-historical survey of Jewish conversion in the modern era is based on two presuppositions, which this study extends to the domain of autobiographical narrative: first, converts' ties to Judaism and Jews persisted after baptism because conversion failed to erase the stigma of their Jewish pasts; and second, conversion should be understood within the framework of modern Jewish history, as yet another strategy of social and cultural adaptation employed by Jews in the modern era. Endelman's work points to a dialectical dynamic in which the post-baptismal lives of former Jews were continuously determined by the very origins they sought to disavow. The present study shifts its focus away from the prevailing preoccupation with the social history of Jewish conversion in order to ask how this dynamic played out in the realm of life writing.

Following Endelman's example, I approach these conversion narratives as "Jewish" historical and literary documents, not because their authors self-identified as Jews, but in the sense that they were conditioned by their authors' Jewish background and attest to an ongoing preoccupation with the problem of Jewish origins. The continuity that Endelman identifies between conversion and other forms of modern Jewish identity is one that *Conversion and Catastrophe* locates in the realm of autobiographical narrative. I explore the rhetorical strategies, motifs, and symbols that Döblin, Hirsch, Kronstein, and Stern employed in their respective efforts to incorporate their Jewish past into their new self-conception as Christians. I ask how the relationship to one's Jewish past materializes in the act of life writing and explore its role in the convert's new self-understanding. I am interested in the literary and autobiographical traces, which Endelman identifies in the realm of social history, for what they tell us about the formation of the convert's identity. How does the struggle away from Jewishness correspond to and reflect broader social and historical concerns that preoccupied their erstwhile co-religionists? In what ways did the political and cultural preoccupations of the convert's former Jewish background continue to shape his or her sense of self? I ask how the rhetoric of conversion employed by these figures relates to larger issues concerning Jewish identity and selfhood in the post-war era. In what ways does the narrative facilitate the author's personal and social reinvention, and how does it continue to bind him to his communal and ancestral past?

Complementing the question of these narratives' relationship to broader trends in modern Jewish history is the social and political context of the conversions they recount. As an act that determines one's social location and public identity, conversion holds a distinctly political significance.[19] These narratives do more than locate the converted self in relation to divine providence and salvation history. They also assume the more pedestrian task of situating the author within a national and political community. The slippage between the rhetoric of religion and that of race that develops in the narratives I discuss in this book reveals the gaps between the conscious intentions of the converts and the stories they tell. The narratives in question contain meanings that outright conflict with the stated self-understanding of their authors. The religious identities constructed in and through these texts are ineluctably tainted by the rhetoric of race and nation they ostensibly disavow. The preoccupation with questions of personal faith and religious commitment is thus repeatedly belied by larger political and social realities that filter through these narratives. These texts illustrate the ways in which the problem of individual conscience and belief becomes entangled with the struggle for political and social self-legitimation.

## The Ideology of Assimilation and Its Diasporic Afterlife

We find another path to reading these narratives as specifically "Jewish" stories in the writings of Hannah Arendt. In her pioneering study of Enlightenment era *salonnière* and convert to Christianity Rahel Varnhagen (1771–1833), Arendt presents Rahel's life as a paradigmatic illustration of German Jewry's failure to grasp the collective and political nature of its historical predicament. According to Arendt, Rahel attempted to isolate herself from the political realities of prejudice and discrimination by fleeing into the ex-territorial realm of the literary salon, which for a brief moment in German history served as a meeting ground for individuals of varied social classes and backgrounds. For Arendt, Rahel's effort to escape her Jewishness by way of baptism and high culture encapsulates the blindness of German Jewry, which never considered the political dimension of its plight.[20]

In Arendt's reading, Rahel responded to the obstacles of social and class prejudice by turning inward and embarking on a path of self-exploration, whose richness and poetic beauty she left to posterity in her letters. By turning to her "inner self" Rahel sought to overcome the external constraints to her freedom. Or as Arendt describes it, "in the isolation achieved by introspection thinking becomes limitless because it is no longer molested by anything exterior; because there is no longer any demand for action, the consequences of which necessarily impose limits even upon the freest spirit."[21] This flight to interiority characterizes the life writing of this book's protagonists, who take the persecution of European Jewry as an occasion to contemplate and reassert their personal faith in a way that effectively elides the political concerns surrounding their actions. Very much like Rahel, Döblin and his fellow converts regarded their Jewishness as an individual problem.

In this regard, the life stories analysed in this study illustrate the constraints and contradictions that characterized the tortuous path towards assimilation as charted in Arendt's *The Origins of Totalitarianism*. According to Arendt, assimilation into non-Jewish society was granted to those who "were clearly distinguished exceptions from the Jewish masses."[22] Admittance into the dominant culture was conceded only to those who proved themselves to be "exceptions." The strategy of assimilation that Arendt identified with Varnhagen emblematized the Jews' apolitical response to the challenges of antisemitism and emancipation:

> For them the Jewish question had lost, once and for all, all political significance; but it haunted their private lives and influenced their personal decisions all the more tyrannically. The adage, "a man in the street and a Jew

at home," was bitterly realized: *political problems were distorted to the point of pure perversion when Jews tried to solve them by means of inner experience and private emotions*; private life was poisoned to the point of inhumanity ... when the heavy burden of unsolved problems of public significance was crammed into that private existence.[23]

The narratives that make up this study confirm Arendt's bleak assertion. My protagonists sought to resolve their "Jewish question" as a personal matter of faith, setting aside its consequential political significance. Although the converts tried to turn the public and political dimensions of their Jewishness into matters of private belief, the external realities they often obscured, ignored, or avoided continued to wield an ineluctable influence on their personal and professional lives.

The "ideology of assimilation" continued to hold sway after 1933, as thousands of Jews sought refuge beyond Germany's borders. Arendt identified the contours of this curious repetition in her 1943 essay "We Refugees." In her polemical analysis, Arendt argued that the defence mechanisms that allowed fellow émigrés to adapt to their new environments simultaneously prevented them from reckoning with the true causes and consequences of their forced migration. The émigrés, she lamented, had decided to forget their past persecution in Europe and pretend they had found a home in their new country of residence. In order to master their traumatic past, they avoided discussing their experiences under Hitler, focusing instead on their promising futures. "We fight like madmen for private existences with individual destinies ... We don't feel entitled to Jewish solidarity; we cannot realize that we by ourselves are not so much concerned as the whole Jewish people."[24]

Instead of fighting for their social and legal status as a group, the refugees opted for a change of identity, as individuals. Arendt understood this desire for reinvention on a psychological level but pointed to the limits of its emancipatory potential, explaining that in seeking to recover "a new personality,"

we reveal nothing but our insane desire to be changed, *not to be Jews*. All our activities are directed to attain this aim: we don't want to be refugees, since we don't want to be Jews; we pretend to be English-speaking people, since German-speaking immigrants of recent years are marked as Jews; we don't call ourselves stateless, since the majority of stateless people in the world are Jews; we are willing to become loyal Hottentots, only to hide the fact that we are Jews ... Under the cover of our "optimism" you can easily detect the hopeless sadness of assimilationists.[25]

According to Arendt, the history of German-Jewish assimilation continued abroad as the refugees followed the failed patterns of adaptation and integration practised by their ancestors since the times of the emancipation. Whether or not one accepts Arendt's critique of the refugees, her polemical approach constitutes an evocative starting point for thinking about the exilic afterlife of German Jewry and the ways in which its cultural dynamics shaped the personal choices made by Jews after 1933.

Arendt's critique of German-Jewish history is based on teleological presuppositions that have, for justifiable reasons, fallen out of favour with scholars. The appeal of Arendt's polemical writings for the purpose of this study is her ability to draw our attention to the dialectical continuities that emerge in the course of German Jewry's path from emancipation to exile. Her analysis of conversion and assimilation offers one interpretative approach to understanding how the narratives surveyed in this book form part of a larger story of the German-Jewish diaspora. I allude to Arendt's panoramic survey of the history of emancipation and its exilic aftermath not to censure the converts but to situate them in the larger context that is often glossed over or only obliquely alluded to in their autobiographical writings. To the extent that Arendt provides us with an interpretative framework for the life stories in question, she also assumes a supporting role in the historical narrative recounted in this book. Her accusatory stance echoes throughout the writings of my protagonists, who devoted their energies to refuting the allegations of desertion and disloyalty.

The turn to Christianity was by no means a pervasive phenomenon among German Jews during or after the war years.[26] Yet Arendt's preoccupation with the question of conversion and its prevalence in the exilic press reveals how large it loomed over the German-Jewish émigré imagination. Their numeric insignificance notwithstanding, the converts in this book merit our attention for what they tell us about how a minority of German-Jewish intellectuals responded to the pressures of persecution and displacement after 1933. Their stories constitute a lesser-known chapter in the history of the German-Jewish diaspora and the transformations of modern Jewish identity in the mid-twentieth century.

**Chapter Outline**

Chapter 1 tells the story of the Hannover-born artist and novelist Karl Jakob Hirsch. Hirsch emigrated to the US after the Nazi rise to power and returned to occupied Germany almost immediately after the war in the hope of re-establishing his literary career. One year after his return, Hirsch published a memoir titled *Heimkehr zu Gott. Briefe an meinen Sohn* (1946), which sought to explain how the great-grandson of the renowned Orthodox Rabbi Samson Raphael Hirsch converted to Protestantism on the eve of his return to Germany. The chapter situates Hirsch's memoir and its reception in the context of the post-war *Schuldfrage* and the re-Christianization of the West German population after 1945. Reading Hirsch's autobiographical writings against the historical backdrop of the immediate post-war years, the chapter reconstructs the political and personal stakes underlying his account of spiritual self-discovery.

Chapter 2 is devoted to Alfred Döblin's 1941 conversion to Catholicism and the story he told about it in his 1949 autobiography *Schicksalsreise*. In the autobiography, Döblin turns his experiences as an exile from Nazi Germany into a story of spiritual awakening in which the predicament of a wartime Jewish political émigré becomes a metaphor for a metaphysical journey culminating in the author's embrace of Christianity. Absent from the autobiography is any mention of antisemitism, the fate of his extended family during the Holocaust, or the annihilation of Polish Jewry he had written about so emphatically twenty-five years earlier in *Reise in Polen*. Despite the narrative's conspicuous silences, I show how the autobiography is deeply, if obliquely, preoccupied with the problem of national identity and belonging that had haunted Döblin since 1933.

Chapter 3 is an in-depth case study of the Bavarian-born psychiatrist Karl Stern, who immigrated to Montreal during the Second World War and published a bestselling memoir called *The Pillar of Fire* (1951) about his conversion to Catholicism. The public avowal of Catholicism in the immediate wake of the Holocaust exposed Stern to accusations of betrayal and callousness among Jews and gentiles alike. I reconstruct the way Stern's memoir harnesses the German-Jewish rhetoric of self-affirmation and the Zionist critique of assimilation to tell the story of his conversion to Christianity. The ingenuity of Stern's conversion narrative is that by aligning his turn to Catholicism with Jewish Orthodoxy and, to a more limited extent, Zionism, Stern presents his religious transformation as an organic outgrowth of his commitment to Judaism.

Chapter 4 focuses on Heinrich Kronstein, an influential legal scholar in the fields of intellectual property and antitrust law, who taught at Georgetown University and the University of Frankfurt. The chapter explores the ways Kronstein's conversion enabled him to gloss over the traumatic effects that Nazism and the Holocaust had on his own biography as a German-Jewish émigré. By recounting the historical events of the 1930s and 1940s through the frame of his spiritual awakening,

Kronstein displaces the centrality of the Holocaust both to his own personal story and to the post-war German context he addresses. Drawing on Eric Santner's concept of narrative fetishism, I argue that conversion in Kronstein's memoir allows its author to reconstitute his self-identity without having to confront the radical ruptures that occurred in his life.

The Conclusion revisits the question of genre and literary form in an attempt to account for the overdetermined character of Christianity in these life stories. I argue that the spiritual epiphanies recounted in these narratives serve as mechanisms of repression and dissociation while at the same time attesting to the unresolved grief and guilt of the authors. What emerges from the autobiographical narratives in question is that the converts' new confessional identity is constructed around the personal loss and psychic injury that remains unarticulated in these texts.

These converts cut highly idiosyncratic figures in the landscape of modern Jewish history. Nevertheless, their life stories were shaped by the political and social forces that governed Jewish self-definition in the wake of the Holocaust. What emerges from the autobiographical narratives is that the converts' new confessional identity was inextricably intertwined with questions of religious renewal, national belonging, and cultural authenticity that preoccupied their Jewish contemporaries. In converting to Christianity, these individuals responded to their respective environments in ways that paralleled and competed with other, more familiar, Jewish responses to the Holocaust. In these narratives, the choice of another religion is explicitly contrasted to other forms of modern Jewish identity. Revealed in these autobiographical accounts is an intricate and ongoing dialogue with alternative Jewish ideologies that were articulated through the confrontation with catastrophe. As such, the vagaries of modern Jewish identity form the indispensable backdrop to understanding the religious self-image the converts constructed in their autobiographies.

# Chapter One

# Conversion and the Question of German Guilt in Karl Jakob Hirsch's *Heimkehr zu Gott* (1946)

In August 1945, the Hannover-born Jewish émigré Karl Jakob Hirsch returned to his native Germany in the uniform of the occupying US Army. Ten-odd years in exile in the US had not been kind to Hirsch, whose life in New York City had been marked by poverty, isolation, and chronic illness. Hoping to turn over a new leaf and leave the disappointments of his American experience behind, the fifty-three-year-old accepted a two-year post as a military censor in Munich. Hirsch returned to occupied Germany secretly hoping to re-establish the promising literary career he had been forced to abandon in 1933. In the years leading up to his immigration, Hirsch, who had already made a name for himself as an Expressionist artist, stage designer, and journalist, found his true calling as a writer, publishing two bestselling novels with the prestigious S. Fischer Verlag.

Hirsch's dream seemed to come true one year after his return to Germany, when he published a memoir, titled *Heimkehr zu Gott. Briefe an meinen Sohn* (1946). Written as a series of letters to his fourteen-year-old son Ralph, the work recounted the main junctures in Hirsch's life, starting with his Orthodox Jewish upbringing as the great-grandson of the renowned Rabbi Samson Raphael Hirsch and culminating in his 1945 conversion to Protestantism. Hirsch's decision to write his memoir in epistolary form seems to have been a homage to his great-grandfather. Rabbi Hirsch's most famous work, *Neunzehn Briefe über Judenthum* (1836), was a religious-philosophical treatise, written in the form of a fictional exchange of letters between a rabbi and a young correspondent. By adopting the epistolary form for *Heimkehr zu Gott*, Hirsch placed his conversion in conversation with his celebrated ancestor. The book became a success in the Western occupation zones, where it garnered widespread praise from the press and the German reading public.[1] The enthusiastic reception of *Homecoming to God* appeared to

Figure 1.1.  Karl Jakob Hirsch, *Selbstportrait* (1920). Nachlaß Karl Jakob Hirsch, Universitätsbibliothek der LMU München.

signal that the author's literary homecoming would be a success. Yet when Hirsch died six years later in 1952, *Heimkehr zu Gott* was still the only work he had managed to publish in post-war Germany.[2]

The recognition that *Heimkehr zu Gott* achieved is especially striking when we consider the German public's general indifference to the autobiographical testimonies of Jewish survivors at the time. According to literary historian Helmut Peitsch, the fanfare surrounding *Heimkehr* stands in stark contrast to the silent treatment accorded to the few German-language memoirs of Jewish survivors and émigrés that appeared in the mid- to late 1940s.[3] In the wake of defeat, Germans were more interested in reckoning with their own losses than in confronting the pain and suffering they had inflicted on others.[4] Why was Hirsch able to break the barrier of German apathy where other Jewish survivors and exiles failed? The German public's enthusiastic reception of Hirsch's memoir was due in no small part to the Christian-theological discourse it employed in broaching the question of German guilt.

In this regard, the early reviews of Hirsch's memoir do much to dispel the mystery surrounding the work's post-war popularity. A critic for the *Passauer Neue Presse* offered a glowing endorsement of *Heimkehr*, crediting the book for "illuminating the tragedy of Jewish existence" from a "religious point of view."[5] The "tragedy" he was referring to was not the systematic destruction of European Jewry but its progressive secularization in the years leading up to it. As the critic went on to explain, "the majority of European Jews were no longer religiously committed, a metaphysical guilt they shared with their exterminators, the Germans of the Third Reich."[6] The reviewer established a moral equivalence between the Jew and the German that seemed to blur the lines between victim and perpetrator. Far from imposing its own agenda on *Heimkehr zu Gott*, the review was merely following the author's line of reasoning, which displaced the politically charged question of German accountability for Nazi war crimes with a fuzzy religious discourse of "metaphysical guilt."

Hirsch's memoir also made a splash in Jewish émigré circles. The scandal surrounding Hirsch's conversion unfolded in the pages of the New York–based émigré paper *Aufbau*. Manfred George, the editor-in-chief of *Aufbau*, argued that Hirsch's conversion had nothing to do with the divine and everything to do with the hardship and loneliness he had endured as an exile. According to George, the memoir offered a "sad picture of a German-Jewish intellectual who failed to find his way in both Germany and America."[7] Noting the author's pedigree as the great-grandson of Rabbi Samson Raphael Hirsch, George added that in the final tally, "Judaism has lost nothing in this man who publicly separated himself from it, for this man never really belonged to it in the first place."[8] George lamented that Hirsch, like many of his Jewish contemporaries, was completely ignorant of "the Jewish concept of God" and thus could not be faulted for abandoning a religion he knew nothing about in the first place. If anyone was responsible for Hirsch's apostasy it was the Jewish community that had failed to impress the uniqueness and greatness of Judaism on their lost brethren. If George's review could be read as generously dismissive, giving Hirsch the benefit of the doubt by attributing his conversion to psychological duress, the satirist and dramaturge Walter Mehring saw Hirsch's narrative as far more pernicious. In its blatantly derisive portrayal of Jews and its reversion to the worn-out accusation of deicide, Hirsch's memoir was not much more than "a theological-antisemitic Sunday school essay."[9]

News of Hirsch's conversion reached the German-Jewish diaspora in Palestine. In a blistering review of his memoir, the journalist Schalom Ben-Chorin called Hirsch a "prototype of the German-Jewish intellectual who … was brusquely disillusioned in 1933."[10] According to Ben-Chorin, Hirsch's "defection" was a decision guided "purely by emotions without any theological substance."[11] The author's vapidity was epitomized in the experience that triggered his conversion in the first place. "And what is it that led him to Christianity in his search for God? Typical for the modern urban dweller: a film, based on the novel *The Song of Bernadette*, written by the Christianizing Jewish poet, Franz Werfel … that is the reality of a faithless Galut-Jew in 1944, tragicomic and devastating at the same time."[12] For Ben-Chorin, Hirsch represented the pinnacle of Jewish deracination. Hirsch's alienation from his own ancestral religion had left him with no other path. The question was "whether we, the Jewish community, are not partly to blame … for the desertion from our ranks."[13] Who was looking after those "Jews on the margins"? Why did German-Jewish émigrés find no pastoral care among their own people?[14]

Writing for *Hazofeh*, a religious Zionist daily associated with the Mizrachi movement, the critic Moshe Ungerfeld noted the generic affinities between Hirsch's memoir and his great-grandfather's influential *Nineteen Letters*. Rabbi Hirsch had sought to "explain the essence of traditional Judaism to his generation," thus bringing scores of young Jews back to "the ancient sources of Israel."[15] A century later, Samson Raphael Hirsch's descendant published a work that resembled the epistolary form of his famed ancestor in order "to lead others down his sinful path."[16] Ungerfeld harshly concluded that "no one will shed a tear for his departure, because a man who responds in this manner to the murder of his brothers and sisters is clearly a person, whose spirit is broken and his soul damaged."[17]

## From Judaism to Expressionism, Communism to Christ

Hirsch began the story of his personal salvation with an account of his early life in Wilhelmine Germany. Karl Jakob and his older twin brother Gottfried were born in Hannover in 1892 to Dr. Salomon and Marie Hirsch. The twins were raised in an observant Jewish household, committed to preserving the path laid down by their famous great-grandfather, Rabbi Samson Raphael Hirsch (1808–1888). Hirsch had been the chief rabbi of Frankfurt am Main and the founder of Neo-Orthodoxy, a movement that advocated religious traditionalism alongside integration into German society. His legacy left a deep imprint on Karl's childhood. Despite growing up in a pious household, young Karl broke with religion at a young age, embittered by his experiences at Jewish Sunday school, which he described as a "prayer mill operation" that turned religious worship into "senseless torment."[18] Hirsch's religious schooling seemed to offer only a "caricature of religiosity" that "could turn even the most pious boy into an atheist."[19]

A childhood episode that heralds Hirsch's gradual move away from Judaism and his eventual embrace of Christianity is his recollection of a visit to a Jewish friend's home around Christmas. Karl and his twin brother Gottfried return from the friend's house and joyously show their father the chocolates they took from the family Christmas tree. Infuriated, the father lashes out in disgust at Karl and Gottfried for having eaten from the forbidden tree and throws their chocolates into the stove. He renounces his paternity in anger over their transgression and what he perceives as a betrayal of their ancestral faith.[20] This event is the first of several passages that paint the Jews in the memoir in unflattering colours – in this case, demonstrating the Jews' aversion to Christianity and portraying Hirsch's father as a capricious tyrant whose conduct recalls the wrathful God of the Old Testament. But if the scene is meant to anticipate Hirsch's eventual break with Judaism, it is also deeply ambiguous, offering a glimpse of the author's unacknowledged sense of guilt. Since the episode alludes to the biblical story of Adam and Eve eating from the Tree of Knowledge, would the analogy not imply that it was Hirsch's tasting from the "forbidden tree" of Christianity that constituted his mortal sin?

The meaningless monotony of religious ritual alienates Hirsch from Judaism. He writes, "So I lost all interest in God. It was for me nothing but a childish memory of ancient customs. For me it was compulsory religious school and having to go to synagogue. God was no longer to be found for me in these things."[21] He finds a substitute for his lost faith in art, a vocation that entices him as a "path to freedom" from the fetters of religious formalism and bourgeois morality he identified with his upbringing. A gifted pianist, the young Karl first hoped to become a professional musician. That dream was cut short after a blood poisoning incident required the amputation of his right index finger. With his father's blessing, Hirsch channelled his artistic talents to the visual arts. In 1910, he moved to Munich to study art at the Debschitz School; however, he ended up spending most of his time hobnobbing with a bohemian crowd in cafés and theatres. He continued his artistic development in Paris, where he lived from 1912 to 1914. Returning to Germany on the eve of the First World War, Hirsch settled in the Worpswede artist colony.

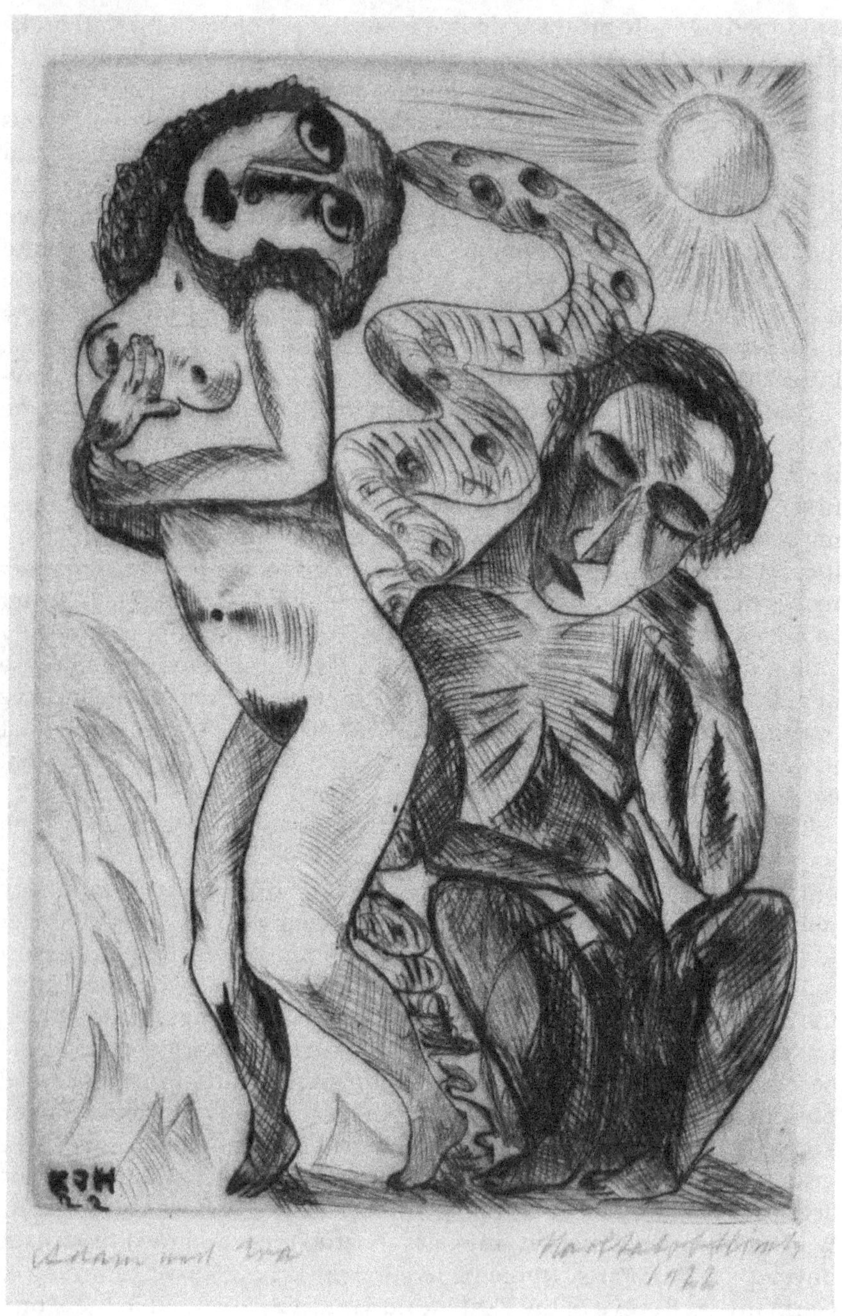

Figure 1.2.  Karl Jakob Hirsch, *Adam und Eva* (1922). Nachlaß Karl Jakob Hirsch, Universitätsbibliothek der LMU München.

Figure 1.3.  Karl Jakob Hirsch, *Baal Schem* (1914). Hirsch's artistic rendition of the charismatic mystical rabbi and founder of the Hasidic movement coincided with a resurging German-Jewish interest in Eastern-Jewish folklore that took place in the early twentieth-century and popularized in the works of Martin Buber. Nachlaß Karl Jakob Hirsch, Universitätsbibliothek der LMU München.

During his time at Worpswede, Hirsch produced a series of illustrations based on Martin Buber's *Legends of the Ba'al Shem Tov* (1915). In his memoir, Hirsch writes that he was strongly drawn to the pantheistic religiosity he found in Buber's book, which went "beyond all synagogues or commercial Judaism" he identified with Western-Jewish life in Germany.[22] His personal acquaintance with Buber temporarily strengthened his "new Jewish consciousness"; even so, he felt like Buber was depicting a world that was foreign to him: "I wanted some form of Judaism to be a part of my life. Yet the Judaism of the Orthodox synagogue had become foreign to me; foreign in its language and in its empty rituals that made no sense to me." Buber's romantic portrayal of Hasidism offered an inspiring alternative to the Judaism he was raised with, but looking back, Hirsch would renounce Buberian Judaism as a false idol in service of Jewish nationalism: "I threw myself into Hasidic Judaism without knowing that I had thereby actually approached National Judaism."[23] Ultimately, with the wisdom of hindsight, the converted Hirsch realizes that it was not Judaism per se that appealed to him at the time but a thirst for religiosity. This thirst was quenched when he discovered Christianity.

Towards the end of 1915, Hirsch left for Berlin to live with his future wife, the physician Auguste Lotz. Soon after his marriage in early 1916, Hirsch was drafted into the army. Due to his poor health and diminutive stature, he was spared from combat and was posted to Adlershof, an airbase outside Berlin, where he served in an administrative capacity. His light clerical duties allowed him to continue his work as an artist. Unlike Karl, a self-declared pacifist, whose health kept him from the front line, his brother Gottfried, an avid patriot, set out to prove his valour on the battlefield; he returned from the war without his left arm. In Berlin, Hirsch befriended Franz Pfemfert, the editor of the Expressionist journal *Die Aktion*.

Between 1916 to 1919, Hirsch's woodcuts and sketches appeared in almost every issue of the journal, which remains a primary source for his surviving artwork. During the early post-war years, Hirsch was active in various avant-garde and radical left-wing movements, such as the well-known November Group and the Council of Intellectual Workers. He designed political placards for the German Communist Party and the Marxist-revolutionary Spartacus League. A staunch supporter of the 1918 German Revolution, he struck a close friendship with Eugen Leviné, leader of the short-lived Bavarian Soviet Republic, who was later murdered by the White Guard.[24] After the Second World War, when Hirsch sought to re-establish himself in West Germany, his prominent left-wing activism would come back to haunt him. The conservative, anti-communist sentiment that pervaded post-war West

Figure 1.4.  Karl Jakob Hirsch, illustrations of the Marxist revolutionaries Rosa Luxemburg and Karl Liebknecht. The portraits first appeared in the left-wing journal *Die Aktion*. During the First World War, Luxemburg and Liebknecht founded the Spartacus League (*Spartakusbund*), which sought to establish a socialist republic in place of the German monarchy. Luxemburg and Liebknecht were murdered on 15 January 1919 by members of the White Guard, a right-wing militia of WWI veterans. Images reproduced from *Revolutionäre Kunst* (1919).

Germany proved to be an insurmountable obstacle for the rehabilitation of Hirsch's literary career.

Between 1918 and 1925, Hirsch worked as a stage designer, first for the Volksbühne theatre. In the mid-1920s, Hirsch transitioned from the visual arts to the written word and began earning his living as an art and theatre critic for papers such as the *Vossische Zeitung* and the *Berliner Zeitung am Mittag*. In 1929, Hirsch divorced his first wife and married the dancer Vera Carus, with whom he had been in a relationship since 1925. They had their only son Ralph in 1932. Hirsch's literary breakthrough occurred in 1931 with the publication of his first novel *Kaiserwetter*.[25]

Set in Hannover, the plot of *Kaiserwetter* begins at the turn of the twentieth century and ends on the eve of the First World War. The protagonist, who resembles Hirsch in his physique and artistic inclinations, is a bespectacled and weakly Jewish boy from an upper-middle-class home named Joe de Vries. His father, Samuel, is a well-respected lawyer and upstanding member of the Jewish community who has little regard for religious custom. This blasé indifference trickles down to his son Joe, who drifts away from Judaism and finds a substitute for religion in art. The novel follows Joe's artistic and moral development as he rebels against the stultifying bourgeois environment of his parental home by becoming an Expressionist musician. Hirsch's antiwar novel depicts imperial Germany in its last decades as a politically corrupt state in the process of moral decline. The work's critique of the nationalism, militarism, and antisemitism that pervaded German society in the years leading up to 1914 also serves as a timely commentary on the political developments of the early 1930s.[26]

The following year, Hirsch wrote and submitted a sequel to the novel called *Die zerfetzte Flagge*, to be published in January 1933. With the Nazis' rise to power, Fischer Verlag thought it imprudent to publish the work of a left-leaning Jewish writer whose previous novel had criticized German nationalism, and decided to delay its publication. The manuscript was lost during the war. (The Nazis would place *Kaiserwetter* on their list of forbidden books, and on 10 May 1933, copies of the novel would be thrown into bonfires across Germany in a book-burning campaign orchestrated by Goebbels.[27]) After the Nazis rose to power, Hirsch's occupational options were severely narrowed. He could no longer publish his literary or journalistic writings in "Aryan" outlets. Hirsch accepted an editorial position with the *Israelitischen Familienblatts*, a Berlin-Jewish weekly that in 1936 also serialized his novella *Hochzeitsmarsch in Moll*.[28] The first instalment of the novella was preceded by the author's "self-portrait," in which Hirsch positioned himself as a proud Jew whose heritage had always been the defining fact of his life: "I can hear the pious hymns and prayers recited at my parents' home. I can hear the chanting of the *Shirhamaalaus* and the *Chadgadjoh* of the Seder Night. I can see the calm piety of my grandfather, the son of Samson Raphael Hirsch ... My Judaism has always been the foundational fact of my being ... It was always something self-evident."[29]

*Hochzeitsmarsch in Moll* is a bildungsroman centring on the figure of Walter Heller, a Jewish youth from a middle-class background, born at the turn of the twentieth century. Recalling *Kaiserwetter*'s protagonist, Joe de Vries, Heller tries to escape the strictures of his bourgeois upbringing by turning to art and adopting a bohemian lifestyle. Heller feels alienated from Judaism and regards it as no more than "a cumbersome burden on my way to Europe." In his search for authentic selfhood, Heller oscillates between artistic self-realization and Zionism. These two options are represented in his two love interests: Marya Rosanski, an observant Jew who embodies the path to Jewish renewal by way of Zionism, and the Danish artist Eva Rasmussen, who represents an emancipated, cosmopolitan European identity. In a passage that captures Heller's inner conflict, he confides to his childhood friend Ernst:

> Being a Jew used to mean being pious. The pious man, like my grandfather, never forgot he was a Jew, but he also never thought about it, because for him it was simply a given. My father … brought me up as a Jew, and I put up with it. Just when I began to passionately love the history and customs of my people, I realized that my father basically despised what he demanded of me. A little childish defiance kept me from immediately throwing overboard everything that still burdened me about Jewish things. But I did it when I decided to become a "free man." I made a brief attempt to emancipate myself from my parents. It failed, because I continued to claim the comforts of bourgeois life … Thus, I lived free and unfree, half-lawyer, half-musician, and perhaps half a husband.[30]

The autobiographical elements in the serialized novel attest to the existential and identitarian crisis of its author, who wrote the work from his exile in Denmark. Progressively distancing himself from Judaism over the course of the preceding two decades, Hirsch suddenly found himself culturally quarantined by the Nazis and forced to reclaim his "primal identity" as a point of pride.

The exact details of Hirsch's trajectory from 1933 onwards are somewhat fuzzy, due in no small part to Hirsch's own prevarications and the inconsistent timeline he drew in his two autobiographies. According to Hirsch's original account, he and his family moved to Denmark in the summer of 1933 and lived there for several months before resettling in Lucerne, Switzerland. Because the Swiss imposed strict prohibitions on foreigners' ability to work, Hirsch was forced to pursue his livelihood elsewhere. He immigrated to America in 1935 ahead of his wife and son in order to prepare the ground for their arrival.[31] Hirsch originally hoped to work as a Hollywood scriptwriter, but when this plan fell through, he became a theatre and film critic for the *Neue Volkszeitung*, a New York-based, German-language newspaper.[32] Hirsch could barely make ends meet on his salary as a journalist and was forced to find other sources of income to support his wife and son. He sought to supplement his meagre salary as a journalist by taking a job as a day labourer in a textile factory in Brooklyn, only to be fired a few weeks later when the foreman discovered that he was receiving help from his workmates in order to reach his daily quotas.[33] He then worked as a doorman, earning three dollars a day and a free meal, at an Upper East Side medical practice run by an acquaintance he had known in Germany. Hirsch's financial situation improved significantly in 1942, when he found employment

Figure 1.5.  Karl Jakob Hirsch, "Ich werde doch keine fremden Briefe lesen" (1948). The image reads "I will certainly not read any foreign letters." The caption refers to Hirsch's frustration with his profession as a military censor. Nachlaß Karl Jakob Hirsch, Universitätsbibliothek der LMU München.

as a civil servant in the Office of Censorship, where he was tasked with reading the correspondence of German prisoners of war. Incidentally, this was also the year that his second marriage fell apart.

During this abysmal period in his life, Hirsch sought comfort in Judaism and, temporarily, tried returning to tradition.

I tried to revert to the time of my childhood, when Jewish piety was part of my daily life. I attended services in synagogues, but when on the highest Jewish holiday, the Feast of Atonement, I saw an armored car parked outside the Fifth Avenue Synagogue to safely drive the funds of pious donors to the bank, I felt very little of the spirit of my great-grandfather Samson Raphael Hirsch. Certainly, there were many Jews who felt very happy and secure in the childhood faith of their fathers. But I could see nothing compelling or redeeming in these prohibitions and laws.[34]

In *Heimkehr*, Hirsch writes that he goes to the synagogue only to discover that it too has been penetrated by the harsh capitalistic realities of the United States. While Hirsch's malicious description of large cash donations being made on Yom Kippur seems highly dubious, it nevertheless corresponds to the antisemitic conceit that runs through his memoir. Hirsch often demonizes the Jews in his narrative, identifying them as a materialistic and loveless community.

In February 1944, Hirsch receives a letter from his niece in Jerusalem, with the unfortunate news that his brother has passed away from a lung infection. Gottfried had embraced the Zionist cause in the early 1930s and had immigrated to Palestine after the Nazi seizure of power. Hirsch reports that although his brother arrived as a convinced Zionist, the ideology failed to sustain him during his final years, which were marked by a deep pessimism and an overwhelming solitude.[35] Gottfried's untimely death at the age of fifty-two is a harsh blow to his twin brother, whose own struggle for survival has taken a heavy toll on his physical health and psychological well-being. Two months later, Karl suffers from a similar ailment that brings him to the verge of death, but over which he ultimately prevails. During his protracted hospitalization, Hirsch undergoes a radical spiritual transformation that revives the faith he had lost in his adolescence and that ultimately leads him to the baptismal font. The contrast could not be clearer: Gottfried Hirsch, who replaced his lost faith by becoming a fervent Jewish nationalist, died an unhappy death in Eretz Israel, whereas his brother Karl Jakob experienced a miraculous recovery from a similar malady when he found spiritual salvation in Christ.

Two months after learning of his brother's untimely death, Hirsch is rushed to the hospital unconscious in what his doctors diagnose as a severe lung infection combined with a cardiac episode. During one of his first nights in the hospital, Hirsch experiences a mystical vision of Saint Bernadette Soubirous. In the preceding chapter, Hirsch had related the deep impression that the 1943 film *The Song of Bernadette* left on him. Based on a novel by Franz Werfel, *The Song of Bernadette* is the story of Bernadette Soubirous, a simple farmer's daughter, whose vision of the Virgin Mary led to the discovery of a miraculous spring near the city of Lourdes. Hirsch is so captivated by the simplicity and sanctity of the figure of Bernadette that he goes to see the film night

Figure 1.6.  Photograph of Karl Jakob Hirsch and twin brother Gottfried Hirsch (circa 1932). In the memoir, Gottfried's fervent Jewish nationalism and immigration to Palestine are contrasted with the author's embrace of Christianity and post-war return to Germany. Nachlaß Karl Jakob Hirsch, Universitätsbibliothek der LMU München.

after night. "I yearned to once again hear Bernadette's simple and wise words that had touched my innermost being."[36] In retrospect, Hirsch speculates that what attracted him to the film in the first place was that it allowed him to re-experience, at least vicariously, the joys of religious piety lost to him since childhood:[37] "It is hard to put it in words, but it was as if something had changed inside me. When I came home, I felt for the first time since my childhood the desire to pray. But I was incapable of deciding in which language to do it. I caught myself reciting the Shema Yisrael prayer aloud. I listened to the sound of my own voice but could hear no echo."[38] The film awakens a long-dormant religious impulse in Hirsch. He first tries to respond to it by reciting the Shema, the most important Jewish prayer, but it fails to elicit the desired effect.

The religious yearning that the film stirs in Hirsch arises again: he is visited by Bernadette in his hospital bed. Teetering on the brink of death, Hirsch recognizes the angelic face of Jennifer Jones, the actress playing

Figure 1.7.  Photograph of Karl Jakob Hirsch in New York (May 1938). Nachlaß Karl Jakob Hirsch, Universitätsbibliothek der LMU München.

Bernadette in the film. Jones/Bernadette addresses Hirsch, reciting her signature line from the film: "There was a lady, I don't know if it was the Madonna, she said nothing of this."[39] Hirsch's vision does not yet lead him to take decisive action, nor is it tied to any specific confession, but it forms a pivotal moment in his nascent religious transformation: "I realized that the true God was not the punishing Jehovah, but the forgiving Christ. And I required forgiveness and love, because I was guilty, as profoundly guilty, as a man who believes he is master of his own destiny can be. Jehovah would have killed me, but the God of love redeemed me."[40]

Reading Hirsch's narrative through the lens of disability sheds light on the social and symbolic meanings he associates with his illness. In the memoir, the author's diminutive stature, deformed hand, and frail health are more than biographical details in the memoir. In fact, they advance the narrative conceit of the author's spiritual and social regeneration through conversion.[41] The tropes of illness and recovery are, of course, common currency in conversion narratives, symbolizing the spiritual revival of the new believer. Yet in this case, Hirsch's frail and diseased body also serves as a metaphor for Jewish difference, symbolizing his stigmatized racial and religious identity. As David Mitchell and Sharon Snyder point out, "stigmatized social positions founded upon gender, class, nationality, and race have often relied upon disability to visually underscore the devaluation of marginal communities."[42] In Hirsch's case, the diseased and disfigured body reads as a mark of the author's racial and religious stigma as a Jew. The author's failing health functions as a shorthand for a flawed identity. It is only through the mystical vision of Bernadette Soubirous that he recovers from his life-threatening illness and the damaged identity it symbolizes. The association of a disparaged identity and the disabled body represent Hirsch's internalization of anti-Jewish prejudice and hatred. The author's disability serves as a marker of his own perceived inferiority. The text's discursive solution to this problem comes in the form of conversion. Hirsch's ability to recover from his illness seems to suggest that his disability – that is, his Jewishness – is not inherent to his character but is a disease that can be overcome, just like a deadly lung infection.

Upon his release from the hospital, Hirsch moves to a guesthouse on Riverside Drive whose residents are mostly German Jews. He hesitates to share his new-found faith with his neighbours, whom he suspects will not receive the news of his religious illumination with the same enthusiasm. Hirsch shows his fellow Jewish émigrés little mercy, indeed, his descriptions of them carry echoes of *völkisch* antisemitism and traditional Christian anti-Judaism:

> In the guesthouse resided the former doctor, the former lawyer, the once-successful merchant with all his familiar characteristics. They and their wives would never recognize that their banishment (*Austreibung*) was a punishment. They were not personally guilty, but there must have been guilt for which they needed to atone. These émigrés were full of hatred and rage towards their former homeland. They hoped for the decisive annihilation of their enemies, but they possessed no positive element in their being. They could not even fathom the fact that their existence was purely negative.[43]

Hirsch characterizes his Jewish neighbours through a series of anti-Jewish stereotypes. Their professions identify them as bourgeois city-dwellers, embodying the threatening qualities of modernity, materialism, and urbanity that were commonly coded as "Jewish" in the German cultural imagination. Hirsch merges this antimodern stereotype of Jewishness with the classical Christian depiction of the Jews as a "hard-necked" people who stubbornly refuse to recognize the divinity of Christ or their role in his death. Lacking a common belief, the only thing that unites these secular, faithless refugees is their shared misfortune. As

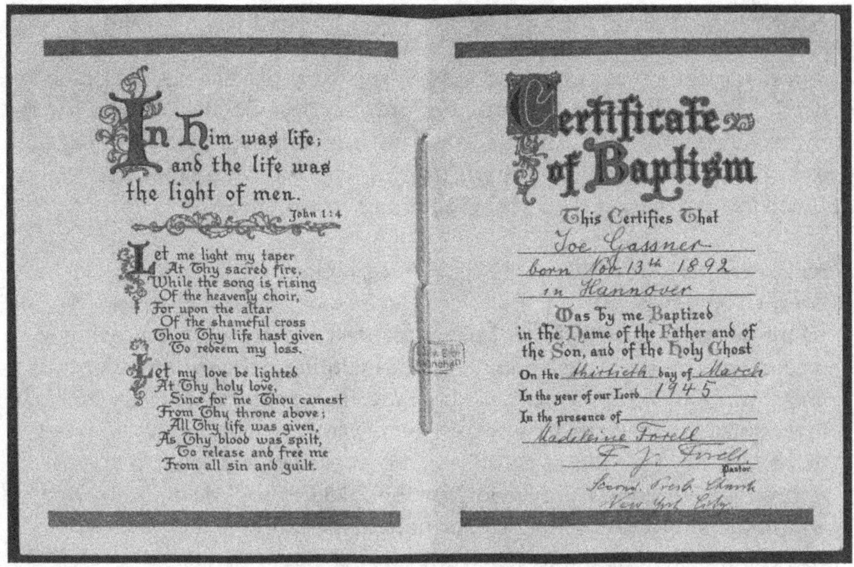


Figure 1.8.  Karl Jakob Hirsch's certificate of baptism (1945). Upon his arrival in the US, Hirsch changed his name to Joe Gassner. Nachlaß Karl Jakob Hirsch, Universitätsbibliothek der LMU München.

Hirsch's allusion to their "banishment" and "punishment" makes clear, it is the Jews' intergenerational responsibility for the crucifixion that renders them collectively and eternally guilty. Their historical suffering, of which the Nazi persecution is only the most recent manifestation, is part of their ongoing expiation for the crimes of their forefathers.

Alienated from the other Jewish exiles, Hirsch finds fellowship with Pastor Frederick Forell, a German-Jewish convert from Breslau. Forell started visiting Hirsch during his time in the hospital and continued to hold regular conversations with Hirsch after he was discharged. Forell conducted Hirsch's baptism in the Second Presbyterian Church in Manhattan on Good Friday of 1945. In the memoir, Hirsch credits Forell for patiently shepherding him towards the Christian truth without pressuring him to convert: "He never said that I needed to let myself be baptized. It was as if he was more concerned with my inner liberation than with my external confession."[44] Three years later, when Hirsch sat down to rewrite his life story, his portrayal of Forell would change dramatically.

On Good Friday of 1945, the day of his conversion, Hirsch goes to hear a performance of Bach's *St. Matthew Passion* in Carnegie Hall.

Hirsch writes that because he was going to be baptized by Pastor Forell that very evening, he knew "that this performance of the St. Matthew Passion would be experienced ... for the first time in its real significance."[45] In the past he had always appreciated Bach's *Passion* for its compositional genius, but this was the first time that he would truly grasp the sacred scriptural event underlying the oratorio – the drama of Christ's suffering. He explains that as a young man,

> religiosity played no role in my life. It was, so to speak, "past history" ... Even when I listened to the *St. Matthew Passion* or the *Christmas Oratorio* by Johann Sebastian Bach, I never realized that the sacred event they recounted was the decisive and significant thing, whereas the glorious music was only a supplement. At that time, it was natural for every music lover to listen to the Passions or the *Ninth Symphony* without caring about the text. Today I see this as an untruth, because how is it possible to experience the "Passion of the Savior" or the "Ode to Joy" as mere musical adornments? Overestimating the formal-artistic aspect of the composition was common among the so-called educated circles at that time.[46]

Hirsch's critique of the "so-called educated circles" taps into an antisemitic tradition of Wagnerian provenance, which faulted the Jews' cold and overly intellectual perception of music for their innate incapacity to fathom the spiritual depths of classical music.[47] Hirsch attributes his pre-Christian inability to grasp the true significance of Bach to the fact that he was too obsessed with the outer form of the work at the expense of its religious-liturgical content. This assertion is a variation of the idea that the Jew is incapable of accessing the inner essence of German high culture. This accusation is encapsulated in Richard Wagner's "Judaism in Music" (1850), in which the composer charges the Jew with being an outsider to the German creative spirit, and thus unable to comprehend the aesthetic and spiritual profundity of German culture. The Jew could mimic the outer form of this musical tradition but was incapable of truly participating in genuine artistic creation. For Wagner, composers of Jewish ancestry such as Giacomo Meyerbeer and Felix Mendelssohn were mere imitators who lacked the aesthetic and ethical sensibilities necessary for them to be an authentic part of the German artistic tradition.

Paul Lawrence Rose explains that Wagner's moralizing approach to the Jewish Question was a "secularized version of the Christian idea that 'the Jew' in every man's soul must be overcome by Christian feeling."[48] Hirsch's trajectory in the memoir subscribes to this logic: it is only through his conversion, that is, the eradication of his "inner Jew," that he overcomes his formalistically "Jewish" approach to music and is capable of genuine feeling, which allows him to plumb the spiritual profundities of Bach's Passions.

During the performance Hirsch undergoes a mystical experience. With the first words of the opening chorus, "Kommt, ihr Töchter, helft mir klagen," Hirsch finds himself transported beyond his immediate reality in New York. He imagines himself in the Garnisonkirche in Berlin, where he heard the Passion performed many times in the past. But this time it is different, because it is not a purely musical-aesthetic experience. This time every word seems to address his own personal fate. He recites the words, which he knows almost by heart, silently along with the performers. He feels as if he is hearing the piece for the first time, even though he had heard it performed almost every Easter.

Hirsch has an epiphany during the second part of the performance, when Pontius Pilate asks the Jewish mob whether he should release Jesus or Barabbas. Despite having heard the crowd's demand to crucify Christ many times in the past, Hirsch is "affected as never before."[49] As the choir sings the words of the Jewish mass demanding Christ's crucifixion, "His blood be upon us and on our children," Hirsch envisions the Jews tortured and murdered throughout the centuries. Although he does not spell it out, the image leaves little room for doubt: Jewish martyrdom is a punishment for deicide. With this understanding, he asserts: "I saw with growing clarity the path to redemption. It had been no escape; it was the way which God had ordered me to go."[50] What began with his feverish visions in the hospital became a reality. "I had found the path that led back, or rather, forward to God … I knew, as I listened to the music that I had finally found a path back to myself."[51] The musical experience serves as a prelude to his baptism later that evening: "When I felt the drops of water on my forehead, I knew that my life had taken on a new meaning. I had come to the end of a long journey, but I was not tired, I was fresh and ready to start on a new path. Pastor Forell asked me: 'Well, how do you feel?' But I answered, 'I don't think I was ever a better Jew than I am today!'"[52]

In recounting the story of his conversion, Hirsch juggles two seemingly contradictory assertions: he has both overcome and somehow preserved his Judaism. Such avowals of faith have a clear theological precedent in Christianity's ambivalent relationship to Judaism, which claims that it fulfils Judaism's religious message even while rendering it obsolete. The assertion that conversion to Christianity is a fuller realization of one's Judaism has been a familiar trope in Jewish conversion narratives going all the way back to Saint Paul. Yet Hirsch's case is also shaped by more immediate ideological concerns that have to do with the desire to appeal to his post-war German audience. To this end, Hirsch's self-presentation as a Jew who "fulfils" his Jewish calling by becoming a Christian works to erase the boundaries of Christian/Jewish difference and thereby blur the distinction between victim and perpetrator. The message of Hirsch's memoir is that the "good Jew" is in fact a Christian.

Half a year after his conversion, Hirsch returned to Germany, where he worked for the Americans as a supervisor of censorship in Munich. During his first year in Germany, Hirsch completed the memoir he had started writing after his conversion. The result, *Heimkehr zu Gott*, appeared with a small Munich-based publishing house, Kurt Desch, in 1946. In the summer of 1947, when his two-year contract with the US government ended, Hirsch reluctantly returned to the United States in order to put his affairs in order, before making his definitive homecoming to Germany in August 1948. Those miserable months Hirsch spent in the US strengthened his resolve to return to Germany as soon as possible. Except for his son, Hirsch's friends and relatives all turned their backs on him after learning of his conversion.[53] Ill, destitute, and unemployed, the fifty-five-year-old found accommodation in various rundown residential hotels and church-run shelters. In a letter to the composer Hans Heinz Stuckenschmidt, Hirsch complained that he was completely unable to bear the hatred he felt upon his return to the US in 1947. Jewish immigrants resented him, and he was similarly "goy-cotted" (*goy-kottiert*) by American publishing houses. "In short, it was not a 'homecoming to God' but rather a hell with all the comforts, except that I slowly but surely used up my savings, and now I am perhaps the poorest person in the richest country." He ends the letter with the exclamation, "The two years I spent in bombed out Germany have shown me once and for all where I belong." He added in English, "I am definitely too European and too German."[54]

Shortly after his return to Munich, Hirsch married Ruth Reinhart-Niemann, a secretary for the American Occupation Forces whom he had gotten to know during his previous stint in Germany. Hirsch held high hopes that his return to Germany would lead to the revival of his literary career. Too sick to type out his own work, the chronically ill Hirsch dictated his literary manuscripts to his devoted third wife. Over the next four years, every one of Hirsch's manuscripts was turned down. The publishers gave various excuses, decrying the lack of paper or the unpredictability of the book market following the currency reform of 1948. The truth was that post-war Germany was simply not interested in hearing from its wartime exiles, especially those identified with the left. Regarded as a left-wing émigré in a political climate that was growing ever more reactionary, Hirsch struggled to find an outlet that would publish his work. In 1951, one year before his death, he wrote to a friend that "I am completely ignored by all publishing houses, radio stations and newspapers, *just like in 1933*."[55]

## The Question of Jewish Guilt

One of the most troubling aspects of Hirsch's 1946 memoir is its disparaging portrayal of Jews and Judaism, which drew on both Christian-theological and modern-*völkisch* forms of antisemitism. This antisemitic dimension is not ancillary to Hirsch's story, but rather its defining feature. It serves as a foil for Hirsch's own self-fashioning as a born-again Christian and shapes the trajectory of the narrative, which is the story of a Jew transcending his "Jewishness." Hirsch resorts to the familiar antisemitic tropes of the modern German literary tradition in characterizing his pre-converted self as "selfish," "egotistical," and "self-centered."[56] His intellectual proclivities, individualism, and social detachment all mark him off as the prototypical Jewish urbanite. This antisemitic imagery signifies the contours of his spiritual transformation from agnostic Jew to believing Christian. This self-characterization strongly resonated with Hirsch's early German critics, who picked up on these tropes in their reviews. *Welt und Wort* hailed Hirsch's conversion as a turn away from "ego-centeredness" and "empty aestheticism," whereas *Das goldene Tor* described Hirsch's early artistic phase as steeped in "aesthetic egocentrism." Other critics characterized the pre-converted Hirsch as "subversive," "radical," and "metaphysically rootless."[57] These terms correspond to a coded language that identified Jewishness with the dislocations of modernity and associated the Jew with such phenomena as political radicalism, avant-garde aestheticism, agnostic-secularism, and crass materialism.

Hirsch's memoir, while ostensibly a straightforward account of one man's path to God, made ample use of an antisemitic "cultural code" that deployed the image of the soulless and superficial Jew as a foil for everything it identified as German.[58] One of the most conspicuous examples of this is Hirsch's depiction of the German-Jewish exiles in America. Upon arriving in New York, he realizes "how hopeless and backward the German-Jewish emigration was."[59] Hirsch portrays the Jewish émigrés as pitiful figures whose tragedy is a consequence of their spiritual deracination. "The Jews," he writes, "did not flee Europe to find God. They came to America and strove to Americanize themselves in the fastest way possible, not to unite as a Jewish people."[60] The German Jews are trapped between two worlds, belonging to neither one. Because of their secularity, they cannot integrate into the American Jewish community, which is largely descended from Eastern Europe, speaks Yiddish, and is still immersed in Judaism's religious traditions.

But they are also barred from fully assimilating into American society, which "was more hostile to Jews than had ever been the case in Europe."[61] If Hirsch's claim that American antisemitism was worse than its European counterpart comes across as highly dubious, it nevertheless captures something of the work's consistent effort to minimize the Holocaust and salve the German conscience.

Hirsch likens his fellow refugees to the walking dead, ambling the streets of New York without any purpose or connection to their present. The descriptions of the émigrés' "ghostly life" and "shadow existence" are remarkable for their lack of compassion or empathy.[62] His portrayal of the Jewish arrivals to America as anachronistic leftovers of a now-defunct world reverts to a mythical register in which they seem closer to Ahasverus, the wandering Jew, than contemporary survivors of a world catastrophe. The religious-metaphysical perspective that Hirsch takes in the memoir decontextualizes the political circumstances that forced them to immigrate to America. Instead, he presents their predicament as the outcome of some timeless curse.

In its medieval and modern manifestations, the myth of Ahasverus, the wandering Jew, represented the Jews as a ghost people, neither alive nor dead. Whereas the medieval Christian myth attributed the guilt of Ahasverus to his refusal to convert and recognize the divinity of Christ, nineteenth-century versions of the myth identified him with the lovelessness and egoism of modern-industrial life that was commonly identified as "Jewish." Hirsch draws on both these traditions in his disparaging depiction of the Jewish exiles. The image of a bitter and backward-looking community recalls the Christian critique of the Jews' obsolescence as a people, whose anachronistic religion had long ago been supplanted by the gospels' message of love. The exiles' predicament goes beyond their "ghost-like existence." They are also guilty of leading a loveless existence in their desire for vengeance.

> I was shocked to realize that there were few who had learned anything from the experience of suffering over the past twelve years other than what is called "retribution," It is natural to hate a murderer, but hatred in turn only gives rise to murder and misfortune. What is needed today is to find a policy that does not seek to avenge, but to make amends. One is almost ashamed to say the word "love" today, because it is the most misunderstood word in the language. Hate blinds, whereas love gives sight![63]

In this cynical reversal of historical events, Hirsch presents the Germans as the victims of blind Jewish hatred. Hirsch's religious rhetoric, which juxtaposes Jewish "vengefulness" with Christian "love," belies a more concrete political and historical issue, specifically the post-war question of German guilt and the Allied policy towards the defeated Germans. By contrasting Christian "love" and "forgiveness" with Jewish "hatred" and "vengeance," Hirsch addresses the controversy surrounding the Germans' accountability for the Nazi war crimes. The memoir takes aim at the call for retribution and suggests that the Allies' treatment of the German population is a continuation of Nazi violence. The analogy between Jewish vengefulness and the Allied policy feeds into the myth that "the Jews" are the ones pulling the strings behind the scenes in the Western occupation zone.

Hirsch justifies his conversion by delegitimizing contemporary forms of collective Jewish existence. According to Hirsch, "Zionism is not a path, but an escape, which has nothing to do with the inner perplexities of Judaism."[64] Hirsch's logic is as follows: since the collective identity of most surviving Jews today is founded on a sense of shared national belonging – an understanding that, having nothing to do with the Torah, radically departs from their religious moorings – the Jews no longer have a legitimate claim to peoplehood. Moreover, "the teaching of Sinai has since become a moral message in which the whole world believes."[65] Hirsch is essentially trying to argue the Jews as a collective entity out of existence. In his own words, "the 'Jewish question' is what the individual Jew conceives as his question."[66] The irony here is that after the Jews were persecuted as a collective, Hirsch is rejecting their right to peoplehood.

This point is expressed most emphatically in the memoir's final letter, where Hirsch writes:

Never did I feel a stronger sense of chosenness than on the night I rose from death to life. "My way as a Jew" is the title of this book, but it seems to me that it would be better and more accurate to call it "The way of the Jew." I experienced the necessity of salvation, which every Jew strives for. The Testament of Moses gives only law and not redemption. The Jew carelessly passed over the figure of the Redeemer; indeed, he delivered Christ to death. *This accursed path of the Jew from the cross in Golgotha to the gas chamber in Auschwitz must come to an end.* A people cannot be destined by the Creator to exist as victims over the course of millennia. Liberation cannot come from outside, no political power on earth is able to free the Jewish people from their curse. I know that what I am doing today is sacrilegious in the eyes of many believing Jews, but I am obsessed and obliged to do this because there is nothing else for me.[67]

This passage captures the gist of Hirsch's work, which argues that the guilt for the Holocaust lies not with the Germans, who were merely minor players in a larger divine drama that had been unfolding since the times of Christ, but with the Jews themselves, whose ghostly existence should have ended long ago. Jewish suffering at the hands of the Nazis was a consequence of the crucifixion and the Jews' subsequent refusal to recognize the divinity of Christ.[68]

This theological justification for the Jews' annihilation served to assuage German guilt regarding the recently publicized crimes committed against European Jewry. In Hirsch's account it is not the Germans who are guilty but the Jews themselves! Punished for its continuous and stubborn survival, this accursed and homeless nation is unredeemable. The Jews' only salvation rests in their conversion to Christianity. As Hirsch asserts, "Today I recognize that there is only one way to ameliorate the plight of the Jews."[69] The memoir offers a vision of "redemptive antisemitism," in which the desired death of Judaism does not take place through the physical annihilation of the Jews, but through their conversion to Christianity.[70]

Hirsch's narrative broached the Jewish fate under National Socialism in a manner that resonated strongly with its German readers. The Christian-theological vocabulary he invoked in order to account for his travails during the war echoed a broader post-war tendency to depoliticize the question of Germany's recent past by confronting it through a biblical lens. As Arendt put it, "The average German looks for the causes of the last war not in the acts of the Nazi regime, but in the events that led to the expulsion of Adam and Eve from Paradise."[71] One reason for the prevalence of such religious reckonings was the central role the Church assumed in German public life in the immediate aftermath of the war. After the Nazi defeat, Germany experienced an unprecedented religious revival, motivated by the search for material and spiritual relief.[72] The "re-Christianization" of the German populace after 1945 reflected a desire to return to more "traditional cultural values after the Nazi experiment."[73] On the assumption that the churches had not been tainted by Nazi ideology, the Allies saw them as potential partners in the process of de-Nazification and re-education.[74] The Protestant and Catholic clergy in western Germany thus played a decisive role in formulating the early post-war response to the horrors of the Holocaust and the crimes of the Nazi regime.

Confronting the question of German guilt was a delicate balancing act that required church leaders to address the recent past without alienating their parishioners, who came to them for spiritual solace. There was also a need to appease the Allies, who expected the Germans to acknowledge their collective responsibility for the crimes committed during the war. The Protestant clergy's confrontation with the *Schuldfrage* during the years of occupation was anything but consistent. It did, however, share in a particular vocabulary that allows us to make generalizations about the German Evangelicals' attitude towards the Holocaust after 1945. Scholars Jeffrey K. Olick and Matthew D. Hockenos note the recurring use of biblical language in the various sermons and declarations devoted to the Nazi past. In addressing the German persecution of European Jewry, Protestant clergy often invoked Christian theological figures of sin, suffering, and salvation. Common to many of their confessions of guilt was the resort to a metaphysically ambiguous language that failed to take the immediate political and social context of Nazism into account. Church leaders acknowledged that horrible crimes had been committed against the Jews, but in framing these transgressions in the language of Christian theology, they undermined their historical specificity. The question of the Germans' agency and accountability – as individuals and as a collective – was watered down and turned into a religious parable of temptation, divine judgment, and forgiveness.[75]

### *Mutter Maria*: Rewriting the Problem of Post-war Return

In the years following his return to Germany, Hirsch drafted a number of manuscripts that grappled with the question of his conversion and post-war return. Not one of these works found its way to print. One of his manuscripts, *Mutter Maria*, exemplifies the personal conflicts that haunted Hirsch in the final years of his life. The novella tells the story of a manipulative and controlling Jewish mother who obsesses over her only child, Aloysius. She is deported to Theresienstadt during the Nazi era, yet miraculously survives the war, returning to her home town in 1945. Maria reunites with her son and daughter-in-law, both of whom were spared deportation but were discriminated against as half-Jews under Nazi law. In contrast to the optimistic Aloysius and Franziska, who have put the war behind them and look forward towards the future, Maria is incapable of resuming her pre-war life. After returning from the concentration camps, she struggles to maintain even the most superficial relationship. Casual conversations make her uneasy. She feels like "a ghost to the people around her" and suspects that all expressions of kindness and warmth from the town's inhabitants are motivated by her interlocutors' guilty conscience and condescending pity.

Before the war, Mutter Maria sought to dissuade her son from leaving her to pursue his university studies in a neighbouring city. After returning from the camps, she again tries to insinuate herself into his life. Surprising the young couple in their home in Erlangen, she announces that she will be living with them permanently. Aloysius and Franziska want to move on with their lives, but the haunting presence of Mutter Maria prevents them from doing so. Upon first arriving in Erlangen to join her son, Maria is disappointed to see so little destruction.[76] In contrast to her son, who is set on rebuilding his life, Maria is consumed with rage and resentment. Having survived Theresienstadt, she tells herself, "I have no more past, no present and perhaps no future."[77] Unable to fall asleep at night, she tosses and turns restlessly as images of moaning Jews crowded together flash before her eyes and the monotonous chant of the Shema prayer recited by an old rabbi echoes in her ears.

Maria exists in a permanent state of grievance and contempt, whose full extent emerges in a heated conversation with Herr Weinzierl, her son's landlord, a good-natured, apolitical German. Over a glass of wine in Herr Weinzierl's living room, Maria accuses the Germans of "self-deception," of wanting to shirk their responsibility for the crimes they committed against the Jews. She is enraged that no one will talk to her about the past. "It often seems to me … that most people in Germany have already forgotten … No one flinches when I say the name Theresienstadt … Six million Jews were killed … But when you start talking about it today, people all say: 'Just be quiet. We didn't know anything about it. How could we?'"[78]

Upset by the uncomfortable topic, Herr Weinzierl asks Maria why she insists on dredging up the past instead of focusing on the present. He protests that the Germans too suffered horrifically during the war. Maria objects to this disingenuous defence, pointing out that while the Germans mourned their dead, they never acknowledged the wrongs committed against her people:

> One is not allowed to speak about the fact that we suffered, that we were tortured and died. I must defend myself against this inhumanity. I know the names of the people who tortured and tormented us in Theresienstadt. I recently learned that one of them now plays a big role again. Do you know what I could do? I could go there and murder him. You have to take revenge, you have to accuse, when you see how injustice is still rewarded.[79]

Maria's appeal to revenge is a protest against the inhuman burden of silence that was imposed on her by the Germans. She is frustrated that the houses, churches, and schools in Erlangen are still standing and that the city bears no hint of destruction of the magnitude the Germans inflicted upon the Jews.

Herr Weinzierl takes Maria's hands and urges her to once again embrace life. "You have to decide whether to live or to mourn the past. You cannot bring the dead back to life ... While you and thousands of others suffered injustice, most Germans knew nothing, nothing at all."[80] In response to her heated tirade against the German people and her burning desire for revenge, he can only offer these words: "You are Jewish. I understand your agitation. But it's all over now."[81] But it is not *all over* for Maria. Her resentment is a revolt against the obtuse reactions of good-natured Germans of Herr Weinzierl's ilk, who fail to acknowledge her suffering or their responsibility for it. The encounter with the survivors is a mere inconvenience for the Germans, who would rather avoid the recent past. "Jawohl, Herr Weinzierl, we returnees are like ghosts you don't like to see."[82]

Maria embodies the resentment and vindictiveness that post-war Germans associated with returning Holocaust victims. The spectre of the vengeful Jew (*der rachesüchtige Jude*) that haunted Germany during the immediate post-war era was a cipher for the unacknowledged premonitions of shame and guilt over the Holocaust.[83] While violent acts of vengeance were exceptionally rare, their predominance in the German popular imagination bespoke a broader sense of insecurity and fear that came in the wake of defeat.[84] The fear that returning Holocaust survivors would exact revenge on their former persecutors was a natural continuation of the Third Reich ideology that saw the Jews as internal enemies of the state. This irrational angst, Frank Biess explains, functioned on psychic and political levels:

> Fear served both as a veiled expression of guilt and as a defense mechanism against it. On the one hand, the extensive knowledge of Nazi crimes and hence a clear sense of guilt were among the causes of fear. Yet, on the other hand, private and public articulations of fear and anxiety may also have blocked a more extensive self-reflection and admission of guilt. The real and imagined consequences of this guilt might have appeared as too catastrophic to many Germans. In this way, the anticipation of a largely fictional catastrophe in an imagined future blocked a more extensive confrontation with the actual catastrophe that Germans had helped to bring about.[85]

Hirsch's portrayal of Mutter Maria resonates with this post-war German fantasy of the unforgiving, vindictive Jew. Mutter Maria is an unsympathetic, cold, and controlling woman. At the same time, this wrathful Jewish mother, unable to let go of the crimes committed against her people, channels the author's own suppressed resentment as a postwar returnee. The struggle between the mother, consumed by rage and possessed by ressentiment, and the son, who is filled with optimism for the future and is set on rebuilding his life in the new Germany, mirrors Hirsch's own moral and psychic conflict in the years following his remigration. Like Aloysius, Hirsch wanted to rebuild his life in the Federal Republic and put the experience of Nazi persecution behind him. At the same time, Hirsch was shocked by the Germans' moral indifference to the Holocaust and devastated by his failed attempts to find an audience for his work.

Mutter Maria ventriloquizes the sentiments of rage and resentment that were never expressed in the author's homecoming conversion narrative. She also seems to speak for the Jewish past that continued to claim its hold over Hirsch. When Aloysius shares his plans to resume his legal studies in Erlangen, his mother lashes out at him: "Are you leaving me alone here? Is this why I came back from Theresienstadt? I endured everything for this?"[86] The mother's accusation of abandonment could equally be directed at Hirsch, who dissociated himself from Judaism in order to rebuild his life as a Christian in the Federal Republic. Mutter Maria is a cipher for the Jewish past that continued to haunt Hirsch after his conversion and remigration.

The work's title clearly suggests that the novella's eponymous protagonist stands in some relation to Mary, mother of Jesus. In the story, Aloysius's absent father evokes the virgin birth. Yet whereas Jesus is purged of his ties to carnal Israel through his virgin birth, Aloysius remains a son of Israel according to the flesh. The allusion to Saint Mary captures something of Hirsch's intractable anxiety over his Jewish origins. As Susannah Heschel notes, Christianity's ambivalence about its Jewish origins finds its expression in the figure of Mary, whose virgin womb represents the desire to preserve Christianity from "Jewish penetration."[87] For Hirsch, the baptized Jew, the virgin birth constitutes a powerfully suggestive symbol for his own yearning to distance himself from his former Jewish self.

The relationship between Maria, the fictional Holocaust survivor, and the mother of God is one of ironic inversion. In the novella's final scene, Mutter Maria can barely suppress her joy over the death of her daughter-in-law shortly after childbirth. The story ends as she secretly rejoices, "Maria knew only one thing, something that made her shiver with happiness. She knew that now she would have her son all to herself. Forever."[88] This selfish and egotistical Maria stands in sharp contrast to the selfless and sorrowful Mary of the Stabat Mater and Mater

Figure 1.9.  Karl Jakob Hirsch, *Josef und Maria* (1923). Nachlaß Karl Jakob Hirsch, Universitätsbibliothek der LMU München.

Dolorosa, who weeps for her son under the cross. The controlling Jewish mother, who wants her son all to herself, is juxtaposed to the saintly mother, who willingly accepts the sacrifice of her son for the sake of humanity. The implied juxtaposition of the possessive Jewish mother and the altruistic mother of Jesus rehearses the anti-Jewish trope that contrasts the Jews' stubborn, jingoistic particularism to Christianity's inclusive universalism.

There are strong antisemitic undertones to Hirsch's novella. It taps into both traditional theological motifs of Jewish tribalism and post-war German fears of the returning Holocaust survivor. If *Mutter Maria* continues the anti-Jewish conceit we already found in *Heimkehr*, when read as an ego-document, it adds a certain level of complexity to our understanding of Hirsch that was absent from the memoir. The mother/son conflict gives voice to an internal struggle that raged in Hirsch's soul, in that he was caught between his loyalty to a disavowed Jewish past and his desire for reinvention as a German Christian. *Mutter Maria* undeniably corroborated the antisemitic image of the returning survivor, filled with hate and resentment towards the German people. But it also drew a compelling psychological portrait of the sources that fed this resentment, depicting the desire for revenge as a desperate cry for recognition. That Maria's indictment of the Germans voiced Hirsch's own convictions becomes clear when we examine his autobiography *Quintessenz meines Lebens*.

**Defeat and Deconversion: Hirsch's Final Years**

In 1946 Hirsch tried to reinvent himself in post-war Germany by writing what was ostensibly the story of his religious and spiritual transformation but in reality was a deeply antisemitic work. In its fuzzy religious rhetoric, *Heimkehr zu Gott* offered an easy-to-consume exculpatory response to the question of German guilt. Despite his attempts to pander to German audiences, Hirsch's career did not stand a chance in the reactionary political climate of Cold War West Germany, which held his pre-war socialist past against him.[89] In 1949, a mere three years after the publication of *Heimkehr*, Hirsch completed another autobiographical work, titled *Quintessenz meines Lebens*. Posthumously published forty-one years after its composition, *Quintessenz* presented a radically different perspective on Hirsch's life than the one found in *Heimkehr*.

Literary historian Helmut Pfanner speculates that Hirsch wrote another account of his life soon after publishing his 1946 memoir because of a critique he received from Alfred Döblin, a fellow writer and wartime convert to Christianity.[90] In a letter to Hirsch, Döblin compliments *Heimkehr*, describing it as a "beautiful document," and adding that

> this little book speaks far too much of external matters and says too little about your internal development. The external events are not the issue, but rather how they were experienced and formulated within … I suppose you will write the book again after some time, starting not with your life, that is, the story of your birth, childhood, etc., … but with the central issues you confronted during your decisive years.[91]

Contrary to Pfanner's interpretation, it appears that the main motivation that drove Hirsch to rewrite his life story was not the critique of a fellow writer but a radical change of perspective regarding post-war Germany, his literary prospects, and his own religious commitments. Although it offers a longer, more comprehensive account of Hirsch's life, the autobiography lacks the thematic coherence and literary flare of his memoir. It also gives vent to a far more pessimistic and cynical Hirsch, who directs his sanctimonious ire at West Germany's political hypocrisy and criticizes its subservience to Western capitalism. Hirsch excoriates West Germany for failing to confront its Nazi past, suppressing free speech, and serving as a vassal state for the US. The Nazi dictatorship, he contends, had simply been replaced by the totalitarianism of the Western Bloc.

Hirsch raised none of these issues in his 1946 memoir. His belated condemnation of Germany's shifty response to its Nazi past suggests that Hirsch's allegations were not motivated exclusively by his political conscience but were also an expression of his personal disappointment at failing to re-establish himself as a writer in post-war West Germany. The indignation and regret that pervades Hirsch's autobiography can be discerned in its opening lines, when Hirsch only half-jokingly confesses that he considered giving it the subtitle "I almost became something" (*Beinahe wäre etwas aus mir geworden*).[92]

The story of a redeemed Jew, graced by the glory of the Christian God, gave way to a bleak account of personal and political disillusionment. In *Heimkehr*, Hirsch enumerated the virtues of Christian love and forgiveness. In *Quintessenz*, he sought to settle scores with the newly established Federal Republic. The Christian message vaunted in *Heimkehr* all but disappears from *Quintessenz*, which replaces the author's earlier search for redemption in Christ with a staunch avowal of socialism. Disenchanted with West Germany's conservative political bent and its oppressive cultural taboos, Hirsch now sets his eyes on a new promised

Figure 1.10.  Photograph of Karl Jakob Hirsch in US passport (1941). Nachlaß Karl Jakob Hirsch, Universitätsbibliothek der LMU München.

land: the German Democratic Republic. *Heimkehr zu Gott* told the story of Hirsch's turn to Christianity, a narrative that resorted to religion in order to communicate its author's desire for another kind of homecoming, his *Heimkehr nach Deutschland*. If the Christianity professed in *Heimkehr* prepared the ground for Hirsch's return to the West, *Quintessenz* made a political pledge of allegiance to the East. The author's avowal of Christian faith only three years earlier was retracted and replaced with a renewed affirmation of his socialist convictions.[93]

*Quintessenz* is divided into three parts, of uneven literary quality and style. The first section offers an elaborate version of Hirsch's life from birth to his 1945 return to Germany; the second, written in the form of a diary, focuses on his first two years in Germany between the summer of 1945 and 1947; the third covers the years 1947 to 1949, beginning with the abysmal year he spent back in the US after his two-year stint in Munich, and follows his definitive return to Germany in August 1948. The third part ends with an extensive critique of the West German political landscape. The most noticeable difference between *Heimkehr* and *Quintessenz* is the shift in ideological orientation, reflected in Hirsch's identification as a socialist and a political supporter of East Germany. We are left to speculate whether Hirsch had decided to reveal his true political colours because he felt he had nothing left to lose or whether he opted for this oppositional stance in response to his rejection by the West German cultural establishment. He acknowledges his transformation with this assertion: "Today I see my life differently than I did four years ago."[94] This change is readily apparent in the socialist perspective he adopts in the autobiography, which substitutes the discourse of religious faith that pervaded his previous memoir. This time around Hirsch accounts for his life as a manifestation of a class-bound "social type" and characterizes his life course from a sociological vantage point. "I was the son of a bourgeois, sophisticated family, brought up without a clue that one had to pay for all things in life ... I was spoiled."[95]

Hirsch reiterates the narrative of German Jewry's pre-war "faithlessness," but in this version the agnosticism of his Jewish milieu is not the problem, but its desire to seamlessly merge with the German bourgeoisie, an expression of its false-consciousness: "The traditional piety was preserved in external terms. But in reality, my father was already a product of that enlightened age which believed in nothing it could not see ... The situation of the bourgeois Jews in Germany was hopeless. They did not grumble aloud, they endured being denied officer and state positions, they all had only one goal: assimilation."[96]

In his 1946 memoir, Hirsch differentiated between the authentic piety of his family and the superficiality of Jewish observance he encountered outside the home. In the second take on his life, Hirsch includes his father among the godless. There are numerous inconsistencies between the two versions of Hirsch's life story, but this particular one can be attributed to the shift in emphasis. The question of faith is subordinate to that of class-consciousness in *Quintessenz*. Pre-war Jewry is faulted, not for its perfunctory observance of an outdated religious tradition or its atavistic guilt, but for its failure to see beyond its narrow class interests and align itself with the progressive political forces that would have prevented the Nazi takeover.

Hirsch illustrates this missed opportunity through a "tragi-comic" anecdote about his father. People of his parents' social class typically regarded the Social Democrats as "subversive" (*umstürzlerisch*).

Figure 1.11. Photograph of Karl Jakob Hirsch in Worpswede (1929). Nachlaß Karl Jakob Hirsch, Universitätsbibliothek der LMU München.

Despite his ostensible aversion to socialism, Hirsch's father once decided to attend a Social Democratic meeting in which August Bebel was slated to be the main speaker – an act that was very rare for someone of Dr. Hirsch's social class. Whatever the reason was that drove Dr. Hirsch to attend the Social Democratic assembly that day, his visit remained short, because just as the gathering was about to convene, a man came to the podium announcing that there was an urgent call for Dr. Hirsch and that he was needed by one of his patients.[97] Hirsch's father never got to hear August Bebel because of a medical emergency. The anecdote serves as a metaphor for the potential alliance that could have been made between the Jewish bourgeoisie of Dr. Salomon Hirsch's generation and that of the working class at the turn of the twentieth century.

In the second account of his life, the "Jewish tragedy" is no longer a consequence of the Jews' collective guilt as Christ killers, but rather of socialism's failure in the years preceding the Nazi power-grab. The problem begins with "the separation between the bourgeoisie and the working class."[98] Bourgeois individualism prevented Jews of his background from truly recognizing the class conflict taking place in the years leading up to the First World War: "We went in circles around our own ego while people around us struggled and fought for their right to live."[99] Yet as the spoiled offspring of the bourgeoisie, "we could not have acted otherwise. We were the heirs to a worldview that no longer existed. We artists never understood how to meet the needs of the masses."[100] In his 1946 memoir, Hirsch presented Jews as an anachronistic people clinging to a superseded religion. This conceit is preserved in the 1949 autobiography, only that the anachronism the Jews are guilty of this time around is that of their false class-consciousness. Members of his generation failed to see that the class they considered their own no longer existed.

This problem manifests itself in the aesthetic outlook that Hirsch shared with his Jewish contemporaries. As children of the upper middle-class, members of Hirsch's generation fled to an aesthetic realm that had little to do with politics. Their revolt against the bourgeoisie was a superficial gesture of bad faith.

> Our life was a protest, but we took our dependence on the bourgeoisie for granted … We were "radicals," but only in art, not in life. I remember very well that at that time I had the dark premonition that a conflict would arise from the contradiction between artistic will and bourgeois life. I only suspected it; I could not describe it exactly. Today I know it much better, it is very clear to me. We were the offspring of rich bourgeois parents that claimed for itself the jester's privilege of ridiculing the institutions of the bourgeoisie.[101]

Hirsch viewed himself as a "pure artist," but one who was naively unaware that he owed his artistic freedom to his privileged bourgeois upbringing and to the fact that he did not threaten the societal status quo. The political indifference of his class of artists manifested itself in the fact that they "lived on the fringes of the bourgeoisie without wanting to intrude into the life of the proletariat."[102] This indifference transformed into a superficial form of aesthetic activism in 1918, when Hirsch and his colleagues joined the November Revolution. In retrospect, Hirsch judges his involvement writing political manifestos and designing revolutionary placards as empty gestures: "Only a few of us thought of joining the socialist parties at that time. We thus remained isolated, and our radicalism was a purely private affair."[103] Thirty years after the fact, Hirsch deplores his noncommittal participation in the November Revolution. He compares his failure to "reach the people" to what transpired in Russia, "where modern art was brought to the people, not only pretending to be revolutionary but actualizing itself in reality."[104] Things were quite different in Germany, where "revolutionary art" was merely lip service paid to the proletariat and funded by the well-established elites. "My affiliation with the Social Democratic Party was only an outward formality, for in reality the former revolutionaries feared the 'radicalism' which they suspected in every intellectual."[105]

The socialist orientation Hirsch takes in *Quintessenz* also leads to a radically different account of the circumstances surrounding his conversion to Protestantism. In this second take on his conversion, Hirsch explains that his illness was a manifestation of an inner crisis caused by the fact that he had been forced to suppress his artistic and political views, which were considered too radical by the Social Democratic *Neue Volkszeitung*. From his present vantage point, Hirsch rationalizes his turn to Christianity as an attempt to reconcile the conflict between his inner convictions and the political compromises he was forced into by external circumstances.[106] He no longer speaks of the gift of divine grace but takes a much cooler and distant tone when accounting for his conversion: "Today I understand it better than I did at the time. I clung to the concept of God, to the appearance of the Saviour, because I fervently hoped that this would allow me to harmonize outer and inner things."[107] He no longer speaks of God, but of the "*concept* of God" and the "*appearance* of the saviour."[108] This cool-headed account also leads to a complete reassessment of his relationship with Pastor Forell. Hirsch explains that he was so devastated by the dissolution of his marriage, the hardships of emigration, and poverty that "any person could have done with me what he wanted."[109] Pastor Forell helped him at his time of need, but he did so with the ulterior motive of bringing him into the Christian fold and adding him to the ranks of his church.[110]

Hirsch seems to walk back his conversion, or at any rate minimize its significance by attributing it to his fragile and impressionable state at the time. For safe measure, he also reinterprets the turn to Christianity as a displaced expression of "my artistic spirit and the desire to devote myself to a greater cause."[111] He downplays the religious significance of his conversion, explaining that it was the result of a misguided effort to give voice to his true artistic and political commitments: "I know that by the grace of a divine power I gained clarity about some things ... But I did not see at the time that my desire was clouding my vision. I heard the music of the divine in me and thought I could hear it again in the words of the clergyman. That was my error."[112]

He may have been graced by God, but this was a completely subjective experience that he mistakenly identified with his Protestant pastor. In the final count, Hirsch asserts that his embrace of Christianity was nothing more than a reaffirmation of his interwar socialist convictions.

How, he asks, could anyone mistake Christ's Sermon on the Mount for anything but what it truly was: a proclamation of social solidarity by a revolutionary bent on remaking the social and economic relations in his society!

In an apologetic effort to clarify the misunderstanding caused by his conversion four years earlier, Hirsch writes:

> The break with my past life as a Jew felt particularly strange. But I did not see things then as I do today, namely that my step toward Christianity was nothing more than a reiteration of my unswerving commitment to socialism, a position I first avowed in 1918. Today it seems clear to me that I correctly understood the figure of the Redeemer ... At the time I hardly comprehended it, but inwardly I knew it ... When I was baptized, I assumed that all Christians realized that Jesus of Nazareth was not only a revolutionary who turned against the tradition of conservative Judaism, but also the proclaimer of a new and active way of life, who refused to turn his back on human suffering.[113]

Authors of conversion narratives often make use of an anticipatory logic that frames their past in light of their present, imbuing it with new meaning. Transformative moments that may have been misunderstood at the time of their occurrence, or only comprehended as a vague premonition, take on their full meaning once the convert reaches his or her state of grace. From the perspective of ineluctable belief, past events become necessary stages on a predetermined path leading to God. This narrative logic was readily apparent in Hirsch's 1946 memoir. It is also there in Hirsch's 1949 autobiography, only that in this case, Hirsch deploys this anticipatory logic to retract and reshape the original meaning he attributed to his religious conversion three years prior. The true, belated significance of Christianity here is as a displaced expression of socialism.

Several of Hirsch's essays from the late 1940s reflect a persistent effort to reconcile his Christian faith with his socialist and Marxist convictions. In "Marxismus und Religiosität" he accuses the Church of distorting the figure of the Messiah. Were Jesus the "soft-hearted, submissive person depicted by the Church, the Jewish fascists would never have handed him over to the Roman military."[114] Hirsch's Jesus is an angry, militant prophet, a champion of the poor and the dispossessed, who revolts against social and economic injustice. Distancing himself from institutionalized Christianity, Hirsch urges believers to purge Christ's teachings of their Roman Catholic and Lutheran accretions so as to restore them to their "original splendor."[115] Hirsch's essay represents a new stage in his evolution as a Christian. It reflects Hirsch's disaffection with the Church, which failed to provide him with the social support and belonging he yearned for when he converted. Jesus is transformed from a source of comfort and consolation, the role he played in *Heimkehr*, into a combative social revolutionary. This metamorphosis is both a throwback to Hirsch's interwar communism and an expression of his progressive identification with the German Democratic Republic after being shunned by the West Germans. Despite the antisemitic references to "Jewish fascists," Hirsch attempts to reconcile his Christian faith with his Jewish ancestry by asserting that Christ's message grew out of the Mosaic social teachings. Both church and synagogue are guilty of falsifying and distorting this common lineage, which Hirsch's Jewish-Christian-Socialist identity recovers. "That Judaism and Christianity are at odds is only because the Jews have always refused to see in the carpenter's son the redeemer and perfecter of the Jewish doctrine."[116]

The final section of *Quintessenz* constituted an elaborate indictment of the nascent Federal Republic and the West German political system. Two years after resettling in West Germany, Hirsch takes stock of his failed attempt to find his place both politically and professionally. He writes: "Today I no longer delude myself; I can see clearly. There is the German Democratic Republic and the occupied part of Germany, which is becoming more regressive and constricted by the day. Because of my illness, I was forced to postpone the practical consequence of this insight."[117] He criticizes the conspiracy of silence surrounding the Holocaust and the Third Reich, writing how an article he submitted to a West German newspaper was rejected by the editor-in-chief, who told him that "we don't want to hear any more remarks against Hitler, our audience has had enough of it."[118] The coyness surrounding West Germany's recent Nazi past and its staunch anti-communist bent constricted Hirsch's freedom of expression and the topics he could touch, to the point that "even mention of Adolf Hitler's little mustache ... was considered too 'embarrassing' by editors of Western newspapers."[119] This event repeated itself when one of his manuscripts was turned down by a publisher, who commented that Hirsch could not judge the Germans because he had not lived in Germany between 1933 and 1945.[120]

Hirsch's archive is replete with rejection letters from presses, newspapers, film studios, and radio stations turning down his manuscripts and requests for employment.[121] Dr. Moritz Hauptmann, the editor of Harriet Schleber Verlag, rejected Hirsch's manuscript *Flucht in die Heimat*, explaining that "you surely know this yourself, the readers from 1930 no longer exist. They either emigrated, died or were corrupted.

Today's youth is completely different."[122] The editor for *Die Deutsche Woche* complimented Hirsch's writing but turned down his work, explaining that his writing was out of touch with the current German and European situation due to his long sojourn in America. "Your point of departure remains that of an author, whose opinions and relations were formed during the Weimar Republic. These conditions no longer exist."[123] Reimund Schnabel of the Bayrischer Rundfunk returned Hirsch's manuscript under the pretext that it was too American.[124]

It was only after Hirsch lost all prospects of publishing his work that he found the courage to criticize the West Germans and point to the parallels between their reactionary tendencies and those that preceded Hitler's rise to power:

> Who are the readers who are so sensitive that they cannot bear the mention of a regime that has produced only misery and sorrow? They are precisely the same people who existed in such frightening numbers in 1932, the so-called "apoliticals," who were indifferent to everything except for the concern that the Weimar Republic was slipping too far to the left ... Today I see that the catastrophe to which this western part of Germany is headed is not only the fault of the occupation, but also the complicity of the majority of the Germans, who put up with Hitler for over a decade ... Today it has become fashionable to blame others for the decline of the German spirit. In reality, the petty-bourgeois elements in Germany are progressively rising to the surface ... and will soon lead this country again ... The frightening thing about the present state of affairs in the Western part of Germany is that the next catastrophe seems inevitable.[125]

The conditions that contributed to the success of his 1946 memoir were also responsible for his subsequent failure to find common ground with the post-war German readership. *Heimkehr zu Gott* succeeded because it whitewashed the Holocaust with its religious-metaphysical rhetoric of universal human guilt and its antisemitic intimations. Hirsch's work pandered to the prejudices of his German audience, depicting his fellow German Jews as loveless beings who nurtured feelings of hatred and vengefulness towards their former landsmen. The memoir's enthusiastic reception can be attributed to the fact that it was a Jewish-authored text that exculpated the Germans for the Holocaust. It accused the Jews and the Allies of vindictiveness and called for reconciliation and forgiveness in the spirit of Christ.[126] Yet it seems that after Hirsch pardoned the Germans, they no longer had much use for him. Like other left-wing Jewish émigré-intellectuals who returned after the war to a very cold welcome, Hirsch found himself isolated, "just like in 1933." As Hirsch carped in *Quintessenz*, "It became clearer to me from day to day that a left-wing or even socialist emigrant was a phenomenon that was in no way desired."[127] Hirsch's utter disappointment with the conservative political climate under Konrad Adenauer led him to consider one final move – immigration to the German Democratic Republic.[128] It is unlikely that he would have found the recognition he was looking for in East Germany, but this fantasy was in any case unfeasible, since by that point Hirsch was too sick to leave his apartment, let alone immigrate to another country. Hirsch died in July 1952, one month after his German citizenship was restored.

# Chapter Two

# The Suppressed Jewish Voice in Alfred Döblin's *Schicksalsreise* (1949)

In an undated letter from the early 1950s, Erna Döblin sought to confront her husband, the celebrated modernist author Alfred Döblin (1878–1957), with the unpleasant facts of his "homecoming" to postwar West Germany:

> You have always been a Jew. You will never be able to deny this fact since your racial affiliation is written on your face. Spiritually speaking, you consider yourself a Christian, rather than saying: "I was born a Jew, I must thus remain one, the Jews must be my community" … You were forced to flee in '33 so as not to be killed by the Germans. You then had to flee from the Germans again to America in '40. You were able to return to Germany and work there after the war solely by virtue of your French citizenship. You are published thanks only to your official position. Most Germans don't even know your name. Everything you have now, you owe to the French. The Germans could well have been your murderers, just as they murdered your son, your brother and millions of others … I am horrified that you don't understand this and feel yourself to be a German again … You can go on telling everyone that you were born a German and a Jew, it makes no difference.[1]

Erna wrote this belligerent letter as part of an ongoing campaign to convince her husband to leave Germany and return to Paris, where the couple had lived between 1933 and 1940, when the Nazi invasion of France forced the family to uproot again and immigrate to the United States. She reprimands her husband for trying to strike new roots in a country that murdered his relatives and would have done the same to him had he not escaped in time. One of their four sons, Wolfgang, a promising mathematician, died fighting the Nazi invasion in French uniform. Erna felt that resettling in Germany was a desecration of his memory. Döblin's "return," she pointedly argued, was realized through the suppression of his Jewish roots. That his books even appeared in post-war Germany did not attest to his growing German readership; it was only due to his official role in the French military administration.

Erna's harsh allegations run counter to the autobiographical account of exile and return that her husband published in 1949 Germany, under the title *Schicksalsreise. Bericht und Bekenntnis*. Döblin's wartime memoir transforms the story of his exile from and return to Germany into a conversion narrative, one that follows the author's path to Catholicism. Curiously absent from the memoir is any mention of antisemitism or the fate of Döblin's extended family during the Holocaust. One suspects that Döblin's focus on the interior drama of faith was meant to sidestep the matter of his Jewishness and the thorny subject of Germany's moral burden, issues that would have hindered his reintegration in post-war West Germany.

Despite his conspicuous silences with regard to the Holocaust, Döblin could not eschew his past altogether. Thus, although the returning author sought to frame his fate during the Nazi years as a personal trial of faith that led him to Christian salvation, the narrative did not hold. *Schicksalsreise* is deeply mired in the problem of national identity and belonging that had haunted Döblin since 1933. Döblin's efforts to suppress the Jewish dimension of his wartime experience notwithstanding, the personal and political predicament of a Jewish émigré's homecoming to Germany filters through the narrative's focus on the author's path to faith.

Döblin tries to fit his wartime experience into the Christian theological and literary template of conversion, but this attempt fails because the external political realities he sought to suppress continued to haunt his narrative. The conversion conceit was meant to serve as the foundation for a coherent and continuous self that would bridge the discontinuities and displacements of the years 1933 to 1945. Yet Döblin's concerted effort to dissociate his wartime experiences from the collective Jewish trauma renders his memoir a rhetorically flawed work. *Schicksalsreise* is marked by its complicit silence with regard to the Holocaust and its author's inability to mourn. Labouring under the dictate of self-censorship, Döblin failed to construct a coherent textual identity. Instead, it is a memoir plagued by thematic inconsistencies and stylistic disjunctures, which reflect the author's inability to find closure through conversion.

Figure 2.1.  Photograph of Alfred Döblin (1930). Leo Baeck Institute, New York.

## Assimilation, Exile, and Jewish Awakening

Born in Stettin in 1878, Alfred was the fourth of five children. His parents, Max Döblin and Sophie Freudenheim, both came from assimilated Jewish homes. The marriage was an unhappy one. Max, a tailor by training, established a series of unsuccessful businesses and failed to live up to the expectations of his wife. In 1888, Max abandoned his wife and five children, immigrating to New York with an employee twenty years his junior. He left the family with a failed tailor's shop that was deep in debt. Lacking any financial prospects in Stettin, Sophie was forced to move to Berlin with her five children, where she relied on her brother's support. The father's abandonment and the family's sudden fall from middle-class respectability were the defining experiences of Döblin's childhood. Despite the adverse circumstances, Döblin managed to obtain an education and go to medical school. After specializing in neurology and psychiatry, he opened his own medical practice in a poor, working-class neighbourhood in east Berlin.

From the 1910s until his hasty departure from Germany in 1933, Döblin led a double life as a physician by day and a writer by night. His literary breakthrough came with the 1916 publication of *Die drei Sprünge des Wang-Lun*, which appeared with S. Fischer Verlag. During the First World War, Döblin volunteered to serve as a military physician in the Lorraine region. After the war, Döblin published a string of novels, *Wadzeks Kampf mit der Dampfturbine* (1918), *Wallenstein* (1920), *Berge Meere und Giganten* (1924), and *Berlin Alexanderplatz* (1929), that enshrined him in the pantheon of literary modernism alongside John Dos Passos and James Joyce.

Although Döblin grew up in a Jewish home, Judaism held a negligible place in his upbringing. His parents' ritual observance involved no more than biannual visits to the synagogue for Rosh Hashanah and Yom Kippur. At school, Alfred received little religious education and acquired only the rudiments of Hebrew. In a ten-page handwritten essay unpublished during his lifetime, Döblin writes that for two or three years he received "some kind of Jewish religious education, but it was not obligatory, so mostly one did not go. It was a boring lesson in which one used to do one's homework in mathematics."[2] Reminiscences of his bar mitzvah, or "confirmation" (*Einsegnung*), crystallize his sense of estrangement:

> Then, however, I enjoyed half a year of monstrous preparation for my confirmation. If the lessons at school were a farce, this "preparation" was a disgrace. The "teacher" was the rabbi of a small synagogue, naturally a good and pious man. The necessary Hebrew verses were given to us in Latin script, along with their translation. We learned them by heart, and then we were given the transcript of a confirmation speech ... This five-page speech was filled with meaningless and moralizing pieties, ornamented with quotations, which we were to deliver to our guests, who were already prepared for it. This nonsense had to be learned by heart, and that was the main purpose of my bar mitzvah lessons. This is how one was accepted into the congregation of Israel.[3]

What defined Döblin's Jewish identity was not his connection to a shared religious or cultural past, but the brute fact of antisemitism. Social prejudice and discrimination accompanied him from childhood, marking his school years, university studies, medical training, and professional career. It was not Judaism as a communal or religious tradition that left its mark on Döblin's early life, but the experience of stigma. "It was from the outside that I learned from an early age that I was a Jew ... the disparagement, the contempt, and the hatred of the persecutors that I got to know and accepted."[4] At school, the fact of his Jewishness "lingered unspoken over every relationship, no matter how friendly it was."[5]

Döblin converted to Protestantism and officially withdrew from the Jewish community in 1912, shortly after his marriage to fellow medical student Erna Reiss, herself a Jew of an assimilated background. Yet sixteen years later, when Döblin deposited a brief *vita* in the archives of the Prussian Academy of Arts in 1928, upon being nominated as a member of the prestigious society, the text's opening lines read "I do not want to forget, I come from Jewish parents."[6] The contradiction between Döblin's formal conversion to Protestantism and the assertion of his Jewish roots in the autobiographical statement he wrote upon joining the Prussian Academy captures the underlying paradox of his relationship to Judaism. Decades after converting to Protestantism, Döblin was still writing about issues pertaining to Jewish culture and politics. These tensions continued to manifest themselves after his conversion to Catholicism in 1941 and his return to Germany in 1945, culminating in the tortured self-reflections recorded in the diaries from the last years of his life.[7]

In his journalistic writings from the early 1920s, Döblin anticipated the disappearance of German Jewry within three generations. He was convinced that "deghettoization" would resolve the Jewish question and that the Jews' assimilation was only a matter of time. In a 1921 essay "Zion und Europa," he lambasted Zionism as a figment of the antisemitic imagination and derided it as a reaction to external prejudice. In his satiric critique of Zionism, Döblin asks "What sort of people is this, that if someone could take away its nose, it would no longer be a people … Can the Jewish question in Western Europe be solved through rhinoplasty? Certainly. But what is to be done with all the straw that comes out of the heads of those who concern themselves with Judaism?"[8]

Döblin's attitude changed dramatically following anti-Jewish riots that broke out in Berlin in 1923. The riots, sparked by the rising cost of bread, took place in Scheunenviertel, a poor neighbourhood in eastern Berlin inhabited by Polish-Jewish immigrants. The police watched on as mobs looted Jewish stores and harassed the Jewish residents. Döblin reported on the antisemitic attacks in the *Prager Tagblatt*.[9] After reporting the attacks in the press, he was invited to participate in a discussion panel organized by a Zionist organization. At the meeting, he contested the idea that the Jews had another homeland besides Germany or that the Jews constituted a national community in any true sense of the word. Surely one had to denounce the pogroms, but he argued that German Jews were already at home, with "Goethe, Kant, Nietzsche,

Figure 2.2. Alfred Döblin sculpted by Harald Kurt Isenstein (1930). Leo Baeck Institute, New York.

Heine and Beethoven as our sole stepfathers."[10] Despite his opposition to Zionism, Döblin came out of the meeting wondering whether the Eastern Jews were closer to him than his German neighbours. Zionist representatives invited him to join the movement and visit Palestine, but he turned down the offer and decided to go to Poland, where he might meet "real Jews."[11] He compares the trip to the remote destinations he had visited in his fiction: "I had mentally made a journey to China in one novel, to the Thirty Years' War in another, to a utopian time in Greenland in a third. Now I wanted to make a real journey to the country of my fathers."[12]

In September 1924, Döblin left on a two-month tour of Poland, visiting Warsaw, Vilnius, Lublin, Lemberg, Kraków, Zakopane, Łódź, and Gdańsk. In the resulting travel diary, published under the title *Reise in Polen* (1925), Döblin shares his impressions of interwar Poland's architecture, culture, and urban life and records his conversations with Zionists, Hasids, Bundists, assimilationists, Yiddishists, and Hebraists. The vitality of Polish-Jewish life in interwar Poland amazes Döblin,

Figure 2.3.  Front cover of *Reise in Polen* (1926). The travelogue's orientalist disposition and its celebration of Eastern European traditionalism is conveyed in the cover art. It shows a young couple of vigorous Polish peasants, dressed in Slavic folkloric costumes. In the background is an Eastern Orthodox church and an industrial factory, symbolizing the tension between tradition and modernity, a motif that runs through *Reise in Polen*. Leo Baeck Institute, New York.

who reaches the realization that the Jews "constitute a nation. People who know only Western Europe fail to realize this. The Jews have their own costumes, their own language, religion, manners and mores, their ancient national feeling and national consciousness."[13]

Döblin, who knew little Yiddish and no Polish, had to rely on German-speaking travel guides and translators to get around. The need for intermediaries and Döblin's foreignness are a recurring theme in the diary, which oscillates between fascination and aversion in its ethnological account of traditional Jewish life. He is shocked by the living conditions of the impoverished Jewish masses but is also impressed by the vitality of the Jewish cultural life he witnesses in schools, theatres, and synagogues. When visiting the Gur Hasidim to meet with Rabbi Abraham Mordechai Alter, he feels as if he has "come upon an exotic tribe."[14] He describes Orthodox customs as primeval and atavistic, yet senses that this is the first time he has grasped the spiritual vitality and national integrity of the Jewish people:

> What an impressive nation Jews are. I didn't know this nation; I believed what I saw in Germany, I believed that the Jews are the industrious people, the shopkeepers, who stew in their sense of family and slowly go to fat, the agile intellectuals, the countless insecure unhappy refined people. Now I see that those are isolated examples, degenerating, remote from the core of the nation that lives here and maintains itself. And what an extraordinary core this is, producing such people as the rich, inundating Baal-Shem, the dark flame of the Gaon of Wilno. What events occurred in these seemingly uncultured Eastern areas, how everything flows around the spiritual! What tremendous importance is placed on spirituality, on religion! Not a minor stratum, an entire mass of people – spiritually united. Few other nations are as centered in religion and spirituality as this one.[15]

Despite his renewed admiration for the Jews, Döblin's tour of interwar Poland did not set him on the path back to Judaism.[16] He appreciated the integrity of Eastern-Jewish life but maintained a certain distance from it, never fully shedding the attitude of a sympathetic ethnologist. He remained estranged from his Jewish roots and continued to regard his ancestral heritage as an exotic, foreign entity. Döblin's inability to access the foreign world of Eastern Jewry is captured in an anecdote he relates about his stay at a hotel in Lublin. He is given two keys to his hotel room. Not knowing which key to use, he tries both but does not manage to unlock the door to his room.[17]

On 28 February 1933, the day after the Reichstag fire, Döblin took his friends' advice and fled Germany, escaping imminent arrest as a vocal member of the Weimar Republic's left-wing intelligentsia. He left Berlin for Switzerland, where he was joined by his wife and sons.[18] After half a year in Zurich, the family resettled in Paris. Döblin's name figured prominently on the list of prohibited works and authors the Nazis published in April of that year. His novels were burned in the bonfires of the Tenth of May. The Nazi takeover and Döblin's forced emigration were the occasion for his renewed preoccupation with Jewish politics and culture. His previous belief in assimilation as the solution to the Jewish question in Germany was overturned by the rise of the Third Reich. During the first years of his Parisian exile, Döblin collaborated with various neo-territorialist organizations, serving as a board member for the ORT (Organization, Reconstruction, Travail), the Freiland Liga, and the Ligue Juive pour Colonisation. Döblin first encountered the Jewish territorialist movement on his trip to Poland. The movement

Figure 2.4.  Front cover of *Jüdische Erneuerung* (1933). Döblin published *Jüdische Erneuerung* with the Dutch publishing house Querido Verlag, which served as the main outlet for German writers in exile from 1933 to 1940. Querido Verlag published dozens of German titles by banned and exiled authors until the German invasion of the Netherlands. Emanuel Querido, owner and founder of the publishing house, was deported and killed in the Sobibor death camp in 1943. Leo Baeck Institute, New York.

sought to establish an autonomous Jewish settlement outside of Palestine and make Yiddish its official language.[19]

Döblin delivered speeches and wrote essays advocating a territorial solution to the Jewish predicament, fully immersing himself in the cause of Jewish spiritual and national renewal. His writings from that period appeared in two volumes: *Jüdische Erneuerung* (1933) and *Flucht und Sammlung des Judenvolks* (1935). In the latter, Döblin repudiated emancipation as a false promise that fraudulently stripped the Jews of their ancestral identity and religious traditions under the pretext of civic equality. The Jews had fallen into a honeytrap that left them spiritually bereft, nationally divided, and physically rootless. The essays in the collection give voice to a deeply wounded author who is disillusioned with the promise of German assimilation and emancipation.

In a lecture titled "I Am Not a Hitler Jew!" that Döblin delivered in England in June 1935, he derided German Jewry for averting its eyes from what he saw as a historical inevitability. He describes

Figure 2.5. "Le-Korai Be-Ivrit" (To My Hebrew Readers). Excerpt from Döblin's *Jüdische Erneuerung* in Hebrew translation. Published in the Tel Aviv-based literary weekly *Turim* (1933). Cornell University Library.

German-Jewish history since the times of the emancipation in terms of "religious suicide" and abandonment. To this narrative of decline Döblin contrasts his own process of Jewish self-discovery during his tour of Poland, where he first recognized his ties to the Jewish people. Döblin's published account of his journey in *Reise in Polen* (1925) had presented a far more ambiguous relationship to Polish Jewry; ten years later, Döblin rewrote the significance of that journey – it was now the starting point of his national and cultural homecoming. In so doing, the assimilated Döblin makes Jewishness the foundational component of his identity. His identity as a Jew is not the result of Nazi persecution or external stigmatization but the product of an affirmative relationship with the Jewish people as a national and historical collective. As Döblin explains:

> While I was in Poland, I came to Łódź, and for the first time I saw in a big European city Jews celebrating a Zionist festival, wearing badges that proclaimed them as Jews, marching with Jewish banners openly through the streets, declaring: We are Jews! They were not ashamed of it as we German Jews were – as I was. I bought one of the flags, but I did not dare to put it on in the street. Not until I was in the train did I put it in my lapel, and I felt that by that action I had finally bound myself up with the Jewish people, that I was one with these Polish Jews whom we in Germany were trying to keep at arm's length. I want to tell you this, because I want you to know that this was the beginning of my return to the Jews. I am not a Hitler Jew![20]

Döblin's declaration captures the personal motivations behind his involvement with the territorialist movement. Branded a Jew and barred from identifying as a German by the Nazis, he sought to transform the stigma of Jewishness imposed upon him from without into an affirmative identity based on collective solidarity and a sense of kinship that drew on a shared cultural and historical past. Döblin rewrites the significance of his journey to Poland yet again in *Schicksalsreise*, where he notes that the Hasidic and Orthodox Jews he saw "wore the costume of the German middle ages ... They were a strange people, from another world altogether. They had their own religion, their own language, their surroundings. I had as little in common with them as they had with me."[21] Curiously, there is no trace of the enthusiasm and fascination with which Döblin described the world of Eastern European Judaism two decades earlier nor any mention of its fate during the war.

Weary of the quibbling among competing factions within the Jewish territorial movement, Döblin broke with the cause in 1937. Despite his deep involvement in Jewish politics during the 1930s, Judaism and Jewish ritual remained inherently foreign to Döblin, who seemed more familiar with Christian lore and symbolism. In a letter to Viktor Zuckerkandl in January 1938 he relayed his decision to break with the territorialists: "I am quite detached from Jewish matters; I devoted much time to the cause; from now on I see no possibility of changing anything. The core problem is that the Jews do not want and cannot reach a solution."[22]

Döblin had turned to territorialism during these difficult times in search of a political and intellectual community that would replace his previous loyalties to German socialism. His conception of Jewish national renewal tended to hyperbolic excess and digressed to philosophical abstraction. Döblin remained oblivious to the constraints of the historical moment and refused to bend to the demands of political pragmatism. His utopian ideal of Jewish nationalism seemed to have been tailored to suit the intellectual and spiritual needs of one man alone.[23] The path to recuperating his ancestral heritage through territorialism failed, just as it had a decade earlier when he travelled to the land of his forefathers.[24]

**Refuge and Redemption**

On 10 June 1940, four days before the Nazis reached the French capital, Döblin fled Paris. His wife Erna and son Stefan had left the city two weeks earlier, for Le Puy. On his journey, Döblin got caught up in the chaotic mass exodus of refugees fleeing the advancing Wehrmacht. It was several weeks before Döblin succeeded in reuniting with his family. During this period of separation, Döblin suffered hunger, humiliation, and isolation. Uncertainty, hopelessness, and the harsh conditions led him to contemplate suicide. He reunited with his family in Toulouse on 10 July. Together they continued to Marseille, then Madrid, then Lisbon, where they boarded a ship to New York. The Alfred Döblin who reached America's shores on 9 September 1940 was not the same man who had fled Paris three months earlier, and he sought to convey the extent of his transformation in a 1949 memoir he published four years after his return to Germany, titled *Schicksalsreise. Bericht und Bekenntnis*.

The memoir consists of three books. The first book is an account of Döblin's flight from Paris and journey to the United States. He wrote the first book after he arrived in Hollywood in 1940. He had planned to publish the story of his escape under the title *Robinson in Frankreich* but failed to find a publisher. He set the project aside until he reworked it into its expanded version in 1948, combining it with the story of his life in America and his return to post-war Germany. *Schicksalsreise*, as its subtitle indicates, is both a "report" and a "confession," alternating between factual testimony, psychological self-reflection, and spiritual contemplation. It is the story of Döblin's harried escape from Paris and desultory passage through southern France in his desperate search for his wife and son. Döblin describes the tribulations of his flight through France, Spain, and Portugal as a "journey between heaven and earth."[25] The story of his emigration takes on a mystical meaning, forming the backdrop to an inner drama that would culminate in his conversion to Catholicism in 1941. As Döblin explains to his readers: "The catastrophe has not robbed me, it has revealed me … I profited in my poverty."[26]

The narrative in the first book follows two parallel and interconnected storylines: Döblin's flight from the advancing Wehrmacht, and the spiritual transformation effected by his journey. Döblin likens his condition during the time to that of Robinson Crusoe: "In the summer of 1940 it happened that I, like Robinson Crusoe washed up on the shore of a distant tropical isle, was shipwrecked in the interior of France."[27] Like Crusoe, an isolated and infirm Döblin undergoes a spiritual crisis and experiences a mystical vision that leads him to God. Döblin's despair as a destitute refugee in search of shelter shakes the foundations of his former self and opens him up to the possibility of faith. The report oscillates between the sceptical rationalism of a trained physician and the tormented soul of a refugee making his first uncertain steps towards Christianity.

During his journey through wartime France, Döblin faces animus and adversity. Even though he holds a French passport, he is repeatedly stopped for questioning because of his German accent and foreign place of birth. The authorities suspect him of being a German spy. When he finally reaches Le Puy, the city where he expected to find his wife and son, he learns that the two left for Bordeaux the previous day. Unable to make the trip, Döblin returns to a refugee camp in Mende, where he had been staying. Over the subsequent two weeks, Döblin undergoes a profound spiritual transformation.

Depressed and destitute, Döblin visits Mende's cathedral day after day, contemplating the meaning of his personal fate in front of a crucifix. This period of contemplation allows Döblin to recognize Christ not as the mere embodiment of human suffering but as a sign of divine salvation that points humanity to the existence of "invisible worlds" beyond its immediate reality.[28] He considers the possibility that the accidents and mishaps that led him to Mende were not the result of mere chance but had a deeper purpose. "It seemed to me the wrong turns I took on my journey were signs, clues."[29] He struggles to believe, hindered by his rational scepticism as a trained physician: "They say you must be trusting, have conviction. But that is precisely what I lack."[30] Döblin contemplates the problem of evil as an obstacle to faith, "How is it," he asks, that God "also takes the form of Nazis and builds concentration camps?"[31] Incredibly, Döblin formulates the traditional challenge of theodicy as an abstract problem, alluding to Nazis and concentration camps as if they had not directly affected his personal fate. This dissociative tendency is the defining characteristic of Döblin's autobiographical narrative. Ultimately, the experience of hunger, isolation, and despair is what allows Döblin to accept the divinity of the suffering Christ. Cut off from all his normal attachments and thrust into the wilderness of wartime France, Döblin confronts the unadorned wretchedness of human existence. He realizes that without Christ human life would be unbearable and comes to the understanding that the crucifix attests to God's ongoing presence in the world.

Scholars have pointed out the similarities between Döblin's spiritual illumination in front of the crucifix in Mende and an event recounted twenty-five years earlier in Döblin's *Reise in Polen*.[32] In his travel diary, Döblin devotes a long passage to his visit to the Marienkirche in Kraków, where he contemplates the crucifix hanging over the altar. In Kraków's cathedral, Döblin concludes that the image of the suffering Christ is meant to crystallize the sorrows and struggles of human existence. He maintains that the image of Christ allows the individual to articulate his emotional agony and find community through the expression of shared suffering.[33] The scene repeats itself in *Schicksalsreise*, where we find Döblin seated in the church pew meditating on the meaning of Christ's death. Yet on this occasion, Döblin replaces his romantic-secular vision of Christ as an "executed rebel" with a religious-salvific conception of his divinity.[34] The identification of Christ as the epitome of human wretchedness and sorrow in *Reise in Polen* – Döblin's most "Jewish" book – is superseded by a new understanding of Christ the Messiah. Döblin's changed perception of Christ as the son of God corresponds to his new self-understanding as a Christian.

Shortly after his spiritual revelation in Mende, Döblin also finds worldly salvation when he succeeds in tracking down his wife and son. After Döblin reunites with them in Toulouse, they continue their journey to Marseille, where they attempt to raise the necessary funds to continue their passage through Spain and Portugal on their way to the United States. They wire friends for money and appeal to the Red Cross for help. Erna Döblin even turns to a Jewish refugee organization, where she speaks with "a rabbi, a well-nourished, well-dressed man," pleading with him to help them in their dire situation.[35] The self-satisfied rabbi turns her down. "He heard her out and smiled superciliously: what was difficult, what was dangerous about it? First of all, the Germans hadn't arrived yet, and second, they weren't in the least concerned with us."[36] The rabbi, the ecumenical embodiment of Judaism, is both indifferent to the suffering of fellow Jews and blind to the impending catastrophe.

Döblin's derisive depiction of Jews continues in his recollection of the voyage to America. He recalls how in 1939, one year prior to his family's escape, he attended a PEN meeting in New York. The ship on which he was sailing carried a large number of German-Jewish emigrants from Berlin. Although they were all fleeing Germany because of the Nazis, they intentionally avoided raising the matter. Döblin adds that "one man was so much like a Nazi himself that I wanted to change my table assignment at our first encounter. It turned out that he was a Jew and had been in a concentration camp."[37] Döblin depicts his fellow travellers as assimilated Jews who either were in self-denial or were as bad as the Nazis. He calls their emigration "a journey following a shipwreck."[38] The shipwreck imagery pervades Döblin's account of his own refugee experience, but Döblin, who likens himself to Robinson Crusoe, has grown from his experience of exile, which has led him to religious enlightenment. This is not the case with the German Jews he meets on his first voyage to the United States. He calls their journey "tragic."[39]

> For, after all, they had been persecuted without having done anything wrong. Would they reflect on their fate now? Would they consider the fact that they had not been persecuted as individuals but as Jews, something they could do nothing about? And they weren't even religious. What, then, did they think and feel? I encountered individuals only, private individuals. Many were embittered, women cried when they told how they had been humiliated. But that was all, it never went beyond that. And what were they concerned about? Business. They worried about how they would earn money in New York. They shrugged their shoulders as if to say: I'm a Jew, people treat you any way they please.[40]

Döblin had disavowed his ties to the territorialist movement in 1937 and was writing his memoir from the perspective of a believing Catholic who rejected both Judaism and Jewish nationalism. Yet his critique of the German Jews sailing to America rings of an earlier ideological phase when he criticized assimilated Western Jews for failing to recognize the collective dimension of their predicament. What is the relevance of this critique in the context of Döblin's conversion narrative? According to Robert Sackett, "hints of disgust for assimilation betray an old passion for Jewish politics from the 30s."[41] Sackett suggests that Döblin's disparagement of the assimilated Jewish passengers is incidental to the story of his conversion and is merely a "throwback to his political phase."[42] For Sackett, this passage exemplifies the fragmentary nature of Döblin's memoir and the author's failure to reconcile his multiple selves. Yet this interpretation misconstrues the role of Döblin's critique. It is not an anachronistic echo of an earlier ideological phase, but an external projection and disavowal of the author's own past as an assimilated German Jew.

The Jewish refugees in Döblin's narrative are not bound by any sense of communal solidarity. Moreover, it would seem that there is

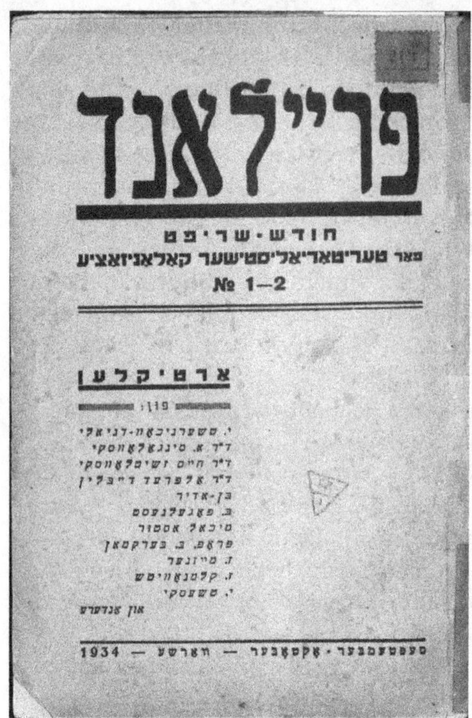


Figure 2.6. Front cover of the September 1934 issue of *Frayland*, a Yiddish-language monthly published by the Territorialist Movement. The issue featured an article by Döblin titled "Gzar din un veg fun di maarav Yidin" (The Verdict and Path of Western Jewry). The Sheridan Libraries at Johns Hopkins University.

nothing to salvage of Judaism, because the only thing that determines the Jewishness of these German Jews is the fact of their persecution. They possess no common religious beliefs or traditions and do not even constitute a community of fate in their shared misfortune. Döblin resorts to stock antisemitic stereotypes in order to describe his fellow passengers as atheistic, individualistic, and obsessed with superficial appearances and wealth. The German Jews on the ship "dressed well" and "elegantly," pretending they were on a deluxe cruise and not a refugee ship. The "handsomely attired men and women" sit at the bar and dance to jazz music.[43] Echoing his earlier critique of German Jewry during his territorialist phase, Döblin depicts his fellow passengers as bourgeois materialists with little grasp of their surrounding spiritual and political realities.[44]

Döblin goes on to compare his first passage across the Atlantic to the one he made in 1940 when immigrating to the US. "This time, on the Greek ship, many of the passengers belonged to intellectual, political, or artistic circles, that is to say, for the most part they were aware of things."[45]

Although politically conscious, these other refugees who fought Nazism in the name of socialism, democracy, and humanitarian ideals are also the object of Döblin's scorn. The Yiddishists and socialists Döblin converses with on his 1940 voyage to America share his post-1933 political views as a Jewish diasporic nationalist. The Jewish political activists represent ideologies that should have been questioned and recalibrated since the war's outbreak, particularly from a spiritual perspective, as Döblin had done. Instead, the "Yiddish acquaintances" he talks to about Jewish matters remain stalwart in their political convictions. "They ransacked the past. They discussed things only superficially, always stayed on the surface. They were crushed. And they wanted only to go to America. I couldn't discuss what I was thinking about. I couldn't articulate it. I was amazed how alien they had become to me."[46] Döblin's encounter with former allies on his voyage to America captures the extent of his transformation and his estrangement from his Jewish past. On his journey to America, Döblin is not only leaving Nazi-occupied Europe behind but also disavowing his former Jewish selves, as an assimilationist, a socialist, and a diasporic nationalist. Whether they are dialectical materialists or just plain materialists, the Jews in Döblin's text play a traditional Christian tropological role as representatives of an unredeemed alterity. They stand in for a former sinful self, against which Döblin makes his claim to a new Christian identity.

Döblin's portrayal of Jews and Judaism in his memoir corresponds to a discursive pattern Sander Gilman analyses in *Jewish Self-Hatred*. Gilman shows how Jewish writers and thinkers in the modern era responded to the stigma of Jewishness not by rejecting the hegemonic view of the Jew but by integrating its rejection of the Jew into their own self-definition. They sought to overcome their position as outsiders by projecting the stigma associated with their Jewishness onto other Jews. As Gilman explains, "in projecting this Otherness onto the world, they select some fragment of that category in which they have been included and see in that the essence of Otherness, an essence that is separate from their own definition of themselves."[47] This dynamic is clearly at work in the narrative, which internalizes the antisemitic perception of the Jew and projects it onto Döblin's fellow passengers.

In a variation on the traditional theme of the Jews' blindness to Christ's divinity, Döblin castigates fellow Jews for failing to comprehend the historical and political contours of their common predicament. The Pauline critique of the Jews' subjection to the letter of the law is echoed in the émigrés' materialist preoccupations. The Nazi-like concentration camp survivor recalls the Christian trope of Jewish vindictiveness. By converting to Christianity, Döblin has overcome the innate Jewish qualities that he identifies with the émigrés. The memoir establishes his distance from the Jews and asserts his metamorphosis. The émigrés sailing to America are "blind" Jews, as opposed to Döblin, the "seeing" Jew who has accepted Christ into his heart. Why the lack of empathy and the disparaging attitude towards fellow refugees? One conceivable explanation for Döblin's unflattering portrayal is the memoir's intended audience in 1949 West Germany. Was Döblin pandering to the antisemitic sentiment of his German readers?

In contrast to Karl Jakob Hirsch and Karl Stern, Döblin does not wrestle with the significance of his conversion to Christianity as a former Jew. He makes no effort to present his Christianity as an outgrowth of his Jewish background or to reconcile his Jewish past with his Christian present, as many converts of his generation were prone to do. There are, however, several telling parallels that allow us to associate Döblin's conversion narrative with those written by Hirsch and Stern. Döblin may not have made his Jewish past the key theme in the narrative, but he nevertheless feels the need to justify the rejection of his ancestral faith. Like Karl Stern, who we will encounter in the next chapter, Döblin criticizes the assimilated Jewish milieu he grew up in and presents German Jewry as a secularized and deracinated community. Having lost its ties to Judaism's spiritual and traditional moorings, German Jewry cannot offer Döblin a viable religious path. He turns his gaze to the East, in the hope of finding a spiritual alternative in Polish Jewry, but feels equally estranged from the traditional lifestyle he encounters there. Döblin immerses himself in the Jewish national cause for several years after his escape from Germany in 1933, but ends up abandoning the movement. Dissatisfied with assimilation, Orthodoxy, and nationalism, Döblin turns to Catholicism as an alternative to the paths he identifies with Jewish modernity. In his polemic against traditional Judaism and its modern-secularized manifestations, Döblin's memoir recalls the apologetic discourse we find in Hirsch's *Heimkehr* and Stern's *Pillar of Fire*.

## The American Years

Alfred, Erna, and their son Stefan reached New York on 12 September 1940 and continued on to Los Angeles, where a one-year contract as a scriptwriter with Metro-Goldwyn-Mayer had been arranged for him. He temporarily forgot about his spiritual experience in Mende, but the question of his religious faith and identity resurfaced when he and Erna discussed their son's education. The Döblins agreed that "it was not right for the boy to grow up without learning about the world and human existence, without knowledge of our fate, without direction or support."[48] Having decided that their son Stefan needed a religious education, they began to take an interest in Catholicism. The natural choice would have seemed obvious, as the Döblins had been nominally Protestant since 1912, but this fact remains unmentioned in the memoir. Instead, Döblin presents there the question of his son's moral and religious upbringing as the occasion that allows him to translate his spiritual illumination in Mende into practice. In the tradition of the conversion narrative, Döblin interprets his path to Catholicism as a journey guided by the invisible hand of God: "But just as God often had given me a sign during my journey, my flight, he did so once again."[49]

On 30 November 1941, Alfred, Erna, and Stefan Döblin were baptized in the Blessed Sacrament Church on Sunset Boulevard. Six months later, they took their first communion.[50] When Erna Döblin shared the news of their impending conversion with her son Peter, who was living in Philadelphia at the time, she urged him to keep it a secret, warning him that "father will inevitably be kicked out of the studio, where the management is essentially in Jewish hands and wants to support Jews. First, we were chased from country to country because of our Jewish descent and now we must keep our faith secret so that we don't lose our means of subsistence. What a strange world!"[51] The Döblins shared the news of their conversion with a small circle of friends, fearing that their new faith would engender resentment from the émigré community and endanger their financial lifeline.

Four weeks after Erna, Alfred, and Stefan's baptism, Peter also converted to Catholicism out of solidarity. Failing to heed his mother's warning, Peter shared the news of the family's conversion with Döblin's friends and benefactors, Elvira and Arthur Rosin. The Rosins were scandalized to learn about the conversion, going so far as to accuse Döblin of "betrayal."[52] In a conciliatory letter, Döblin sought to play down his conversion, describing it as a "private affair" that had grown out of his readings of Kierkegaard and the Christian mystics. These religious matters, he explained, had already found their expression in his novels. One might speak of betrayal if he had publicly declared his Christian faith and denounced his Judaism in the open, but he had not done that. "I have always had the same conception of Jewishness, nothing has changed: we are a people in the process of full dissolution."[53] He reminds them that he had already converted to Protestantism in 1912, but that the fact had never stopped him from advocating for Jewish causes or speaking publicly as a Jew.

Figure 2.7. Photograph of Alfred Döblin by Eric Schaal (1939). Deutsche Nationalbibliothek, Deutsches Exilarchiv 1933–1945, Frankfurt am Main. Copyright Eric Schaal/Weidle Verlag.

Although Döblin initially kept his conversion a secret, he did not want to remain silent about his spiritual transformation. He opened up about his new religious outlook during an event held in honour of his sixty-fifth birthday at a small theatre in Santa Monica on 14 August 1943. That evening 180 guests gathered at the El Pablo Rey Playhouse in Santa Monica to celebrate his birthday.[54] Tasked with organizing the event was Helene Weigel. Hans Eisler composed music for the occasion, and Heinrich Mann gave the opening speech. Among the guests were Thomas Mann, Arnold Schönberg, Franz Werfel, Lion Feuchtwanger, and Bertolt Brecht. Congratulatory letters from prominent émigré artists were read aloud before Döblin stood up to deliver a few impromptu words. The exact content of Döblin's speech did not survive, but its dramatic reverberations can be found in the second-hand accounts of the night left by some of its participants. Recollecting the event in his autobiography, Ludwig Marcuse describes it as the "most grotesque among the many strange émigré birthdays" he had attended. He writes that "the jubilant old man spoke obstinately of his God, with a thousand tongues, of which we did not understand one, but it was certainly no longer Jehovah."[55]

Another telling testimony of the scandal Döblin's words unleashed is recorded in Bertolt Brecht's work diaries:

> Döblin gave a speech against moral relativism and for firm measures of a religious nature, thereby hurting the irreligious feelings of most of those celebrating. A fatal feeling gripped the more rational listeners, something of the sympathetic horror at a fellow prisoner who had succumbed to torture and was now testifying. Indeed, particularly hard blows knocked Döblin down: the loss of two sons in France, the unprintability of a 2400-page epic, angina (the great convert), and life with an unusually stupid and stuffy wife.[56]

According to Döblin's own account of the event, he had pronounced himself and his fellow writers complicit in the rise of National Socialism and declared that deliverance demanded a decisive turn to the religious domain. Reflecting back on the event in his memoir, he recalls: "What I said was received in silence. It was not the speech to deliver at a birthday party."[57] Whatever was said that night, it clearly missed the mark with the predominantly secular, left-leaning audience of German émigrés that had come to celebrate Döblin's birthday. Döblin's impromptu religious confession was met with complete misunderstanding, marking his growing estrangement from the literary and intellectual community of his Weimar years.

What benefits did Döblin hope to reap by converting to Catholicism in Los Angeles in 1941? It endangered his standing in the German émigré community, which was overwhelmingly Jewish and secular. We can only speculate about Döblin's true motivations, which could have been the result of a deep personal crisis, as Brecht dismissively described his friend's new religious mindset, or the consequence of a genuine spiritual revelation of the kind Döblin attributed to his time in Mende. Klaus Müller-Salget argues that Döblin's conversion was a personal decision that must be accepted as such.[58] The problem with this assertion is the public character that Döblin's decision assumed after he shared his conversion with German readers and turned his Christian faith into the pillar of his public persona in the post-war years.

Arguing against what he considered reductive psychological interpretations of Döblin's conversion, Helmuth Kiesel insists that Döblin's turn to Catholicism must be understood in political terms. Kiesel views Döblin's conversion as an ideological act that grew out of the author's political and philosophical convictions – mainly, his belief that reason was insufficient to guarantee the morality and political stability of modern civilization.[59] Christoph Bartscherer makes a similar argument, explaining that

Döblin's Christianity can be seen as a response to the "hegemonic intrusions of Fascism and Stalinism that menaced the private sphere in those years."[60] Kiesel and Bartscherer interpret Döblin's Catholicism as an intellectually informed and ethically driven decision that grew out of the author's understanding of the challenges of the historical moment. Döblin, according to this argument, realized that the depersonalizing effects of totalitarian politics could only be combated by making the Christian humanistic tradition the foundation of contemporary politics.

While the interpretations by Kiesel and Bartscherer are consistent with Döblin's own assertions in *Schicksalsreise*, other passages in the memoir tell another story, one that complicates the narrative's religious conceit. Döblin's path to Catholicism was intertwined with the painful disillusionments he experienced after his 1933 exile from Germany. If *Schicksalsreise* celebrates Döblin's Christian faith, it also subtly acknowledges the author's failure to identify as German, French, American, and Jewish. By 1935, Döblin seems to have accepted that his ties to Germany had been severed for good. He describes the insurmountable challenge of rooting himself in a new society and culture:

> Language had caused problems for me often since 1933 and I had lost much of my enjoyment of it, now that I had the land of the Nazis behind me. I had entered France as a foreigner, of course, but I happily would have liquidated – at least externally – all of what was foreign in my character, just as the Nazis had liquidated me by forcing me to expatriate. The only way would have been to speak French. And if I could not penetrate the heart of the language, I would at least learn it superficially. That was difficult enough, but understandable in someone who continued daily to write in the German language.[61]

Döblin tries to assimilate into his new homeland and become French, yet he cannot shed "all of what was foreign in my character." The Nazis' attempt to liquidate his Germanness by chasing him out of the country is followed by his own attempt at "self-liquidation," to eradicate the linguistic foreignness that was the defining attribute of his identity as a German writer. The impossible dictate of self-abnegation would repeat itself upon Döblin's return to post-war West Germany.

The family was naturalized in 1936, and Döblin's two sons Klaus and Wolfgang were drafted into the French army. Döblin himself began serving in the French Ministry of Information's counterpropaganda offices shortly after the Nazi invasion of Poland. However, the German invasion revealed the tenuousness of his ties to his adopted homeland despite the seven years he spent there. As Döblin fled the Nazis to southern France in search of his wife and son, he was treated with suspicion and outright hostility by the French. He spoke French poorly and with a strong accent that immediately gave away his German origins. As a result, he was repeatedly stopped for questioning and mistreated along his journey. The country that had given him shelter in 1933 seemed to be turning against him. The war had inflamed nationalistic sentiments, and this turned Döblin into a foreigner again. The problem of foreignness continues to haunt Döblin in America, where he finds himself socially isolated, culturally estranged, and chronically unemployed.

Döblin recognizes that unlike other exiles, "who carried the flag with an iron fist," he cannot claim any national or ideological home. Having been driven out of Germany and then France, Döblin can find no deeper meaning to his predicament. The problem, he realizes, is "the flag, it all has to do with the flag. Which flag have I carried? Which flag do I carry? And the others, can they tell me which flag they are carrying, have they answered for that flag?"[62] After his flight from Germany, Döblin identified with the Jewish territorialist movement, but he turned away from the cause some years later: "I travelled, wrote, and spoke out in support of this movement. But I remained outside it. My words meant nothing, and I felt nothing. It was yet another flag I could not carry."[63] Döblin ultimately finds his "flag" in Christianity. The irony of Döblin's private solution to his "Jewish question" is that only a few years prior, he had written to Nathan Birnbaum, "From my understanding of the Jewish past, the return to Orthodoxy is as unhistorical as baptism, which only allowed individuals to reach a private end to the difficulties of emancipation. It was not a solution to the problem of the people."[64]

Whatever his motives were in 1941, the more pertinent question is what the conversion meant in the context of the narrative's 1949 publication. *Schicksalsreise* is more than an autobiographical account of the author's exile and return. It was intended as a work of self-justification, in which the returning émigré sought to shape his public image in post-war West Germany. It was no coincidence that Döblin, who left Germany as a persecuted Jew in 1933 and returned as a Christian in 1945, made his conversion to Catholicism the central theme of a memoir that culminated in his homecoming. It reflected the calculated strategy of a returning émigré of Jewish ancestry, who sought to reclaim his place in the German cultural sphere by distancing himself from his origins. Aware of the German public's antipathy to Jews and émigrés, Döblin sought to find common ground in Christianity.[65]

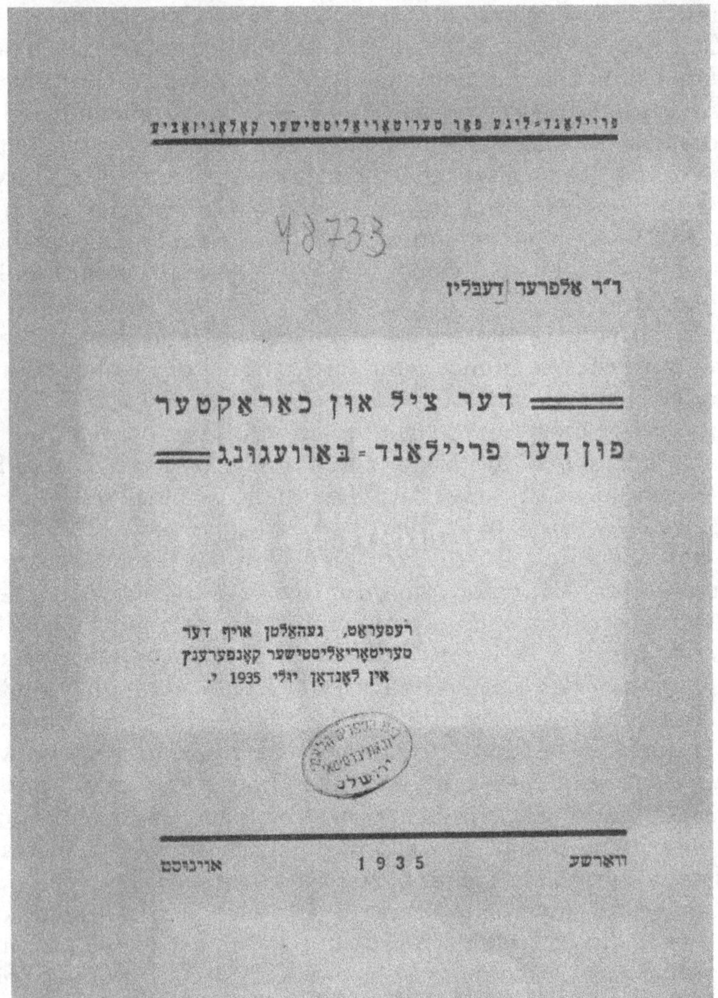


Figure 2.8. Yiddish translation of a lecture delivered by Alfred Döblin on the goal and character of the Jewish Territorialist Movement. The Yiddish title reads "Der tsil un kharakter fun der Frayland-bavegung: referat, gehaltn oyf der teritoryalistisher konferents in London, Yuli 1935" (The Goal and Character of the Frayland Movement: Presentation Delivered at the Territorialist Conference in London, July 1935). Published in Warsaw by the Freeland League for Jewish Territorial Colonization (1935). As Schalom Ben-Chorin and Ilse Blumenthal-Weiss note in their reviews of *Schicksalsreise*, Döblin never mentions his deep involvement with the movement in his autobiography. The National Library of Israel.

## Return to Post-war Germany

Döblin's five years in Los Angeles were marked by financial hardship, artistic disappointment, and social isolation. He never fully integrated with the west coast's émigré circles. While Döblin struggled to find an American publisher for his work, he saw other émigré writers establishing literary reputations on American shores. Thomas Mann constructed a new Bauhaus-style villa in Santa Barbara with earnings from book royalties and lecture honorariums. Lion Feuchtwanger purchased a twenty-room, castle-like estate in Pacific Palisades, in which he hosted large gatherings for Hollywood's high society and the émigré intellectual elite. Döblin, in contrast, never mastered the English language and failed to establish his presence in American literary and intellectual circles. His experience of exile in the United States was even harsher than that of his years in France.

To secure a US entry visa for Döblin and his family, the Emergency Rescue Committee had arranged a one-year contract for him as a scriptwriter at MGM. When his contract was up, the studio did not renew it. Döblin received unemployment payments for several months, but once those benefits ran out, the family was forced to rely on charity. From 1942 to 1945, Döblin depended on financial support from the Writers' Fund, a philanthropic organization that supported émigré artists. In August 1945, Döblin was notified that the fund had dried up and that he would receive no further disbursements. Having failed to find publishers for his manuscripts and incapable of supporting his family, Döblin shifted his gaze back to Europe. He hoped to revive his position as a prominent writer and intellectual in post-war Europe and to contribute to Germany's reconstruction. As early as 1942, he was plotting his return.

After the war, Alfred and Erna finally received news of the fate of their son Wolfgang, who had been drafted into the French army in 1938. Wolfgang had been separated from his unit in the Vosges Mountains while fighting the German invaders. On 21 June 1940, to avoid falling into German captivity, he shot himself. After learning of her son's death, Erna Döblin refused to resettle in Germany, for she felt that treading on the accursed German soil would be a betrayal of her son's memory.[66]

Döblin returned to Europe with his wife in October 1945, well before any other German writer, thanks to his French citizenship and his position as censor and cultural liaison for the French military government. While Erna stayed behind in Paris, Döblin resettled in Baden-Baden as a diplomatic envoy in the French occupation zone. He was tasked with approving literary manuscripts for publication and judging whether various works of fiction, philosophy, and theology were ideologically suited for the German reading public. In 1946, he launched a literary journal called *Das goldene Tor*, which set out to rehabilitate the humanistic heritage of pre-war German letters.[67]

As *chargé de mission* for public education in the French military government, Döblin was given the rank of colonel and wore the uniform of the French army. Wearing his uniform to all official events he attended, Döblin elicited the animus of his German audiences. A testimony from 1947 describes the reaction to Döblin during an event at the Charlottenburg Palace in Berlin:

> We all looked anxiously toward the door as Döblin came in. Yes, there he was, the little bespectacled man. Some were already beginning to clap their hands, when suddenly everyone became silent. The man who appeared at the door had Döblin's face, but it was a French major in uniform. The hands sank down in amazement … Was this really our Döblin? Was this a homecoming, or was it the fleeting visit of an Allied officer? Our gratitude towards the author of *Berlin Alexanderplatz* did not find the right expression. Döblin acted like a foreign dignitary, and he soon departed again.[68]

Döblin's disavowal of his Jewish past and communal affiliations is reflected in the detached, benevolent tone of the returning émigré's account of post-war Germany in *Schicksalsreise*. His "report" of Germany's spiritual and physical condition after 1945 is completely dissociated from his own personal experience of 1933 to 1945. Upon crossing the French–German border on the way to Baden-Baden, Döblin notes that the date is 9 November, the day of the 1918 revolution. His sees this as an auspicious sign marking a new beginning for Germany.[69] Another symbolic date Döblin might have alluded to was that of *Kristallnacht*, which took place on the same day, 9 November 1938. Döblin's reticence in this regard is a telling sign of the memoir's self-imposed silence concerning the fate of the Jews during the Nazi years.

Döblin in his memoir avoids confronting his readers with the question of German collective guilt or complicity during the Nazi period. Instead, he portrays the Germans as victims of National Socialism, writing, "Very few influences from the outside world reached them during those twelve years, and those that did were harshly controlled. They were subjected to systematic propaganda, an uninterrupted flood of official lies, and it levelled them, the educated and uneducated alike."[70] Döblin laments the traumatic events the Germans underwent during the war, writing that "Germany has suffered what I was able to escape."[71] He raises concerns over their inability to work through their traumatic experiences, positioning himself as a benevolent spiritual guide who has come to their rescue: "And then I see their pain and see that they have not yet experienced what it is they have experienced. It is intolerable. I want to help."[72] Instead of presenting himself as a victim of the Nazi regime, a Jew forced to emigrate, Döblin positions himself as a German who was able to elude Germany's tragic fate during the war years and is thus best situated to help redeem the nation's moral standing by reviving its suppressed Christian heritage.[73] As Döblin explains, "It was important to replace the military mentality with something better, by returning to its rightful place the European, Christian, humanistic traits that had once existed in Germany."[74]

Döblin's idea of re-education and de-Nazification was a decidedly religious project that did not involve confronting Germans with the crimes of National Socialism but instead consisted of re-Christianizing the nation. Questions of moral agency and historical accountability were glossed over in favour of a depoliticized critique of the religious-metaphysical causes of the war's atrocities: "No one can deny that this era is marked by original sin. Each death, each illness and conflict, is a reminder of this atrocious original sin that brought misery into the world."[75] In the aftermath of the war the Germans saw themselves as victims rather than perpetrators. Döblin's account in the memoir fed into the regnant narrative of German victimhood. Witnessing Germany's levelled cities, Döblin recalled the Book of Lamentations and "the volcanic destruction of the Roman cities of Pompeii and Herculaneum."[76] In comparing Germany to Pompeii, Döblin removed the fault for the German catastrophe from the realm of human agency, suggesting that Germany's devastation was as inevitable as the eruption of Mount Vesuvius. His allusion to the Book of Lamentations was similarly suspect. The book's accusing prophet lays the blame for the destruction of Jerusalem on the city's inhabitants, whom he faults for turning away from God. The Germans, by analogy, seemed to be guilty of a similar sin: godlessness. As Döblin explained, "the German mentality, no longer clothed in Nazi uniform, proved to be fundamentally heathen."[77] In narrating the German catastrophe as a natural disaster or alternatively as a tragedy rooted in the religious-metaphysical realm, Döblin was unburdening the Germans of any specific crimes committed by the Nazi regime.

Döblin makes no reference to the Nazi campaign against the Jews, nor does he mention the death camps, where he lost numerous friends and relatives. Helmuth Kiesel attributes Döblin's silence to the traumatic magnitude of the events, arguing that his literary works confronted the legacy of the Holocaust in more nuanced and subtle ways.[78] The claim that the fate of the Jews during the war was too difficult to broach directly and required a coded, oblique language of prayer is patently contradicted by the fact that Döblin engaged with the Holocaust, Germany's post-war amnesia, and the stubborn persistence of the Nazi legacy in his private correspondence and diaries. A simpler explanation for this glaring lacuna is that Döblin was aware of the resentment that Germans harboured towards returning Jewish émigrés, who served as living reminders of their unabsolved guilt. In a letter from December 1948, Döblin warned his friend, the writer Hermann Kesten, to watch out when writing for German audiences: "Do not use the word 'Jew' too often and preferably not at all. It was and remains a term of abuse in this country. Use it only if you wish to satisfy the antisemites. Sadly, this is no joke. Antisemitism is deeply rooted here and even more malignant than it was in our time."[79]

In the immediate aftermath of the war, the persecution and systemic murder of European Jewry was not a particularly popular topic in the West German book market. Very few testimonies of Jewish survivors and émigrés were published in the 1940s and 1950s, and those that were received scant attention. It is likely that if Döblin had framed his memoir as the account of a Jewish survivor addressing his erstwhile German persecutors, it would not have found an audience. Döblin was by then struggling to find publishers for his manuscripts, which were passed over by the likes of Fischer Verlag and appearing instead with minor publishing houses and printed in limited editions.[80]

In translating his wartime experiences into a depoliticized, Christian idiom, the memoir relinquishes all claim to Jewish rage and political accusation. Döblin took this route with the understanding that this concession was the prerequisite for his participation in the culture of post-war West Germany. Yet the suppression of his Jewish voice comes at a cost, which manifests itself in the work's flawed structure and inconsistent aesthetic. There is a marked stylistic inconsistency between the memoir's first and third books. The first book, which recounts Döblin's flight from France, tells the story of the author's spiritual crisis in a probing, introspective tone. This confessional mode all but disappears in the third book, which is presented as an objective report. The first book's introspective focus and the third book's impersonal and dissociative narration represent two complementary strategies, which together have the effect of silencing the collective Jewish dimension of the author's wartime experience.

The inconsistency in narrative tone and perspective makes evident the author's split self as well as his inability to weave together his disparate wartime experiences in a coherent way. Döblin's inability to mourn his dead or acknowledge his victimhood as a German Jew results in a gap in the narrative that precludes autobiographical closure. His adoption of the trope of conversion was meant to establish the continuity and stability of a coherent self across time. The narrative template Döblin employs to recount his years in exile fails for two primary reasons that have to do with the incompatibility between the materials of his life and his choice of literary genre. As a literary archetype, the Christian conversion narrative revolves around the inner transformation of the isolated individual and the total renewal of the self that occurs in its wake. Yet Döblin's war years were of a different order of experience, corresponding to a collective-historical predicament that he shared with European Jewry but that is largely absent from the narrative. The "Jewish dimension" of his story could not be glossed over by the flight to interiority in the first part of the memoir, just as it could not convincingly be disregarded as irrelevant to its third part, which focused on the author's return. The memoir's fragmentary form is revealed in its lacunae and the arbitrary shifts in narrative perspective.

The author's failure to reconcile his past as a Jewish survivor of the Nazi years with his identity as a returning Catholic convert finds its symptomatic expression in the work's closing pages, in which Döblin recounts the cold and sceptical response to his new religious worldview. In 1948 Döblin returns to Berlin, the city of his youth and the backdrop to his most celebrated novel *Berlin Alexanderplatz*, in order to deliver a public lecture. During his talk, Döblin entreats his audience to recognize the necessity of spiritual renewal in combating "the brazen nationalistic and atheistic arrogance" of the Nazis.[81] The vituperative response to Döblin's religious appeal recalls the misunderstanding that arose during his sixty-fifth-birthday speech in Santa Monica. Döblin recounts how one newspaper mocked his "total surrender to mysticism" while another characterized his speech as a "flight from reality."[82] Döblin bleakly concludes that "no real communication" is possible with his former interlocutors on the left.[83] The event of miscommunication with which the book ends reads like a synecdoche for *Schicksalsreise*, an author's botched attempt to re-establish himself as a Catholic intellectual in post-war West Germany.

**Return of the Jewish Repressed**

*If the Jews are to be able to stay in Europe, then they cannot stay as Germans or Frenchmen, etc., as if nothing had happened. It seems to me that none of us can return (and writing is surely a form of return) merely because people again seem prepared to recognize Jews as Germans or something else. We can return only if we are welcome as Jews. That would mean that I would gladly write something if I can write as a Jew on some aspect of the Jewish question ... I don't know if you would be able to print something of that nature under the present difficult circumstances.*

– Hannah Arendt to Karl Jaspers (29 January 1946)[84]

Döblin's attempt to reinvent himself in post-war Germany in the guise of a Catholic writer and intellectual failed because the Germans continued to identify him with his Jewish ancestry and his left-wing political persona from the Weimar years. Even conversion could not erase the stigma of his origins. As a German writer of Jewish ancestry, who was a former socialist, Catholic convert, and uniformed French officer, Döblin faced the impossible task of juggling multiple identities. The complexity of his situation could hardly be accommodated by a society whose recently toppled regime divided the world into opposing camps of friend and foe. As Erna Döblin wrote Theodor Heuss, the first president of West Germany, when she informed him of her husband's death: "He was the first to return because he wanted to help ... In spite of his efforts ... he experienced only ingratitude from all sides, some saw him as a Frenchman, others as a German, some considered him a realist, others as a Catholic – he fell through the cracks ... Your country silenced him for a decade. He often said to me: 'All my work for this people has been in vain.'"[85]

The few works Döblin managed to publish in Germany after his return sold poorly, and the sales for *Schicksalsreise* were no exception. The press either ignored or dismissed his work, and the scarce positive reviews he received were mostly limited to the Catholic press. Analysing the lukewarm reception of Döblin's 1948 novel *Karl und Rosa*, Wolfgang Weyrauch explained that the press ignored the work

> because ... Karl Liebknecht and Rosa Luxemburg ... are communists, or socialists, or in any case, something that should be hushed up ... And what's more, they are Jews ... Alfred Döblin delights in reviving their story. He himself is a Jew and an old socialist ... He is also an emigrant. He later became Catholic in order to conceal his origins ... Döblin is somehow connected with the French military government ... In prison – where she clearly belongs – Döblin's Rosa speaks to angels; what a strange affair, a communist talking to angels.[86]

Weyrauch's *ad hominem* attack captured the resentment Döblin faced as a former Jew and uniformed representative of the French military government. For Weyrauch, Döblin was a Jew, a communist, and a French occupier on German soil, an outsider who was trying to camouflage his foreignness by assuming the guise of a Christian.

Reviews in the GDR were no less critical. The East German writer and exiled dissident Bodo Uhse found *Schicksalsreise* "curiously implausible," arguing that it reflected the author's inability to grasp the war through the broader perspective of dialectical materialism.[87] Döblin's narrow focus on his personal struggles during the Nazi invasion of France belied his bourgeois sensibilities. According to Uhse, Döblin's account was representative of a broader sociological phenomenon: "For a certain intellectual class … conversion to Catholicism became a kind of fad during the postwar years. In most cases, conversion was preceded by a fleeting encounter with socialism, which then turned to psychoanalysis. In search of a stronger means for soothing the soul, this path ended in [an] attempt to find refuge in Catholicism (*beim Katholizismus Zuflucht zu suchen*)."[88]

The accusation of insincerity was echoed in a review of *Schicksalsreise* written by Carl Seelig: "The seventy-five-year-old gives an account of the inner transformation, which led him to convert to Catholicism. To us it seems more like an escape from Judaism. The former fighter has become a penitent, whose final spiritual moulting will probably remain a mystery."[89] Seelig was accusing Döblin of betraying the Jews, yet another reviewer faulted the author for abandoning the German people when he immigrated to America. Ignoring the fact that Döblin was forced into exile as a Jew and political dissident, the critic noted that "the Germans, who stood by him in the hardest years of our nation in unbreakable loyalty, have their own thoughts about the value and dignity of a man who left Germany, whose sons fought against Germany in foreign uniforms, and who found his way back to the devastated and foreign homeland, after he was rejected in America."[90] This reviewer, even while alluding to Döblin's Jewishness by referencing his "ahasveric wanderings," faulted him for abandoning Germany in its time of crisis, feigning ignorance of Döblin's fate had he remained in Nazi Germany.

The Jewish responses to *Schicksalsreise* were no less critical. Schalom Ben-Chorin, an independent scholar and journalist who immigrated to Palestine in 1935, published a scathing review titled "Abschied von Alfred Döblin." Despite being a staunch post-war advocate of Jewish–Christian rapprochement, Ben-Chorin took a harsh stance towards Döblin, whose biographical omissions he found suspect: "We do not want to judge when it comes to decisions of faith. But the fact that Alfred Döblin, a returnee to Germany, deliberately conceals who he was and is from his readers; that he lists his books but does not even mention *Jüdische Erneuerung* with a single word, that is … a 'forgetfulness' which we cannot forget."[91]

The poet and Holocaust survivor Ilse Blumenthal-Weiss voiced similar reservations, decrying "the zeal of the renegade mind that has moved so far away from its origins."[92] Recounting their time together as refugees in Zurich during the 1930s, she recalled heated conversations with him about the Jewish fate. The contrast between Döblin's professions of loyalty to the Jewish people at that time and his new-found attraction to Christianity could not be more shocking: "In that simple boarding house room on the side of the Zürichberg, Alfred Döblin revealed himself as a conscious Jew. And now this book I hold in my hand celebrates the homecoming of the 70-year-old to German-ness and Catholicism!"[93] Blumenthal-Weiss concluded that Döblin's embrace of Catholicism and his return to Germany revealed the sad truth about the émigré fate: "It was the broken ones who returned and the nonbelievers who clasped the cross."[94]

News of Döblin's conversion even made waves in the Hebrew press, where the journalist Yeshayahu Klinov ironically quipped that the Catholic Church had scored a great victory with the famed author's baptism. Reflecting on Döblin's passionate attachment to Polish Jewry in the 1920s and 1930s, Klinov wondered whether his religious and ideological commitments were nothing more than manifestations of Döblin's "literary extravagancy."[95] Aharon Zeitlin took a far harsher position, writing that after his flirtation with the Jewish national cause in the 1930s, "Döblin finally found a way to distance himself from Judaism and join its destroyers, its cremators, stranglers, and execu-tioners. In his search for a solution to the Jewish problem, Döblin came to those who 'solved' the problem in the gas chambers ... He is now showered with honours by those who perpetrated the worst crimes against our people."[96]

In the polarized political climate of Cold War West Germany, Döb-lin's Christian credentials were not enough to absolve him of his ideo-logical past as a member of the much-maligned left-wing intelligentsia. His reputation as a socialist, atheist, and avant-garde modernist during the Weimar era haunted him after the war, casting his conversion in a questionable light.[97] Regarded with suspicion in conservative Chris-tian circles, Döblin was similarly estranged from his former colleagues on the left, who denounced him for betraying his political convictions and artistic integrity. Döblin's problem, as Günter Grass put it, was that "he was too Catholic for the progressive left and too anarchistic for the Catholics."[98]

Döblin's failure to reach German audiences seems puzzling, consider-ing the Christian tenor of his later works. In the first years after the war, the West German occupation zones experienced a religious renaissance.

Döblin's theological treatises and religiously themed novels seemed especially suitable for a society flocking to the church pews. Contemplating his failure to relate to German Christian readers after the war, Döblin wrote: "I read a lot of Christian books and magazines, and I confess, despite my best efforts, I could not appeal to them. The word regional custom (*Brauchtum*) is fitting here. They were Germans and practiced Christian custom ... In Germany, Christianity is the exclusive patrimony of the nation and tribe."[99]

Döblin denounced the Catholics he encountered in post-war Germany as Pharisees and identified them with the "synagogue."[100] He compared German Catholicism to the "Mosaic faith," a religious tradition growing desiccated under the weight of "strict custom."[101] The irony of a Jewish convert accusing German Christians of Jewishness seems to have eluded Döblin. Döblin's meditations reveal his awareness of the extent to which religious persuasion and national identity were inextricably intertwined. While Döblin criticized German Catholicism of being a nationally tinged religious persuasion, the observation suggests that the author might have considered his own conversion in similar light, as a measure benefiting his reintegration in post-war Germany.

These melancholy meditations reflect the reality of Döblin's failed homecoming and his inability to find a Christian community. What is missing from this reckoning is Döblin's own role in the story. His Catholicism, like his brief time as a Jewish diasporic nationalist, was the product of a deeply personal and philosophical quest. His Catholicism was not rooted in the traditions or liturgy of a particular Catholic community; rather, it was the idiosyncratic, intellectual artefact of his solitary readings of Pascal, Kierkegaard, Augustine, and Aquinas in the Bibliothèque Nationale and the Los Angeles Public Library.[102] Döblin had failed to find his place in a Catholic community – be it in Germany or France – because his religious identity was the product of isolated self-reflection that grew out of a private intellectual journey.

Faced with the bleakening prospects of integrating into the culture and society of the young Federal Republic, Döblin left Germany in January of 1953. To a friend, Döblin wrote that he did not want to be buried in Germany out of fear that "Jewish graves will soon again be desecrated."[103] Contemplating the seven years he had just spent in Germany, Döblin expressed his disappointment with the Germans and considered his contribution to the task of re-education a failure. Writing in his diary while his train crossed the German border on his journey back to France, Döblin recorded his bitter disillusionment. He had believed at first that Hitler and the Nazis "represented a malignant foreign element in the German body."[104] But he later came to realize that the Nazis and the Germans were one and the same. He contemplated the futility of re-education, when "it was always the old teachers or those with the old mentality who taught" at the schools. "The teachers, like the rest of the population, remained the way they were. You don't change that quickly. Certainly, the biggest Nazi banners were set aside, the facade had changed … But the hatred and desire for revenge continued to burn in many."[105]

Döblin's posthumously published journals from 1952 and 1953 offer a stark contrast to the restrained account he gave of his return to Germany in *Schicksalsreise*. In his 1949 memoir he could still imagine himself reintegrating; by 1952, he seems to have abandoned all hope of that, conceding that "my departure from this country is approaching. Yes, we will leave this country again, and the whole thing was not supposed to be a homecoming … it became an extended visit."[106] The tone in the diaries veers from despondency to regret to outrage. Burdened by poor health and preoccupied with the infirmities of old age, Döblin is given to bouts of self-pity and thoughts of death. He is haunted by the memory of his deceased family members: "The faint moving images of my dead come to me as I lie here in bed, for the second and third month. They dance around me, take me into their circle."[107] The entries present us with an aggrieved author who feels spurned by his readers, misunderstood by his former colleagues, and spited by the very cultural institutions he had helped rebuild. They reveal a man plagued by guilt and riddled with self-doubt about his contribution to German reconstruction. Döblin, who had failed to take root again in his former homeland, harbours strong misgivings about the Germans' capacity for change and suggests that the Nazis "are already stirring again, in different costumes."[108] Contemplating his time in Germany in late 1952, a melancholic Döblin concludes: "It has remained as it was. I can't find the air to breathe here."[109]

In a journal entry titled "Meine Toten," Döblin meditates on the friends and family members he has lost over the years. In this private Kaddish for his dead, Döblin refers explicitly to the victims and perpetrators he glossed over in *Schicksalsreise*. He mentions his oldest brother Ludwig's wife and daughter, who "were seized by henchmen, taken to Auschwitz and gassed."[110] His youngest brother Kurt tried to flee Germany with his family, but, lacking the means to escape, they too were murdered in Auschwitz. Döblin's dirge for the dead transforms itself into enraged accusation, wholly absent from *Schicksalsreise*: "With what indifference, or rather cynicism, did one allow masses of serious, righteous, and capable people to be deported, expelled and exterminated."[111]

Reading *Schicksalsreise* alongside the author's private diaries and letters gives the impression that there were two Döblins: the convert to Catholicism, who addressed his German audiences in the language of faith and forgiveness, and the Jewish survivor, burning with rage and resentment towards his former countrymen. The returning convert addresses his fellow Germans under the seal of silence, dissociating himself from the Jewish dead, whereas the Jewish survivor rails against the Germans' post-war indifference to the Jewish fate. After resettling in Paris, Döblin spent the last four years of his life shuttling between France and Germany, where he was hospitalized for Parkinson's disease. On 26 June 1957, Döblin died in a public psychiatric hospital in the Black Forest. According to his final wish, he was buried in northeastern France in the commune of Housseras, beside his son Wolfgang, who died in combat as a French soldier in the Second World War.

# Chapter Three

# Mixed Metaphors of Jewish Blindness in Karl Stern's *The Pillar of Fire* (1951)

In 1951, the Canadian psychiatrist Karl Stern (1906–1975) published a memoir titled *The Pillar of Fire*.[1] It recounted the life story of a Bavarian-born Jew's tortuous path to the baptismal font at the Church of the Franciscan Fathers of Montreal in 1943. The spiritual journey that led Stern to Catholicism began with an adolescent revolt against his assimilated parents through a rekindled commitment to Judaism. By the time Stern fled Nazi Germany in 1935, he had undergone several transformations as a Zionist activist, Orthodox Jew, Marxist radical, and devotee of psychoanalysis.[2] The memoir became an international bestseller, reprinted seventeen times and translated into German, French, Spanish, Dutch, and Italian. It received enthusiastic praise from the likes of C.S. Lewis, Reinhold Niebuhr, Thomas Merton, Dorothy Day, and Graham Greene.[3] *The Pillar of Fire*'s success turned Stern into a sought-after speaker on the Catholic lecture circuit in North America.

Stern's stardom in Catholic circles stood in stark contrast to the Jewish responses to his public avowal of Christianity.[4] Erich Fromm called Stern "an insecure and confused man," suggesting that the author was not straightforward about his motives for conversion.[5] Grudgingly recognizing Stern's literary talent, Rabbi Bernard Heller went so far as to write an entire book debunking Stern's missionary agenda and rebutting his portrayal of Judaism.[6] The London-based Reform Rabbi Ignaz Maybaum, himself a refugee from Nazi Germany, panned the book as "nothing but words, cliches, sentimentalities," asserting that any "true Christian" reading it would immediately recognize that "this man has not become a Christian, he is merely a deserter."[7] While the dust jacket spoke of Stern's "spiritual voyage from Judaism to Catholicism," Maybaum argued that it more accurately described "the voyage of a Jew, marrying out of the faith, finding in Canada social contacts exclusively in non-Jewish circles, and becoming a Catholic in the process of assimilation which he styles conversion."[8] The scandal of Stern's conversion even reached Israel, where Aharon Zeitlin berated *The Pillar of Fire* as a "stupid book that is completely ignorant of Judaism and filled with self-hatred. His main goal is to find new converts for his apostasy."[9]

The autobiography's negative reception among Jewish audiences seems understandable in light of the sensitive timing of its publication, only a few years after the Holocaust. Keenly aware that many Jews would regard his turn to Catholicism as a craven act of betrayal, Stern acknowledges this problem from the outset, noting that just uttering the words "I have become a Catholic" immediately raises "a cloud of estrangement" between him and his Jewish interlocutors.[10] Stern summarizes this problem as follows: "How can you with your Jewish consciousness leave the Jewish community at the time of its most terrible persecution, and join a community in which there are many enemies of the Jewish people?"[11] He attempts to resolve this conflict by framing his conversion less as a defection from his ancestral community and more as a reaffirmation of his Jewish heritage. As he explains,

> When I meet a friend with whom I used to work in the Zionist Youth Movement or in a group of radical students, I realize the extraordinary fact that, when we come to the bottom of things, I have not really departed from their ideals. There is a core to their beliefs which I still share with them. It is contained in my belief. *What must appear to them as a betrayal, is to me a fulfillment.* I still understand everything they are talking about, but they cannot possibly understand me.[12]

This passage captures the memoir's overarching claim in a nutshell: Stern's turn to the Church is in fact a fuller realization of Judaism, one that has been tragically met with the incomprehension of fellow Jews. He has written his memoir in order to address this misunderstanding and convince readers of the sincerity of his spiritual transformation.

Stern's stated desire in the narrative is to reconcile himself with the Jewish community by laying out his religious and personal motives. Yet this gesture of rapprochement is tainted by an ineluctable ambiguity, in that his memoir presupposes the incomprehension of its Jewish addressees. The assertion of Jewish incomprehension rehearses a longstanding Christian conceit: that the Jews stubbornly refuse to recognize that their role in history culminated in the arrival of Christ. This polemic is epitomized by the trope of Jewish blindness, which recurs throughout the New Testament and the writings of the Church Fathers.[13]

Figure 3.1.  Photograph of Karl Stern (circa 1955). Simon Silverman Phenomenology Center, Duquesne University.

Recourse to the worn trope of Jewish blindness is only to be expected in the conversion narrative of a Jew turned Catholic. Yet Stern's autobiography is far savvier in the way it deploys this metaphor, which it interweaves with another *topos* of Jewish blindness, that of German Jewry's failure to anticipate its own impending destruction. This second trope of blindness runs throughout the writings of Stern's better-known intellectual contemporaries, such as Gershom Scholem, Günther Anders, and Hannah Arendt, who challenged the status quo of nineteenth-century German-Jewish liberalism and criticized the political quiescence of their elders. The *topos* of blindness in face of the Shoah is especially pronounced in the writings of Zionists such as Gershom Scholem, who decried German Jewry's "adventure of assimilation" as a betrayal of its ancestral heritage, arguing that there was a causal relation between the Jews' attempts to integrate into German society and their subsequent destruction.[14] Whereas Stern's conversion to Catholicism would seem to place him outside the boundaries of modern Jewish identity politics, the parallels with Scholem demonstrate the extent to which his memoir is steeped in the post-liberal and anti-assimilatory rhetoric of his German-Jewish contemporaries.

Stern's narrative skilfully conflates the Christian-theological and Jewish-political tropes of blindness so as to link his conversion to the post-Holocaust critique of German-Jewish assimilation. The ingenuity of this move is that in binding together these two figures of blindness, Stern frames his conversion as a revolt against the inauthentic Jewishness of German Jewry. Stern, who flirted with Zionism and Orthodox Judaism in the 1920s and 1930s before he made his decisive turn to Catholicism, presents himself as a member of the same "post-assimilatory" generation that sought to affirm its Jewishness as a proud sign of communal difference and as an expression of political and moral revolt against the liberal worldview of its parents. The appeal to Jewish authenticity was juxtaposed with the self-denial of the German-Jewish bourgeoisie, who had supposedly betrayed their origins for the political pipe dream of integration. Interweaving these two tropes of blindness allows Stern to fashion his conversion as a rejection of the German-Jewish ideology of assimilation and frame it as an act of Jewish self-assertion.[15] By aligning his turn to Catholicism with Jewish Orthodoxy and to a more limited extent Zionism, Stern presents his religious transformation as an organic outgrowth of his commitment to Judaism.[16]

**Bavarian Childhood circa 1900**

Stern's autobiography opens with an account of his idyllic childhood in rural Bavaria. He describes growing up in a prosperous and close-knit family that lived peacefully with its non-Jewish neighbours. The one thing that casts a pall over his childhood and youth is his family's tenuous ties to Judaism. The family's assimilationist trajectory begins with the grandfather, Moritz Stern, who abandoned his Orthodox Jewish upbringing and quit his rabbinic studies to become a peddler, later establishing himself as a successful textile merchant. Moritz Stern was one of the few members of Cham's small Jewish community who could lead the services other than the synagogue's cantor. Although familiar with Jewish law and liturgy, Moritz "was not at all orthodox, and assumed the somewhat lax attitude of compromise frequent with Western Jews."[17] If Moritz Stern possessed any residual attachment to traditional Judaism, he was careful not to pass it on to his children. As a result, "the people of my parents' generation were almost entirely cut off from Jewish tradition. They hardly understood Hebrew, and therefore were unable to follow the liturgy."[18] Stern describes a generation unsure of its Judaism, whose eclectic identity "consisted of a strange mixture of political liberalism, agnosticism, Lessing's religion of tolerance, Goethean, and even Nietzschean ideas."[19]

In Stern's account of his family history, we find a familiar vignette of German-Jewish modernity: exodus from the ghetto, followed by a socio-economic ascent to the ranks of the bourgeoisie, and culminating in the enthusiastic immersion into the culture of the *Bildungsbürgertum*. This ideological trajectory has been traced by the historians George Mosse and David Sorkin, who argue that the cultural development of German Jewry beginning in the nineteenth century was indelibly marked by the Enlightenment values of autonomy, rationality, and tolerance, which prevailed during the time of the emancipation. These values were encapsulated in the concept of *Bildung*. The *Bildungsideal*, as propounded by figures such as Lessing and Goethe, called for the moral and spiritual cultivation of the individual through lifelong learning. Its appeal to the Jews was that in its focus on individual development, *Bildung* transcended all barriers of race, religion, and nationality, thus constituting an ideal of citizenship that did not exclude them.[20] This ethos continued to inform German-Jewish self-understanding even after it no longer held much currency among the rest of the German population. As Mosse writes, "such lack of realism in politics was strikingly characteristic of the Jewish bourgeoisie. It must be explained in large part by their commitment to a German-Jewish identity which no longer corresponded to the realities of German life."[21]

The disconnect between German Jewry's self-perception and the surrounding political climate is illustrated by the figure of Stern's mother. Opposed to Jewish nationalism, she argues with her son about his membership in the Jewish Youth Movement. In her naive embrace of cosmopolitan humanism, she fails to see that his classmates regard the Jews "as an alien people." She wistfully follows the utopian universalist ideas of Romain Rolland and Bernard Shaw, "instead of accepting the fact that we were not regarded as Germans in Germany or Frenchmen in France."[22] The adolescent Stern is taken aback by his mother's naivety: "There seemed to be nothing very noble about the fact that so many Jews had a blind spot for their Jewishness."[23]

Stern's account of his childhood and youth contains a pointed critique of the German-Jewish ideology of assimilation. He describes his superficial religious upbringing in a household that lacked much appreciation or knowledge of Jewish tradition, custom, or lore. His parents and grandfather represent the misguided generations of post-emancipatory German Jews, who deluded themselves into believing they could become full-fledged Germans and who sacrificed their Jewish heritage in pursuit of an illusory Germanness. Like the Zionist youth of his generation, Stern criticizes his elders for their political naivety, accusing them of self-abasement and of betraying their Jewishness. Stern's critique of German-Jewish liberalism is encapsulated in his description of the drawing-room in his childhood home:

> The salon was hardly ever used. It contained a cupboard with books and thick easy chairs with useless tassels. Its only window, curiously enough, had been walled off and one had to turn on the electric light even during the day. Outside a fake window had been painted, a meaningless artificial eye facing the street. In the salon there were three huge albums called *The Nineteenth Century*, with pictures of Beethoven, Alexander Graham Bell, Wagner, Verdi, Napoleon, Lincoln and Goethe.[24]

The family drawing room is a largely abandoned ornamental space that is rarely used. The room's only window is walled off so that artificial lighting is required. Substituting for the blocked window is a painted one on the apartment's exterior, described as a "meaningless artificial eye." The room with its blocked-off window serves as an evocative emblem for the stodgy irrelevance Stern identifies with the German-Jewish liberal heritage passed down to him by his parents and grandparents. The room's darkness and the artificiality of its décor suggest a stifling atmosphere, and the random assemblage of great figures who adorn the coffee table albums attest to the family's incoherent cultural identity. Stern's critique of his family and the diminishing Jewishness of post-emancipation Jewry strongly recalls Gershom Scholem's derisive portrayal of German Jewry in his memoir *From Berlin to Jerusalem*.

Scholem's memoir reads like a conversion narrative in that it tells his life story as if it inevitably led to his embrace of Zionism and immigration to Palestine. As Scholem explains in the opening lines of his book, "I am describing the life of a young Jew whose path took him from the Berlin of his childhood and youth to Jerusalem and Israel. This path appeared to me to be singularly direct and illuminated by clear signposts; to others, including my own family, it often seemed incomprehensible, if not vexatious."[25] Like Stern's, Scholem's childhood recollections emphasize the family's tenuous observance of Jewish custom. His parents remembered some Hebrew prayers they learned as children but had no idea what they meant. The family did not keep kosher, and "there were only

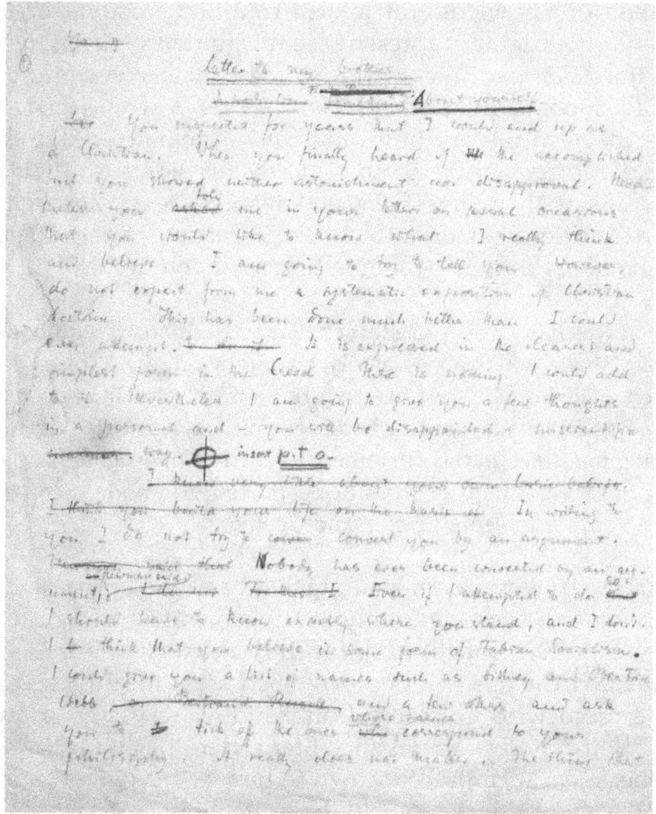

Figure 3.2. First page of longhand manuscript for *The Pillar of Fire* (undated). Simon Silverman Phenomenology Center, Duquesne University.

a few perceptible relics of Judaism" in his childhood home.[26] The Judaism his parents sought to pass on to him was a watered-down version of tradition abstracted to the idea of "pure monotheism and a purely rational morality."[27] Scholem depicts his growing interest in Judaism against the backdrop of assimilation, "which loomed so large in the life of German Jewry of my youth."[28] He describes a "deliberate break with the Jewish tradition" that was motivated by the hopes for social emancipation.[29] What Scholem finds inexplicable is that the desire for full integration stood in direct conflict with the rising tide of antisemitism: "Only wishful thinking could suppress this experience."[30] He views the discovery of German Jewry's "self-deception" as "one of the most decisive experiences of my youth."[31] Although their religious and ideological trajectories diverge, Scholem and Stern are working with a similar cultural script that pits their respective conversions to Zionism and Catholicism against the assimilated milieu of liberal Judaism. Beyond the biographical parallels, Scholem and Stern share a master plot of spiritual and political awakening that is staged through a conflict with their familial and cultural environment. What these affinities demonstrate, above all else, is the extent to which Stern's memoir is indebted to a specifically Jewish narrative logic, one that is shared by a post-assimilatory generation of German Jews.

Stern's religious and personal trajectory matches the generational profile of Weimar Jews, whose coming of age occurred against the backdrop of the First World War and the crisis of liberal Judaism. Like Gershom Scholem, Stern defines his identity "in opposition to mainstream liberal, 'bourgeois' Jewry."[32] His religiosity resonates with the same post-*Bildung* sensibilities that were shared by advocates of the Jewish Renaissance of the 1920s and 1930s. The young Jews who participated in the Jewish revival of the interwar era rejected the secular-rationalist conception of Judaism held by their parents and grandparents. Stern's embrace of Catholicism follows a path parallel to that of a generation that came of age during the interwar era and whose resolute turn to a messianic-tinged Judaism grew out of the crisis of German-Jewish liberalism.[33]

Stern goes on to recount the stilted religious instruction he receives as a child. Once in school, Stern starts studying with the town's cantor, "a man of vices, full of pride and vanity."[34] The dreary lessons consist of mechanical repetition and rote learning, which utterly fail to convey the spiritual treasures of Judaism. The next religious teacher Stern studies with, during his first year of high school in the drab, industrial city of Ebenburg, is not much of an improvement: "He had hardly any religious education, and there was not very much of the living fire of the Torah ... The tie of such cantors with Jewish tradition was only external and historical, their function purely social."[35] The teacher is not so much a man of God as a "religious professional" good for circumcisions and funerals. Fellow Bavarian Alfred Neumeyer, an art historian who fled to California in 1935 and converted to Catholicism in exile, would share similar memories of his Jewish education. Revolted by his teacher, "a red-haired Eastern Jew, who spoke a foreign guttural German," Neumeyer found the study of religious texts in Hebrew "repugnant."[36]

For his bar mitzvah, Stern reads the *haftorah* at the local synagogue – a makeshift prayer hall set up in the town brewery. Stern quotes the weekly portion he read from Ezekiel 37, which depicts the exiled People of Israel's revival and return to the Promised Land. Ezekiel's vision of the Valley of Dry Bones starkly contrasts with the atmosphere of spiritual decay that Stern attributes to his surroundings. He recalls that "nobody understood Hebrew or knew anything about the meaning of the texts."[37] His aunt Clara sarcastically remarks that his reading moved her to tears. The gifts he receives to mark the event similarly attest to the family's remove from its religious moorings: "There was a gift table with the collected works of Schiller, Kleist, Uhland and Eichendorff, and numerous works on Polar expeditions and on Tibet."[38]

Stern's discontent with his family's superficial Jewishness was a sign of the times. As an adolescent in the early interwar years, Stern joins the Jung-Jüdischer Wanderbund, a Zionist youth movement modelled on the Wandervogel. The movement's members share "a rebellious attitude against their parents' generation, or at least against the mode of living of that generation."[39] Looking back at the uncompromising battle his generation waged against anything it considered "bourgeois," Stern mocks the juvenile self-righteousness of his peers. He nevertheless accedes that this youthful rebellion was nourished by "a profound spiritual restlessness," which emerged as a "reaction against middle-class culture, against a parent-generation, against a colourless form of liberalism and assimilation, against the 'German citizen of Jewish denomination.'"[40]

Feelings of dissatisfaction with the youth movement's ideological ambiguity and the noncommittal stance of its members lead Stern to experiment with religion. As a high school student in Munich, Stern boards with the Kohens, an Orthodox Jewish family, whose lifestyle stands in stark contrast to the vapid religiosity Stern identifies with his own upbringing. Recalling his Sabbaths with the Kohens, Stern writes, "It was as if time and space had become a spiritual enclave … there was an atmosphere of peace and enchantment."[41] The Kohen family belongs to the Canal Synagogue, an inconspicuous structure that lacks the pomp and grandeur of Munich's liberal congregation, whose "synagogue resembled a big, fashionable Protestant church, and contained an organ." [42] What the Orthodox synagogue lacks in splendor it makes up for in its liveliness and religious devotion. Unlike the liberal congregation, whose services and architecture imitate their Christian neighbours, the Orthodox synagogue has preserved its authenticity, observing Judaism's perennial traditions. The young Stern is struck by the pious atmosphere, the all-encompassing nature of the Jewish-Orthodox lifestyle, and its communal character: "Everybody seemed to know the liturgy by heart … The synagogue was an organic continuation of religious life in the family.[43]

Stern's turn to Orthodoxy comes as a great shock to his family. Fearing for their son's sanity, his parents call a family council to bring him back into the fold: "The entire world, Spinoza, Goethe, Voltaire, Heine ... political liberalism, and the Age of Reason seemed to be denied by an act of lunacy. For some obscure and repellent reason I had turned my back on progress. I am sure mother was afraid I was going crazy."[44] To his parents' great relief, Stern's interest in Orthodox Judaism turns out to be a passing phase, but this does not exhaust its symbolic role in the overall narrative, in which it signifies an authentically Jewish counterpoint to the noncommittal religiosity the author identifies with German Judaism.

The critique of German-Jewish assimilation and the inauthenticity of Reform Judaism we encounter in Stern's memoir recurs in the narratives of Alfred Döblin and numerous other converts. In his fictionalized autobiography, *Memoiren eines Banquiers* (1836), the writer and critic August Lewald (1792–1871) describes entering a "so-called German-Israelite temple" (*einen sogenannten deutsch-israelitischen Tempel*) after his conversion.[45] He recalls hearing "an enlightened speech, delivered in pure German," and beautifully orchestrated music and song, in stark contrast to "the confused, stupefying noise" and "incomprehensible murmuring" of the synagogues he attended in his youth.[46] Lewald bemoans the artificiality of this modernized Jewish service, seeing in it "nothing but ostentation meant to imitate the Christians."[47] One hundred thirty years after Lewald, actor Ernst Ginsberg takes up the same issue in his memoir *Abschied* (1965). Describing the religious identity of his grandparents in Berlin, he writes that "they belonged to the so-called Jewish Reform community and rarely went to the synagogue, where a kind of washed-out liberalism prevailed, which, for example, made it possible for me to hear a glorifying sermon on Nietzsche's Zarathustra. In a Jewish synagogue!"[48] Ginsberg wonders why assimilated Jews who lack any deep religious ties to their ancestral religion are nevertheless so resentful towards anyone who distances himself from Judaism.

## Jewish Catastrophe as Christian Revelation

In contrast to his own growing Jewish self-awareness, Stern presents his parents as completely oblivious to the antisemitic chauvinist tide that washed over Germany in the wake of the First World War: "During this time my parents received a large amount of literature, mainly periodicals, which seemed to emphasize that German Jews were Germans."[49] The drama of German-Jewish self-deception becomes even more acute when Stern's narrative reaches 1933. His recollections from the period offer an overview of the different Jewish responses to the rise of National Socialism:

> The National Socialist Revolution had, not only materially, a devastating impact upon German and European Jewry. It acted like an earthquake and flood because the masses of Jews were, in spite of years of gathering clouds, psychologically and ideologically utterly unprepared. Most people think of us as cunning, foxy, with a great amount of practical foresight. The years after 1933 proved us to be as sentimental in our attachments, as emotional and stupid in our practical decisions, as much given to wishful thinking and self-deception as any other people.[50]

Underscoring German Jewry's ostrich-like response to the Nazi takeover, Stern describes middle-class families listening to foreign radio stations, in search of "every little scrap of story or anecdote that resembled a small-scale Nazi defeat."[51] Others reason that the Nazi regime will be unable to sustain itself economically and will collapse in a matter of months. "Most of those who deceived themselves in this way had in the end to emigrate without any material goods whatsoever."[52]

Even members of the intelligentsia and the liberal professions, who ultimately managed to relocate and rebuild their lives outside of Germany, "retained a profound feeling of uprootedness and insecurity."[53] The existential upheaval they experienced as émigrés fleeing National Socialism toppled their faith in "the peculiar nineteenth-century brand of liberalism … characteristic of the social strata to which they belonged."[54] For Stern, the true tragedy of the German-Jewish middle class was that the belated realization of its imminent doom left it in a state of moral crisis. The rise of National Socialism revealed that the liberal culture to which the majority of German Jews had subscribed was nothing but a "hollow structure."[55] "Most of them had no roots whatsoever in Jewry. Its positive values, its great traditions, its spirit were entirely unknown to these people. A senseless and cruel stigma was all that Jewry had become to them."[56]

In Stern's account, German Jewry is both ignorant of its religious heritage and unaware of its impending destruction. Once struck by the magnitude of the events, this community, which has fooled itself into believing it is secure, is incapable of coming to terms with its existential crisis. The only mark left of the Jewishness it so eagerly disposed of is its victimhood. The crisis is particularly acute for those Jews who long believed they had completed the path towards acculturation: "There was a particularly small group of those who had identified themselves so much with German culture, not only the Germany of Goethe but the Germany of Bismarck, that their forcible exclusion struck them as an explosion strikes a child. They *groped blindly around* in some sort of no-man's-land. Among these were the first cases of suicide of which we heard."[57]

There is a direct line connecting Stern's portrayal of German Jewry and Gershom Scholem's outspoken rejection of the "German–Jewish dialogue." Scholem's harshest critique of the post-Shoah idealization of German–Jewish relations appeared in a letter titled "Against the Myth of the German–Jewish Dialogue" (1964).[58] Scholem, who is never one to mince words, belligerently declares, "I deny that there has ever been such a German–Jewish dialogue in any genuine sense whatsoever," and asserts that the much-celebrated dialogue died before it even began.[59] According to Scholem, this dialogue never occurred for the simple reason that "it takes two to have a dialogue, who listen to each other, who are prepared to perceive the other as what he is and represents, and to respond to him." The Germans never accepted the Jews as interlocutors, and in those rare cases where a dialogue took place, it was always contingent upon the Jews' "expressed or unexpressed self-denial" of their Jewish identity. As Scholem later explained, one could not speak of a "German-Jewish dialogue," not only because the Germans never collaborated in this idealistic endeavour, but also because those Jews who devoted themselves to realizing this dialogue had already sacrificed their Judaism and were thus no longer Jews "in the full sense of an unbroken historical consciousness."[60]

Scholem's denial of the "dialogue" corroborated his negative verdict on the legacy of German Jewry and its historical trajectory since the time of the Enlightenment. Evaluating the Jews' attempt to acculturate from a post-Shoah perspective, Scholem believed that this collective effort was doomed from the start. The Jewish project of the Enlightenment, from the times of Moses Mendelssohn up until the rise of National Socialism, was nothing but a misguided and illusory aspiration that spelled out the Jews' tragic end. The "'adventure' of assimilation" had led to the inner disintegration of Judaism; indeed, according to Scholem, it was intricately linked to the Jews' physical destruction at the hands of the Nazis.

Scholem construes the course of German-Jewish history as a teleological process whose culmination in the Shoah was inevitable. His deterministic approach to German-Jewish history enacts a certain kind of logic that literary critic Michael André Bernstein calls "backshadowing." Bernstein coined the term to describe "a kind of retroactive foreshadowing in which the shared knowledge of the outcome of a series of events … is used to judge the participants in those events as though they too should have known what was to come."[61] It is only by positing the Shoah as the preordained outcome of German-Jewish history that Scholem can deride German Jews for their blindness and wilful self-deception.

Much as in Scholem, in Stern's account there is a sense that the German-Jewish fate in the Nazi era was inevitable. He too faults the Jews for tenaciously holding on to the fantasy of their Germanness. But whereas the critique of German-Jewish blindness serves as an ideological justification for Zionism in Scholem's case, it functions as a theological confirmation of the Christian truth in Stern's autobiography. Stern implicitly juxtaposes German Jewry's fumbling response to the rise of the Nazis against his own probing spiritual search, which leads to his single-minded embrace of Christianity. What convinces Stern "of the absolute truth of Revelation" is his growing conviction that there is a messianic meaning to the collective suffering of the Jews that surpasses their communal predicament. He comes to believe that "the fate of European Jewry, was either meaningless, or else its meaning was transcendental."

Daniel Burston points out that Stern, in his idealized portrayal of Cardinal Faulhaber and his 1933 sermon on Jewish–Christian relations, omits the fact that Faulhaber was not seeking to defend the Jews from Nazi persecution; rather, he was making a theological argument concerning the continuity of the Old and New Testaments. His homily was actually reiterating the supersessionist idea that Christianity had succeeded Judaism. In contrast to Stern's enthusiastic response, most Jews regarded Faulhaber's sermon as a direct attack on their community of faith. As Burston explains: "Faulhaber never incited Catholics to commit violence against Jews. The problem was that his sermon provided Catholics with the perfect justification for passivity and indifference to the fate of the Jews in the years leading up to the Holocaust, thereby helping to seal their fate at the hands of Hitler's minions."[62]

Cardinal Faulhaber delivered his homily at Saint Michael's Church in December 1933. Stern attended it with his brother. Arriving at the sermon, Stern was encouraged by the large turnout at a gathering that was meant to be a show of anti-Nazi solidarity. In his sermon the cardinal asserted the Jewishness of Jesus, reminding his audience of the organic unity that bound the God of the Church and the God of the biblical Patriarchs.[63] Stern would remember Faulhaber's address as a personal revelation:

The sermon came as if it had been specially timed and written for my personal consumption. It had a profound, irrevocable influence on me. I remember well that, with the few meager hints he gave of the Paulinian idea with regard to post-Christian Judaism, he opened up an entirely new Vista. I felt like a child who had known its own house from the garden, and who is now, for the first time, shown it from far away as part of the landscape.[64]

The sermon reframed Stern's perception of Judaism and the historical predicament of European Jewry, revealing a whole new and broader perspective on the events unfolding in Germany. It allowed Stern to grasp the larger significance of the Jewish catastrophe, which extended beyond the confines of the Jews' communal existence. As Stern would later explain, "under the indescribable dread of persecution, I began to see the meaning of the mystery of Israel … Christ is not only the Messiah to Israel. If He means anything then His meaning transcends all national destiny."[65]

True to the literary tradition of the Christian conversion narrative, in which near-death experiences either anticipate or follow the convert's revelation, Stern is seized by a severe case of miliary tuberculosis from which he nearly dies. The fatal illness and miraculous recovery, which occur shortly after he attended the cardinal's sermon, symbolize the rebirth that comes with Stern's spiritual transformation. Like Paul, who was blind for three days and could not eat or drink after his fateful encounter on the road to Damascus, Stern endures a long period of recovery and suffers from chronic weakness in the months following his brush with death.

Stern's valorization of Jewish suffering as bearing a transcendental meaning draws on a distinctly Christian-theological understanding of the Jews' role in the history of salvation. The theological problem faced by the Church Fathers was how to explain the survival of the Jews after Judaism's supersession by Christianity. To justify the persistence of Judaism after the coming of Christ, the church cast the Jews in the role of "witness-people," whose mysterious survival confirmed the truth of the New Testament and attested to God's active involvement in the course of history. The Jews' exile was interpreted as a punishment for their role in the crucifixion and their refusal to acknowledge Christ's divinity, but it was also seen as a confirmation of Christianity in two important ways: first, the Jews' historical degradation was understood as a sign of Christianity's theological superiority, and second, the Jews, who stubbornly clung to the Old Testament, served as a living reminder of Christianity's origins. This theological interpretation of Jewish suffering and survival had nothing to do with the Jews' self-understanding as a people, but instead served to explain the meaning of their continued existence within a Christian framework.[66]

The symbolic role that Jewish suffering and survival plays in the Christian imagination is epitomized in *The City of God*, where Augustine explains that the Jews were "uprooted from their kingdom" for killing and then renouncing Christ. For Augustine, Jewish exile is a sign of both punishment (for the Jews) and salvation (for the Christians):

> By the evidence of their own scriptures they bear witness for us that we have not fabricated the prophecies about Christ ... It follows that when the Jews do not believe in our scriptures, their scriptures are fulfilled in them, while they read them with blind eyes ... It is in order to give this testimony which, in spite of themselves, they supply for our benefit by their possession and preservation of those books [of the Old Testament] that they are themselves dispersed among all nations, wherever the Christian church spreads.[67]

The Jews in this passage serve as the ultimate witnesses to a divine message of salvation, which they have denied and from which they are subsequently excluded. They remain a "chosen people," not as the purveyors of the living word of God but as a historical relic that confirms the truth of Christianity. By stubbornly clinging to the Old Testament, they serve as the "slave-librarian" for the Church. The ingenuity of this theological construct lies in the fact that it responds to the doctrinal threat posed by Judaism by subsuming its religious significance and redefining it in accordance with Church doctrine. Rather than disproving Christ's prophecies, Jewish suffering and survival is interpreted as an integral part of the unfolding drama of the Christian history of salvation. In most versions of this myth, the Jews will continue to live in exile until the end of times, when many of them will finally convert to Christianity.

Stephen Haynes argues that Augustine's account of Jewish survival reflects an ambivalence characteristic of all subsequent versions of the "witness-people myth," in which the Jews are cast in the role of an eternally guilty people, who paradoxically also represent the work of divine providence. This paradoxical Christian construct underlies Stern's Holocaust theodicy. He presents the Jews as a people who have gone astray through their secularization and assimilation. The blindness that Christian theologians attribute to the Jews due to their inability to recognize the divinity of Christ is reproduced in Stern's claim that German Jews have lost sight of their religious mainstay yet continue to fulfil their divine vocation in ways unbeknown to them. German Jewry is portrayed as a hollow relic of the Jewish past, a people lacking in religious and communal vitality who nevertheless continue to play an important and mysterious role in the history of salvation. Their suffering attests to a higher metaphysical truth, the meaning of which is unavailable to them.

While Stern's account of Jewish suffering builds on a long-standing Christian theological tradition, what makes his "revelation" so rhetorically compelling is the manner in which it merges with the post-Holocaust critique presented by Scholem. Stern interweaves the Christian imputation of the Jews' theological blindness with the Zionist charge of European Jewry's political blindness. In coupling these two accusations together, Stern harmonizes his Catholic identity with Zionism's anti-assimilatory critique of German Jewry. By presenting his turn to Catholicism as the culmination of his youthful revolt against his parental milieu and its superficial Judaism, Stern fashions his spiritual development as the result of a deep commitment to Judaism. A young adult who was passionately involved with the Zionist cause and attracted to the communal lifestyle and spiritual treasures of Jewish Orthodoxy, Stern wants to convince his readers that his deep ties to Judaism are what motivated him to convert to Christianity. His Catholicism is not a rejection of his past Jewish self, but a perfection and evolution of a drawn-out and probing spiritual search for the ultimate. He cannot accept Zionism or Orthodoxy because both betray the universalistic message of Judaism, perfected in the form of Christianity.

**The True Israel**

The two exceptions to Stern's portrait of German-Jewish self-deception are Orthodox Jews and Zionists. Stern writes that in all the "uproar, bewilderment and confusion" of the years after the Nazi rise to power, the path offered by the Zionist Youth seemed the most "realistic and positive." For the Zionists, "the German turmoil was an almost welcome pretext ... to shed the clothes of Western Jewish bourgeoisie, the position of economic intermediators which it held in a capitalistic world, its pale abstract existence in the foam of a drying-out current of civilization."[68] Stern takes part in the activities of various Zionist groups in Munich, where he helps organize courses in Hebrew language and culture. Yet he remains sceptical of Zionism, writing that "pure Zionism with the somewhat noncommittal appendix of 'Jewish culture' left me dissatisfied and with the definite sense of a void."[69] He does not deny that the Zionist movement tackled "the immediate practical necessities" of Germany's persecuted Jews, but he remains uncomfortable with the solution it offered: "I felt at the bottom of my heart that a mere withdrawal into a national culture was not a solution for the Jews, and what we needed in the end was a universal solution, a solution which was equally applicable and equally binding on those poor devils around us who persecuted us."[70]

Stern's critique of Zionism echoed the viewpoint of many German-Jewish liberals, who argued that Jewish nationalism betrayed the Jewish people's "universal mission." This tradition may well have informed his analysis. But in the context of his autobiography, the significance of this critique is in the way it prepares the grounds for his turn to Christianity – a religion that universalizes the biblical revelation that the Jews mistakenly interpret as a tribal affair.

The dissatisfaction with Zionism's secular nationalism leads Stern back to the synagogue. Stern is once again enchanted by the piety and deep devotion of Orthodox Jewry, whose lifestyle revolves around study, prayer, and religious observance. During his frequent visits to the synagogue, he devotes his time to studying the Prophets in the Hebrew original with the traditional biblical commentators.[71] He tries to balance his commitment to Zionism and Orthodoxy in face of Zionist friends, who "saw no necessity at all for religious tradition in any form."[72] What the Zionists failed to recognize was that the extraordinary self-sacrifice they exhibited in their own lives was a direct result of the tradition they denied. They "did not realize that they themselves were actually living on the immense treasure of Orthodoxy."[73] The Zionists here exemplify another type of "Jewish blindness" in their inability to see that their movement is nurtured by the very religious traditions they rebel against.

In 1932, around the same time that Stern is deepening his ties to the synagogue, he befriends two devout Christians working with him at the German Research Institute for Psychiatry in Munich. The first, Frau Bertha Flamm, is a middle-aged lab technician and single mother, residing in one of Munich's poorer residential districts with her daughter and eighty-year-old adoptive mother. A fervent Catholic and anti-Nazi, Frau Flamm supports Stern's growing interest in Orthodox Judaism. The other believer at the institute, who takes to Stern, is a visiting researcher by the name of Dr. Yamagiwa, a Japanese veterinary pathologist. The pathologist and his wife are Protestant converts and avowed pacifists, who are shunned by the other Japanese researchers at the institute, whom they describe as "fanatical nationalists."[74] The Yamagiwas are fascinated by Stern, the first Jew they have ever met. Like Frau Flam, they do not try to convert him; indeed, they encourage him to deepen his ties to Judaism.

The friendship with Frau Flamm and the Yamagiwas exemplifies the interethnic fraternity that Stern finds in Christianity and that he juxtaposes against the tribalism of his Zionist and Orthodox Jewish peers.

> Here were people of the Japanese and the German race who thought the same thoughts as I, and felt the same feelings as I – entirely different from the pagans around us but also different from those of my Jewish brethren who were agnostic or irreligious. Here I … found people of a strange nation who had the words of David and Isaiah engraved in their hearts. This was a miracle. I felt it to my innermost depth but I refused somehow to admit it in its fullness and in all its implications.[75]

Stern's friendships with Frau Flam and the Yamagiwas mark his growing realization that Judaism is contained within Christianity. Stern struggles with this insight, because he cannot bring himself to abandon the Jewish community at its time of crisis. "I seemed to cling to the stark overwhelming reality, to the call of the Jewish communion which had become the tragic communion of Fate. I intensified my study of Hebrew … I took part more frequently in study courses and in the services at the synagogue."[76]

He frequently visits the house of Dr. Eugene Fränkel, a leader in Munich's Orthodox community, who "was a true example of Jewish piety" and who "seemed to personify the spirit of the Torah."[77] He regularly dines with the Fränkel family on the Sabbath, yet he suffers from a deep sense of conflict between his attraction to the Christian world of Frau Flamm and the Yamagiwas and the Orthodox Jewish world of Dr. Fränkel. He wants to share his thoughts with Dr. Fränkel, but fears that Dr. Fränkel "was so deeply rooted in tradition that he would not have understood me."[78] Confessing his dilemma to Fränkel would only confuse and scandalize him. Torn between the world of Dr. Fränkel and that of Frau Flamm and the Yamagiwas, Stern eventually realizes that the two are not so different from each other. In the evenings with Frau Flamm and the Yamagiwas, Stern finds "a harmony of spirit which equalled that of the Friday evenings with the Fränkels. There was no doubt, it was the same atmosphere of peace and understanding … It was really the spirit of Judaism I rediscovered in this strange setting, enriched by remote peoples, and cleansed of its purely ethnic elements."[79]

The difference between the two worlds was that Frau Flamm and the Yamagiwas understood and accepted the world of Dr. Fränkel, whereas he was incapable of comprehending theirs. "Thus, I made another important discovery. Christianity confirmed and believed everything which Jewry believed but added one fundamental assertion which

Jewry rejected."[80] According to Stern's formula, Christianity is Judaism minus the ethnocentrism. He thus emerges from the synagogue to discover a living embodiment of the message of the Jewish Prophets in the non-Jews, who offer him their friendship and spiritual support. Stern comes to feel that the "Jews who reacted to nationalism around us with national vigour were closer to the Nazis than these people who believed in the God of Abraham, Isaac and Jacob."[81]

Stern establishes a moral equivalence between Nazism and Judaism in order to justify his turn to Catholicism. The Jews, he contends, were in "perfect agreement" with the Nazis in that both parties "maintained the racial wall around the God of Sinai."[82] Judaism "was racial exclusiveness in its noblest form – in its metaphysical form, so to speak. It was a racism exactly opposed to that of the Nazis, but it was racism just the same."[83]

## The Jonah Complex

There would be a ten-year lag between Stern's spiritual epiphany at Cardinal Faulhaber's 1933 Christmas Eve sermon and his formal conversion to Catholicism in December 1943, when he was finally baptized in Montreal's Church of the Franciscan Fathers. During this decade, Stern agonized over his religious loyalties, vacillating between his ever-growing attraction to Christianity and his residual attachment to Judaism. He felt caught between the Church and the Synagogue, unable to make the final step towards Christianity. This dilemma constitutes the central drama of Stern's memoir, one that unfolds through intimate soul-searching conversations with historically renowned figures such as the Jewish philosopher Martin Buber, founder of the Youth Aliyah movement Recha Freier, and Catholic theologian Jacques Maritain.[84] Convinced that he cannot abandon the Jewish community in its time of need, Stern is paralysed by what he calls a "traitor complex."[85] Stern elaborates on this "complex" through his recurring allusions to the Book of Jonah, which serves to illustrate the conflict between Jewish particularism and Christian universalism.

Stern invokes the Prophet Jonah not only as a biblical metaphor for his own ongoing reluctance to convert to Christianity, but also as a critique of Judaism. In this short scriptural narrative, traditionally read on Yom Kippur, Jonah is enjoined by God to go and warn the inhabitants of Nineveh to repent, lest they be destroyed in forty days. Jonah, "a proud Jew," according to Stern, refuses to fulfil his divine mission because it "hurt his feelings of national dignity."[86] In his attempt to flee God and his responsibility as a prophet, Jonah is thrown overboard

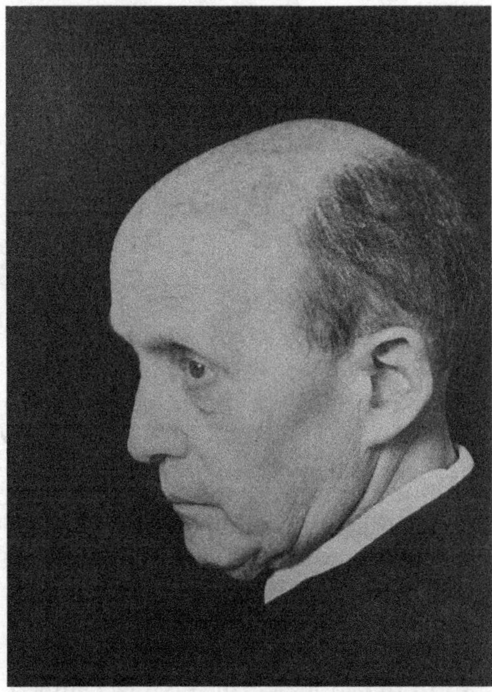

Figure 3.3.  Photograph of Karl Stern (undated). Simon Silverman Phenomenology Center, Duquesne University.

on his voyage to Tarshish and is swallowed by a large fish. After three days and nights of praying for mercy, the fish spews out Jonah, and he returns to Nineveh in order to fulfil his divine mission. Jonah grudgingly goes to Nineveh and shares the prophecy with the city's inhabitants, who duly repent and are subsequently spared divine retribution. The story ends with Jonah, sulking outside the city gates, disappointed that God did not fulfil his prophecy and inflict his wrath upon the denizens of Nineveh.

According to Stern's interpretation, Jonah is averse to sharing God's prophecy with the nations. "To be a Prophet and in his function of a Prophet not to be associated with the idea of the nation is so horrible that he would rather drown than fulfil his mission. It is the enemies of his people whose conversion is at stake, and to sacrifice his national pride for the conversion of others is more than his human nature can take."[87] For Stern the story of Jonah is the story of the Jewish people's stubborn refusal to share their revelation with the non-Jews. The Jews, like Jonah in Stern's reading, fail to grasp the universal scope of the divine message with which they have been charged.

An important reservation to Stern's reading is that his critique of Jonah is intrinsic to the text, that is, it is already contained within the Jewish tradition. By identifying Jonah's mulishness with Judaism as a whole, Stern superimposes an archetypal interpretation that is part of a long-standing Christian hermeneutic tradition, whose exponents include Augustine, Luther, Johann David Michaelis, and Bruno Bauer. Yvonne Sherwood traces the evolution of this interpretative tradition and its underlying anti-Jewish polemics in *A Biblical Text and Its Afterlives: The Survival of Jonah*. For Augustine, the Ninevites represent the Church and gentile repentance. The Ninevites embody Israel of the Spirit in opposition to Jonah, who in his refusal to universalize God's prophecy represents Israel of the Flesh. The image of Jonah as a stiff-necked Jew re-emerges in Luther's writings. For Luther, the fish that swallows and then spews out Jonah serves as a metaphor for the birth of Christianity out of the Jewish tradition. In preaching to the gentiles, Jonah is "the first to make Judaism contemptible and superfluous."[88] In 1782, the biblical scholar and opponent of Jewish emancipation Johann David Michaelis interpreted the Book of Jonah as a critique of "the Israelite people's hate and envy towards all the other nations of the earth."[89] In similar vein, the theologian and philosopher Bruno Bauer claimed that the book dramatized the struggle between the principles of particularism and universalism. For Christian readers of the book, Jonah thus encapsulates the Christian supersession of Judaism. As Sherwood explains, "the supersessionist drama of the humiliation of the Jew is performed in the exchange between the ungodly Hebrew and the godly sailors ... the superiority of the Ninevites, who act like saints and shine forth as pure angels of God. Allegedly, as Jonah unwittingly invalidates his own tradition, so he condemns his own race."[90]

During his last months in Germany before fleeing to England, Stern attends a seminar on the Book of Jonah delivered by Martin Buber at the Jewish Congregation of Munich. He nostalgically recalls the heated debates between the different Jewish factions in attendance. Stern conjures up a sentimental scene of Jewish learning, in which Jews of all political and religious denominations argue over the meaning of scripture, as Jews have done for two millennia. "The scene was outside time. Here were young Jews in the middle of Germany, an island engulfed by contempt, hostility and danger ... At that moment the only important thing was the significance of the written word."[91] This turned out to be the last time that Stern was in close contact with the German-Jewish world of his youth: "Oh, how I should like to be able to see them all once more, my friends of those days, and tell them the story of a journey which seems to have taken me infinitely far away from them, but in reality has led me right into their midst."[92]

This tender portrayal of German-Jewish spiritual resilience in its ongoing commitment to the study of scripture is marred by Stern's earlier interpretation of the Book of Jonah, which criticized the Jews as a tribal holdout to Christian universal brotherhood. Buber and the members of the Jewish congregation discussing this biblical story are metonymically implicated in Stern's critique of "Jonah the Jew." By this reading, the Jews in Nazi Germany are likened to the rebellious prophet caught in the storm on the ship to Tarshish. Their inability to fathom the impending catastrophe parallels that of Jonah sleeping below deck on his way to Tarshish, wholly indifferent to the storm raging outside.

The Jonah parallel extends to Stern himself, who like the disobedient prophet avoids realizing his religious convictions through conversion to Christianity. The power of the Jonah metaphor in Stern's memoir can be illustrated through Abraham Maslow's notion of "the Jonah complex." Maslow coined the term to describe the psychological fear of self-realization, when such change threatens one's existing sense of selfhood.[93] According to Pierre-Emmanuel and André Lacocque, Jonah "is also a paradigm of our resistance to election by God, for nothing is more repulsive to us than to be designated (elected, chosen) by the Outer Voice for a self-transcending task, when we would rather follow our inner voice and our biological dictates for our self-satisfaction and our self-aggrandizement."[94] Like Jonah, Stern suffers from an unresolved conflict between his newly gained insight into Christ's divinity and his fear of breaking away from the Jewish community. Even though his religious transformation has the potential to open up new spiritual vistas, he consistently evades his divine destiny out of fear of standing alone. He hesitates to make the existential decision and prefers the warmth of the Jewish hearth over Jesus.

Stern's spiritual dilemma is exacerbated when he thinks of his brother Ludwig, who immigrated to Palestine in 1939, where he changed his name to Shimon and founded Kibbutz Kfar Szold. Stern romanticizes the collective lifestyle of the Jewish pioneers and is once again drawn by "the lure of belonging."[95] He rationalizes his renewed attraction to Jewish communitarianism by the fact that "Providence had made me a Jew." Despite his nostalgic yearning for "the sheltering warmth of blood," Stern recalls his debt to "those Christians in Munich who had suffered for us and with us during the night of annihilation, with whom I had for the first time seen a super-national Israel – they seemed to beckon me not to betray them."[96] The conflict between Israel of the Flesh

Figure 3.4.  An aerogram sent from Ludwig (Shimon) Stern, who lived in Kibbutz Kfar Szold in northern Israel, to his brother Karl Stern in Montreal (1951). Despite Karl's conversion to Catholicism the two brothers remained in contact over the years. Simon Silverman Phenomenology Center, Duquesne University.

and Israel of the Spirit is exemplified in Stern's opposition between Jonah's "Jewish tribalism" and "Ninevite universalism."

Recalling the literary strategy employed in Hirsch's *Heimkehr zu Gott*, which contrasts the diverging paths taken by the twin brothers Karl Jakob and Gottfried, Stern uses his younger brother as a foil for his conversion to Catholicism. The book's final chapter, "Letter to My Brother," addressed to Ludwig Stern, sets out to explain the reasons for the author's conversion. The choice of epistolary form is one we are already familiar with from Karl Jakob Hirsch and will encounter again in the next chapter of this book, on Heinrich Kronstein. The appeal to a concrete addressee, who in this case is also a close family member, creates a sense of intimacy and proximity. The dialogical effect of a memoir written as a series of letters or concluding with a letter to one's brother creates the illusion of artlessness and simplicity, when in fact the stories it recounts are highly stylized and sophisticated works of rhetoric. Stern's letter to his brother is not so much an attempt to convince Ludwig to turn from *kibbutznik* to Catholic as it is a formalistic device serving the purpose of self-justification. Stern juxtaposes his devout

Catholicism against his brother's secular socialism in order to affirm the paradoxical Jewishness of his confessional choice. "The fact remains that you live in a co-operative community not far from Lake Genezareth, and when you talk you do so in the language of Isaiah. I talk Isaiah, but in the language of Bertrand Russell ... and in a place four thousand miles away from Lake Genezareth."[97] The appeal to the brother demonstrates how Stern fashions his Catholic identity in relation to his Jewish past and *against* the Jewish present, as an alternative to the prevailing paths of post-Holocaust Jewry.

It is only when he overcomes his inner resistance to breaking away from the supposed insularity of the Jewish community and opens up to the "Ninevites" – that is to say, Christianity – that Stern is reborn. The fish's belly is the mother's womb. It is comfortable and protective, but ultimately inhibiting to one's freedom. Stern is a Jonah figure in that he runs away from his responsibility, his calling. He has recognized the divinity of Christ and the error of the Jews, yet he fears the growing pains that this transformation calls for. He wants to regress to the womb of Judaism. Like Jonah, who seeks relief from the crisis at sea by going to sleep, Stern temporarily rejoins the Orthodox Jewish community after Hitler's rise to power and is drawn by the lure of Jewish-national regeneration in Palestine.

In a striking reversal of the biblical version, Stern isn't thrown overboard by the sailors, but jumps ship and manages to save himself from the sinking vessel of Nazi Germany. The isolation he experiences during his years of indecision, while he vacillates between Judaism and Christianity, correspond to Jonah's desperate solitude in the belly of the fish. The Book of Jonah thus functions as an evocative intertext for Stern's own spiritual struggles, summarized in the book's closing sentence: "Towards Him we had been running, or from Him we had been running away, but all the time He had been in the centre of things."[98] Like Jonah preaching to the Ninevites, Stern has turned to the gentiles to share the story of his spiritual regeneration in Christ. Yet unlike Jonah, he does so willingly. He has joined the Ninevites instead of moping alone under the dead gourd vine.

**First Communion and the Fantasy of Incorporation**

Stern deftly incorporates the Book of Jonah as the guiding intertext to narrate his passage to Catholicism. In this reading, Jonah's flight from God corresponds to Stern's own efforts to avoid the truth of Catholicism and the ultimate necessity of conversion. This compelling interpretation excludes another unacknowledged possibility, which the

Jonah parallel seems to call for: that the flight recounted in the narrative is that of the author's own escape from Judaism and the Jewish fate. This act of disidentification goes hand in hand with Stern's failure to confront the trauma of survival and his inability to mourn his friends and family members murdered by the Nazis. The narrative never fully registers the psychic injuries that the author sustained as a bereaved survivor and victim of Nazism. Traces of this unsettled grief and guilt find their expression precisely in those places in the memoir that supposedly point to the plot's resolution.

The narrative concludes with Stern's First Communion on 21 December 1943. During this sacramental rite, the bread and wine consumed by the believer are transformed into the body and blood of Christ through the miracle of transubstantiation. This sacrament is a re-enactment of the Last Supper prior to the crucifixion. Ingesting the body and blood of Christ is a way to relive and commemorate his sacrifice on the cross. Stern describes the morning of his First Communion as an event that bridges the different moments in his life, bringing them all into harmonious unity. He experiences the Holy Communion as a moment of totality that transcends the Jewish–Christian divide: "Our lives … had converged, and had converged with those unknown ones around us. And it was as if others were there: my parents, and Kaspar Russ, and the Kohen family, the Jews from the Canal Synagogue, and Jacques Maritain and Dorothy Day, and the pious old maids of our childhood homes."[99]

The figures Stern conjures up in the context of his First Communion are highly suggestive of the psychic reality that is deflected through his consumption of the Eucharist. The sacrament represents Stern's assimilation into the Body of Christ through his ingestion of that very body. At the same time, this sacramental rite fulfils another fantasy of incorporation, in that it reunites Stern with a Jewish past that was lost to him in the Holocaust. What is being consumed here is more than the body of Christ, it is also the world of German Jewry destroyed in the death camps.

It is not merely the association of dead Jews and the dead (and resurrected) Jesus that drives my reading here. It is also the symbolic and literal operations of the Eucharist that illuminate Stern's forced attempt at closure. Supporting such a reading is Nicolas Abraham and Maria Torok's "Mourning *or* Melancholia: Introjection *versus* Incorporation." In their influential essay, the psychoanalytic theorists Torok and Abraham describe a defence mechanism they call "the fantasy of incorporation."[100] This fantasy is enacted through the incorporation of a lost love object into one's body, thus allowing the subject to circumvent "the reality of a loss sustained by the psyche."[101] The acceptance of, or conscious confrontation with, such a loss would require a readjustment that the subject is unprepared to make. Instead, this profound psychic transformation is simulated through the fantasy of incorporation. In literally ingesting one's loss the subject incorporates it without processing its psychic meaning. The fantasy of incorporation operates "by implementing literally something that has only figurative meaning. So in order not to have to 'swallow' a loss, we fantasize swallowing (or having swallowed) that which has been lost, as if it were some kind of thing."[102]

The fantasy of incorporation works on two levels: "demetaphorization (taking literally what is meant figuratively) and objectivation (pretending that the suffering is not an injury to the subject but instead a loss sustained by the love object)."[103] The fantasy frees the subject from registering his own psychic pain and confronting its consequences. In this regard, Christianity proves to be the "cure" for Stern. When he takes in the Eucharist, he is ingesting the love object he refuses to mourn. As Abraham and Torok explain, "incorporation is the refusal to reclaim as our own the part of ourselves that we placed in what we lost; incorporation is the refusal to acknowledge the full import of the loss, a loss that, if recognized as such, would effectively, transform us ... The fantasy of incorporation reveals a gap within the psyche; it points to something that is missing just where introjection should have occurred."[104]

The metaphoric logic that Abraham and Torok outline here helps illuminate the contours of Stern's ambivalent mourning of the Jewish social and spiritual world he lost in the war. Communion allows Stern to substitute his unarticulated grief with the body and blood of Christ. The act of swallowing as a guiding metaphor in the memoir brings us back to the Jonah motif, where the prophet is swallowed by a large fish. Communion, in Stern's case, is not merely the event of spiritual salvation, it similarly conveys the author's own unresolved grief and unarticulated guilt. In imagining his deceased friends and relatives present with him on the occasion of his First Communion, Stern seeks to incorporate their memory along with the body and blood of Christ, while circumventing the work of mourning.

The underlying irony of the Communion scene that closes the memoir is accentuated by the biblical passage with which Stern associates it. Following his First Communion, Stern realizes that the daily missal includes a passage from the Gospel of John in which Thomas the Apostle insists on touching the wounds of Jesus before accepting his divinity. When Jesus appears before him and invites him to touch the stigmata, the sceptical Thomas recognizes him as God and forgoes his demand.[105] Stern quotes John 20:24–29 in order to mark his transformation into a

Christian believer. Yet the passage seems no less evocative of the open wounds that were left untouched in the memoir.

## Beyond Conviction and Convenience: Conversion as Literary Conceit

Stern's literary skill allows him to shed light on the inner drama that accompanies his dilemmas of faith. Yet in focusing on Stern's personal and spiritual plight, we lose sight of how commonplace such conversions actually were during that period. As Todd Endelman has shown, thousands of European Jews underwent baptism during the years of the Second World War in hope of saving themselves. In the immediate aftermath of the war, thousands of survivors and refugees joined the ranks of the converted. Endelman argues that those who converted, while they no longer faced any imminent danger, "wished to rid themselves once and for all of a marker that, in the war years, almost ended their lives … Restarting life in a foreign country offered them the chance to make a clean break with their Jewish past and the suffering and turmoil associated with it."[106] The pervasiveness of this phenomenon is attested to in a scathing editorial the English historian Cecil Roth published in the *Jewish Chronicle* in 1941. Lamenting that so many German-Jewish refugees underwent baptism once they reached the shores of Great Britain, Roth vented that they were "carrying to its logical conclusion the process interrupted at home."[107]

How should the prevalence of conversion during the war and its immediate aftermath affect our understanding of Stern's memoir and its credibility? Expecting that his affirmation of Christianity would be received with some scepticism, Stern mounted a defence of his motives, explaining that

> during the Nazi persecution, for the first time in Jewish history since Christ, the Jews were not persecuted on account of their religion but only on account of their race. In fact, in Germany I had seen that Jewish Christians were frequently worse off than we who were also Jewish by religion. They were rejected by the "Christians" as Jews, and the Jews as renegades. They shared the fate of Christ, of whom Pascal says that He is equally undesired by pagans and by Jews. Thus baptism as an escape from the fate of Jewry existed no longer. In this respect Hitler had, unwittingly, helped to clarify a spiritual issue.[108]

By defining the Jews as a race the Nazis precluded the possibility of conversion as an escape from persecution. Thus Stern's conversion to

Christianity during the war could have had no ulterior motive but true belief. In fact, he reminds his readers, Christian Jews often fared far worse than their Jewish brethren because socially and politically, they were regarded as outsiders by both Jews and Christians. The problem with Stern's self-justification is that he did not convert under Nazi rule, but after immigrating to Montreal, where Catholicism was the majority religion. When Stern converted in 1943, antisemitism was palpable in Quebec's cultural and social life. During this period there were undeniable benefits to unburdening oneself from the stigma of Jewishness. Conversion in this context possessed the assimilatory appeal Stern sought to deny. Stern himself seemed acknowledge this when he described how Catholicism served as a vehicle for ethno-national identity in Montreal, and how the city was divided along ethnic and religious lines: "We did not have any feeling of 'belonging.' We felt like rabbits who turn up accidentally in the middle of a fox-hunt ... Some Catholic people let us feel anti-Semitism for the first time since leaving Germany ... It was as if these ethnic groups had brought along with them all their ancient animosities."[109]

Although we cannot possibly fathom Stern's true motives, it would be naive to read his memoir as a straightforward testimony of his path to Catholicism. There is an undeniable gap between Stern's stated avowal of pure faith and the unacknowledged worldly rewards he reaped from his conversion. But are spiritual salvation and socio-economic opportunism necessarily mutually exclusive? Endelman points out that the distinction between Jews who converted out of belief and those who converted for more utilitarian reasons is misleading in that it disregards the shared historical and political context in which all conversions occurred, regardless of their "true" motive. As Endelman explains,

it is difficult to believe that the "true believers" were ignorant of the social and emotional advantages of abandoning Judaism ... The fact that some Jews saw Judaism in a negative light and Christianity in a positive light was the outcome of historical circumstances, not spiritual yearning and speculation alone. Moreover, even if it were true that these conversions were spiritual transformations pure and simple, exceptional events removed from the common run of human experience, the language the converts used to describe their journey toward Christianity was rooted in the time-bound attitudes of the period. The invidious way in which they contrasted Judaism and Christianity, and the terms they used to disparage the one and exalt the other, emerged from the same negation of Jews and Judaism that motivated strategic conversions. Thus, conversions of "convenience" and conversions of "conviction" were not altogether dissimilar.[110]

According to Endelman, conversion is not an either/or phenomenon that allows us to distinguish between converts on the basis of one singular driving motive, but a messy and overdetermined affair. Against the binary distinction between conviction and convenience, Endelman emphasizes the complex nature of human behaviour, which easily gets forgotten when we seek to reduce conversion to one determining factor. Even if he did not acknowledge this fact, Stern could not have been immune to the "emotional and social disabilities of Jewishness."[111]

The conflict between the idealized image Stern presents in his memoir and the more complicated reality he eschews should not lead us to discount the work's "autobiographical truth." Literary scholars such as Roy Pascal and Karl Weintraub employ this concept in order to describe the way autobiographers rearrange their past so as to fit it into an overarching pattern and structure of meaning. As Weintraub explains, the "truth" of an autobiographical text is not found in the details, but in the prism through which the author looks back on his life. The autobiographer takes certain liberties with his past because he is trying to fit into a particular pattern of meaning. The reader cannot grasp the autobiographer's "truth" if she cannot capture the autobiographer's point of view.[112]

Harvard philosopher Harry Austryn Wolfson offers a somewhat less benevolent interpretation of the gap between the facts and fiction of the autobiographer's life in his reflections on the phenomenon of conversion:

> We are sufficiently acquainted with the phenomenon of actual conversion to know that it is not always the result of an intellectual quest for truth, but rather of a spiritual quest for a new God, which is only a vague and illusive term to dissemble so many of our real wishes and desires. Conversion is seldom a triumph of truth over falsehood; it is most often the restoration of peace to a mind that has been disturbed, and as the mind's disturbance is never due to a single cause, conversion must be explained by a variety of causes and motives. Not that there are no true converts, but the true convert is he who, unconscious of his motives, genuinely believes that he has found the truth when he has merely found his peace.[113]

According to Wolfson, "genuine" conversion inevitably involves an unconscious act of dissimulation. The victim of this deception is the convert himself, who suppresses the multifaceted motives underlying his conversion. Wolfson's patronizing tone notwithstanding, his approach reminds us that *The Pillar of Fire* presents us with an idealized image of Stern's conversion rather than a factual account of it. His

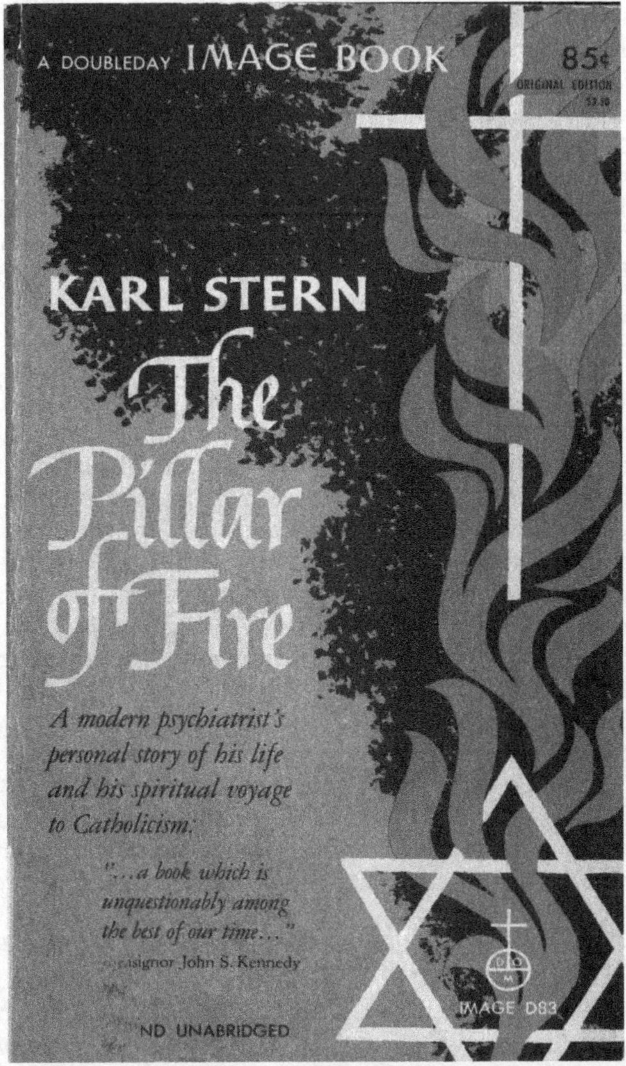


Figure 3.5.  Front cover of the paperback edition of Karl Stern's *The Pillar of Fire* (1959). The artwork adorning the paperback of Stern's memoir offers a visual metaphor for the narrative's supersessionist conceit. It shows a cross and, beneath it, a Star of David engulfed in a blaze of fire with smoke billowing in the background. The work's title alludes to the pillar of fire that guided the Israelites through the desert on their exodus from Egypt (Exodus 13:21). The book's cover art merges this biblical reference with a visual allusion to the smokestacks of the crematoria, suggesting that the Holocaust is the divine event that leads Stern towards Catholicism. Roesch Library, The University of Dayton.

memoir should be regarded not as an objective recollection of the personal and historical circumstances that brought him to Christianity, but as a retroactive interpretation of his conversion.

In Stern's chronicle the conversion to Christianity becomes the central axis of his life story, endowing it with a sense of linear continuity, when in reality it was repeatedly disrupted by the political and historical crises of the twentieth century. Catholicism allows Stern to tie the loose ends of his life together into a coherent narrative that culminates in his conversion. As Peter Stromberg explains, the conversion narrative is not a factual account of past events, but a reorganization of those events according to a predetermined symbolic logic. It is a performance of identity in which the actor's self-transformation is inseparable from the telling itself.[114] Stromberg's observations help clarify the proper approach to Stern's narrative, not as a literal re-enactment of his past but as a reinterpretation of it that was shaped by his convictions at the time of writing. The autobiographical recollections of his path to Christianity do not constitute a straightforward record of his past, but rather a self-conscious articulation of his life as he wanted it to be seen. Taking this fact into account, it seems more productive to ask how Stern integrated the idiosyncrasies of his life into a unified and coherent whole by resorting to the symbolic language of the Christian conversion narrative.

Instead of trying to resolve the question of Stern's motivations, we might look at the conversion narrative itself as an attempt to create a sense of continuity and closure in face of the traumatic experiences of exile, migration, and displacement. Reading Stern's conversion as a literary conceit allows us to grasp its organizing role in the narrative, which endows Stern's life with a unity of direction and purpose that renders it existentially and morally meaningful. The conversion that concludes the memoir provides the narrative with a clear teleology, which allows the author to synthesize the different turning points in his life and place them together as necessary stages on his path to faith. In this regard, we might say that Stern undergoes a series of conversions, each one serving as a stepping stone towards his discovery of the ultimate truth. Before converting to Christianity, Stern embraces different ideologies and outlooks. The sequence of "negative identities" Stern passes through include Zionism, Orthodox Judaism, Marxism, and psychoanalysis. Stern turns to these ideologies at different stages in his life in an effort to resolve his existential predicament. The partial fulfilment he finds in each of these paths is offset by their respective limitations.

He rebels against his parents' liberal-assimilatory tendencies by embracing Zionism, but is discontent with its disavowal of traditional

Judaism. He adopts an Orthodox Jewish lifestyle in response to the secular-nationalism of Zionist ideology, but finds Jewish ritual law restrictive and anachronistic. His adherence to Marxism during his years in medical school expresses a desire for a universalistic vision of human redemption that transcends the tribal confines of the Jewish communitarian movements of his youth. Stern's turn to psychoanalysis after his brush with Marxism can effectively be interpreted as a rejection of its materialist and deterministic view of human history and a reaffirmation of individual agency. The partial truth Stern finds in each of these worldviews is contained in Catholicism, which unites the disparate ideological phases he has passed through. It is a religion that "fulfils" his Judaism, and advocates a universalistic vision of justice on a scale no less ambitious than Marxism, while acknowledging the depths of the human soul like psychoanalysis. Stern's ultimate identity as a believing Catholic reconciles all the different episodes in his life and merges them into one organic unity.

# Chapter Four

# Judeo-Christian Reconciliation and the Inability to Mourn in Heinrich Kronstein's *Briefe an einen jungen Deutschen* (1967)

In 1967, legal scholar Heinrich Kronstein published his life story under the title *Briefe an einen jungen Deutschen* (Letters to a young German).[1] Written in epistolary form, Kronstein's narrative is a spiritual autobiography that interweaves the story of his religious journey towards Catholicism with that of his exile from Nazi Germany and post-war return. A glowing review of Kronstein's work in *Der Spiegel* opens on a note of exasperation: "What haven't we in Germany been forced to hear about our past, from claims of collective guilt to complete self-justification!"[2] The reviewer observes approvingly that Kronstein rejects such blanket incriminations of the Germans and identifies the cultural nihilism of the pre-war era as the root cause of National Socialism. He goes on to praise the author's sober impressions of his time in the United States, dwelling on Kronstein's portrayal of the country's "coldness and emptiness" and its "widespread ignorance about Europe."[3] Concluding his column, the reviewer summarizes the book's optimistic message: "Despite all the disappointment and devastation, we do not have the right to bitterness and resignation; we need to think of reconstruction with a healthy sense of what is possible."[4] The appeal of Kronstein's autobiography to this reader rests on three points: its exculpation of the Germans, its critique of the American victor's spiritual vapidity, and its author's renunciation of resentment over past historical injuries. The critic makes a passing remark about the author's frequent references to his conversion to Catholicism, noting that these "remain somewhat obscure to the non-Catholic reader."[5] While this observation suggests that Kronstein's Christianity is almost incidental to the story he tells in his autobiography, the conversion conceit is central to the work's structure and the messages the critic found so appealing.

Several months after the article on Kronstein's memoir appeared in *Der Spiegel*, another less benevolent review was published in *Die Zeit*.

Its author, Francis Mann, was an exiled German Jew and fellow lawyer, who re-established himself in England. Mann expressed a deep scepticism towards the work, noting that despite the book's "interest to a wide audience … the reader cannot shake off a feeling of deep unease."[6] Mann's apprehension stems from the same aspects that the *Der Spiegel* reviewer singled out for praise. He questions the author's determined resolve to exculpate the Germans. But what Mann finds most troubling about Kronstein's book is what it leaves out:

> The most unique fact, however, is that the author for whom politics is a realization of our moral values says close to nothing about the struggle that marked our century and was aimed at preserving our fundamental values. Was not the eradication of the greatest evil the world has ever seen the basic precondition for guaranteeing our physical and moral existence … ? Did Mr. Kronstein's heart not tremble for the future in 1940? Was there no event, no war measure, no battle that brought him close to despair or inspire him with hope? Did he hear no speech worth mentioning? Did nothing draw a tear of sorrow or joy, pain or emotion from him? Apparently not, because the book makes no mention of it. Karl Jaspers's dreadful exclamation – "That we are still alive is our fault" – finds no echo in Kronstein's work.[7]

Mann points to a curious lacuna in Kronstein's memoir – the author's complete dissociation from the events of the war. Kronstein refuses to judge his German persecutors, rejects punitive measures against German industry during his tenure in the Department of Justice, and seems almost indifferent to the war, as if its outcome did not affect him personally, as an exiled German of Jewish ancestry. Kronstein's enigmatic stance troubled Mann not only because it dissimulated the author's own personal past but also because it corroborated a falsified version of history that positioned the Germans as Nazism's victims.

The appeal of Kronstein's autobiography to some and its distaste to others derives from the way it utilizes the author's conversion as the organizing principle of the narrative. Conversion enables Kronstein to dissociate himself from fellow Jewish victims and gloss over the traumatic impact that Nazism and the Holocaust had on his own self-understanding as an exiled German Jew. By recounting the historical events of the 1930s and 1940s through the frame of his own spiritual awakening, Kronstein displaces the centrality of the Holocaust both to his own personal story and to the post-war German context he addresses. The text subordinates the life events it recounts to a religious conceit that effectively contains and mitigates the historical realities that conflicted with the author's self-presentation as a devout Christian who had successfully reintegrated in his native homeland after the war.

I argue that Christianity in Kronstein's autobiography functions as a kind of "narrative fetishism" that works to repress the traumatic effects of the war and maintain the fiction of an integral and undamaged identity in the wake of the Holocaust. Eric Santner, who coined the term "narrative fetishism," uses it to refer to

> the construction and deployment of a narrative consciously or unconsciously designed to expunge the traces of the trauma or loss that called that narrative into being in the first place. The use of narrative as fetish may be contrasted with that rather different mode of symbolic behavior that Freud called *Trauerarbeit* or the "work of mourning." Both narrative fetishism and mourning are responses to loss, to a past that refuses to go away due to its traumatic impact. The work of mourning is a process of elaborating and integrating the reality of loss or traumatic shock by remembering and repeating it in symbolically and dialogically mediated doses; it is a process of translating, troping, and figuring loss … Narrative fetishism, by contrast, is the way an inability or refusal to mourn emplots traumatic events; it is a strategy of undoing, in fantasy, the need for mourning by simulating a condition of intactness, typically by situating the site and origin of loss elsewhere. Narrative fetishism releases one from the burden of having to reconstitute one's self-identity under "posttraumatic" conditions; in narrative fetishism, the "post" is indefinitely postponed.[8]

Narrative fetishism, according to Santner, involves a repressive response to trauma and loss that refuses to acknowledge their devastating impact on the self-image of an individual or a collective. In contrast to the Freudian "work of mourning," which entails the subject's recognition of traumatic loss, narrative fetishism maintains the fiction of the subject's intactness. Conversion in Kronstein's autobiography realizes the fetishistic task of "simulating a condition of intactness" by allowing its author to reconstitute his self-identity without registering the traumatic effects of exile and persecution. Kronstein only alludes to the destruction of German Jewry in passing, and never mentions the loss of friends and family members during the war, nor does he acknowledge the historical rift that came to separate émigrés of Jewish ancestry from the Germans, who remained behind. The religious rhetoric that infuses his narrative functions as a fetishistic device that absorbs the radical rupture of the Holocaust and glosses over the living legacy of Nazi anti-semitism in post-war Germany. By adapting his life story to the Christian conservative discourse of restoration Germany that valorized the country's return to its "Judeo-Christian" origins, Kronstein suppresses the historical complexities of reclaiming his German identity in the wake of the Holocaust.

## Christian Recollections of a German-Jewish Childhood and Adolescence

Heinrich David Kronstein (1897–1972) was born in Karlsruhe into a non-observant, middle-class Jewish family. Recounting his childhood, Kronstein dwells on his mother as the religious role model, whose life he sought to emulate when he converted to Catholicism. An avid German patriot of Russian-Jewish origins, his mother "understood the concept of Judeo-Christian unity better than most."[9] Better than the Zionists who believed that the national element was essential to Judaism, and the assimilationists, "who renounced the peculiarities of their past for the sake of career advancement."[10] She was raised in a Jewish Orthodox household but turned away from its strict rules of observance in her youth. He explains that for Orthodox Jews, "the external rules of conduct, especially all the rules of eating, were at the centre of their conversations and lives."[11] His mother, in contrast, "believed that it was only possible to realize her religiosity by turning away from the strict principles of rabbinic teaching."[12] By contrasting his mother's Judeo-Christian convictions to assimilation, Orthodoxy, and Zionism, Kronstein anticipates his own conversion as an alternative to other, misguided paths of Jewish modernity. His mother's philanthropic activities on behalf of the German working class – activities that extended beyond the Jewish fold – were seedbeds for the universalist religious impulse that Kronstein would rediscover in Catholicism.

His father, a chemist by profession, "lived completely for chemistry and had no understanding for the world of my mother."[13] Kronstein's mother was a woman of faith and works, whereas his father was wholly engrossed with the material side of reality, convinced that "everything in existence could be proven in a test tube."[14] Complementing his father's materialistic leanings was his unflagging commitment to Jewish custom.[15] In classic Augustinian fashion, the text's opposition between the two parental figures fashions Kronstein's turn to Christianity as a rejection of the world of the father and a recuperation of the mother's religious outlook. The stereotyped portrayal of the father's "Jewish" stubbornness and materialism, encapsulated in his inability to grasp the spiritual side of human existence, represents the hypocritical cultural inheritance of

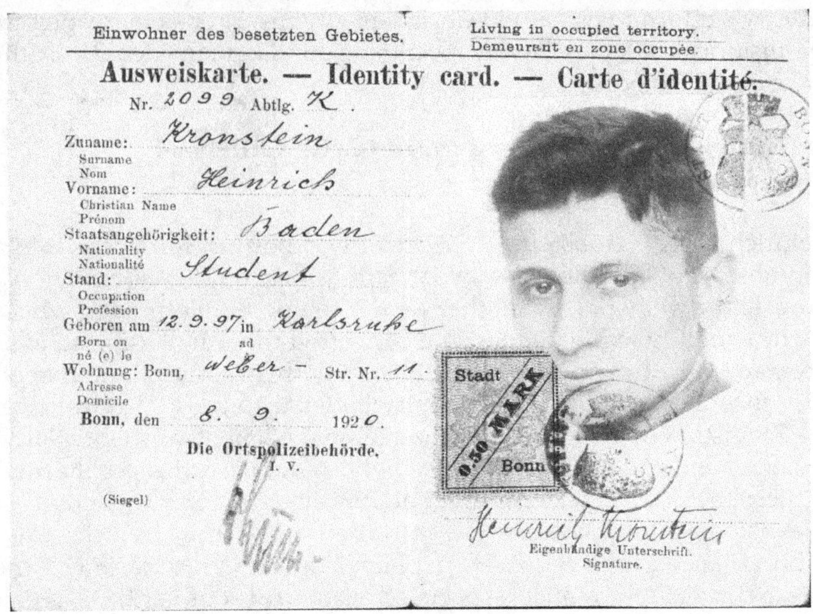


Figure 4.1.  Heinrich Kronstein's identification card (1920). Booth Family Center for Special Collections, Georgetown University.

pre-war German-Jewish liberalism that Kronstein disavows through his conversion to Christianity.

As a seventeen-year-old, Kronstein was a member of the Jugendwehr, a youth organization that prepared adolescents for their military service. During the organization's night exercises in the forest, Kronstein was often paired with a youth named Dieter Siebert. These night-time drills came to mean a great deal to him. Later in life, Kronstein remembered the soft-spoken, intimate discussions the two had while camping alone in the verdant hills surrounding Karlsruhe. Over the course of the night, accompanied by the distant sound of church bells and cannon fire, Dieter would share his love of Christ and liturgy with Kronstein:

Again and again our conversations led back to the Church. Each time he explained new parts of the Mass to me. As a boy he was connected to the Benedictine monastery of Beuron ... And in the spirit of those fathers, he introduced me to the liturgy. These memories shaped my sense of home (*Heimatgefühl*) ... My readiness to sacrifice my life for Germany in the First World War should thus not surprise you.[16]

It is striking here that Kronstein's description of how the seeds of Christian devotion were first planted in him is set against a militaristic backdrop before shifting to a heartfelt confession of his avid German patriotism. The author's nascent religiosity is woven into the fabric of his national identity and *Heimatgefühl*. Kronstein served on the Western Front in a field artillery regiment and was severely wounded at Verdun. After the war he studied law in Heidelberg, Bonn, and Berlin, where he completed his doctoral studies in 1924.[17] In 1925 he started a private practice specializing in patent law in Mannheim, until the Nazi racial laws forced him out of the profession.

**Finding Faith in Flight**

Kronstein immigrated to the United States in 1935 and converted to Catholicism shortly thereafter. In his book, he discusses at length his decision to convert and contrasts his choice with the various Jewish responses to the rise of National Socialism. He contends that the Zionist and Orthodox Jews, despite their ideological differences, were two camps that tried to transform the experience of persecution into a positive form of self-understanding. The Orthodox understood "suffering as a religious task," while the Zionists saw it as the "foundation for the establishment of a Jewish nation-state."[18] Both camps were able to preserve their self-respect in the midst of persecution. He identifies a similar phenomenon among the Christian Jews, "who saw their destiny as a necessary part of divine salvation. They, too, were strengthened through their recognition of the redeeming quality of suffering."[19] The ones who had the hardest time adapting to the reality of National Socialism were the assimilated. Kronstein reserves his scorn for secular Jews, explaining that "philosophical liberalism had destroyed their religious and national ties to Judaism. The only principle they lived by was *carpe diem*. As the catastrophe neared, they failed to grasp the demands of the hour and only lived to seize the day. *Their conduct only increased the hatred*."[20]

He writes that before they decided to immigrate to the US, he and his wife had considered moving to Palestine. "Of course, I too was infected by the young pioneers' anticipation and excitement … And I prepared the grounds for many who emigrated to Israel. I was prepared to embark on this journey myself. But as I grew more aware of my situation, I became progressively disenchanted with this path."[21] After spending hours with members of Mannheim's Zionist movement, Kronstein came to realize that for all its youthful optimism, Jewish nationalism simply mirrored the ideological premises of National Socialism.

**Der Präsident**
des
**Landgerichts Mannheim**

Mannheim, den *6. Juni 1933.*

Nr. *2009*

## Ausweis.

Rechtsanwalt *Dr. Heinrich Kronstein*

geboren am *12. September 1897* und wohnhaft in

*M a n n h e i m* ist bei dem Landgericht Mannheim

als Rechtsanwalt zugelassen.

(Rechtsanwaltsordnung und Gesetz über die Zulassung zur
Rechtsanwaltschaft vom 7. April 1933 –R.G.Bl.I S. 188.–).

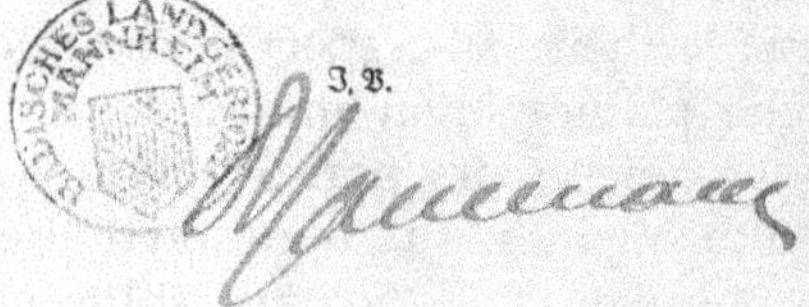

J. V.

*Das nebenstehende mit Dienstsiegel versehene
Lichtbild stellt den genannten Rechtsanwalt dar.*

Figure 4.2.  Heinrich Kronstein's licence to practise law. The document, dating to 6 June 1933, restored Kronstein's right to practise law after the *Berufsbeamtengesetz* of April 1933 barred Jews from serving as lawyers. It is likely that he was readmitted to the bar because he was exempted from this law as a veteran of the First World War. Booth Family Center for Special Collections, Georgetown University.

The Nazi threat to the Jews' physical existence could be combated in one of two ways: by affirming the Jews' *völkisch* existence against the Nazi-German one, or by rejecting the *völkisch* principle altogether and substituting it with a higher religious ideal. The latter option reflected the universalism to which Kronstein aspired and that he identified with Christianity. "Somehow it was the image of the individual standing before Christ that allowed me to overcome the *völkisch* idea, whether in the form of National Socialism or in the form of Zionism."[22] Kronstein's choice of destination was, he asserts, determined not by economic considerations but by moral principles. The US, he believed, "embodied a historical society that transcended racial and ethnic belonging."[23]

Describing his forced displacement from Nazi Germany in 1935, Kronstein writes: "As difficult as these times were, I was certain that my survival had a purpose and that my life was meant for the fulfilment of some greater calling. I understood that all of my personal sacrifices would one day bear fruit."[24] This statement captures the trajectory of Kronstein's narrative: the bane of migration turns into a blessing in disguise, one that reveals a new spiritual path. According to Kronstein, "it is a great advantage if the emigrant has been so inwardly broken by expulsion that he is capable of shedding all externals and dares to embark on a truly new beginning."[25] Like Hirsch and Döblin, Kronstein contrasts his growing awareness of a new religious calling to the psychological and political responses of other Jewish émigrés in his situation. These other emigrants were too attached to their pasts and their worldly belongings to recognize the significance or magnitude of the events. They sought to perpetuate the pretence of continuity in their new environment and thereby perished in their illusory world. The "inner hardships" of immigration were further augmented by the fact that the Jews who left Germany after 1933 were overwhelmingly secular.[26] Unlike earlier waves of Jewish refugees, who were "bound together by a shared religious past," German Jews were completely cut off from their ancestral history.[27] They were so preoccupied with worldly concerns that when the catastrophic events of 1933 unfolded, they failed to confront the true existential meaning of their collective fate. Like the other Jewish refugees, Kronstein and his wife were at first oblivious to the profound significance of the catastrophe that was enveloping them, but once they reached New York, the demands of daily life "could no longer cover up the inner emptiness of our existence. Sooner or later, we would have to deal with the true substance of our lives."[28]

Kronstein's religious awakening occurred on a winter day in 1936, when he and his wife attended the funeral of a fellow exile who succumbed to suicide. While still in Germany, this woman had devoted all her energies to aiding Jewish émigrés fleeing their homeland. In her total commitment to the Jewish cause, she had failed to remember that persecution was all that tied her to her Judaism. Thus, when she reached the safety of America's shores, she lost her identity and sense of purpose. "In her despair, she ended a life that no longer contained any substance for her."[29] According to Kronstein, her death was the inevitable result of her commitment to a cause that lacked deeper spiritual foundations. He saw the meaninglessness of her existence reflected in the funeral: "The evening ceremony held for the deceased was the culmination of the emptiness and the nullification of all that makes us human. It was a manifestation of the most flagrant nihilism. The vacuity of the event was reflected in the blank faces of those present ... They stood helplessly, incapable of comprehending the tragedy and dignity of death."[30]

Kronstein's account of the funeral plays a key role in the narrative of his spiritual awakening. The use of a fellow Jew's funeral as the staging ground for the convert's disparagement of Judaism as a spiritual dead end can similarly be found in Edith Stein's autobiography. In *Aus dem Leben einer jüdischen Familie*, Stein relates attending her uncle's funeral. The account serves as an occasion for her to reflect on the nature of Jewish-Christian difference. Recalling the rabbi's eulogy for her maternal uncle Jakob Courant, who took his life following a devastating bankruptcy, Stein writes:

> I have heard many such talks. They gave a resume of the life of the deceased, recalling all the good things he had done, thereby rousing the sorrow of the bereaved all the more; there was nothing consoling about them. To be sure, there was a prayer pronounced in solemn tones: "And when the body returns to dust, the spirit returns to God who gave it." However, nothing of faith in a personal life after death, nor any belief in a future reunion with those who had died, lay behind these words. Many years later, when for the first time I attended a Catholic funeral, the contrast made a deep impression upon me. The one then being buried was a very well-known scholar. But no longer was mention made of his achievements or of the reputation he had won in the world. Called by his baptismal name alone, the humble soul, in all its poverty, was commended to divine mercy. But how consoling and calming were the words of the liturgy which accompanied the deceased into eternity![31]

Stein's contrasting of the Jewish and Christian funeral orations evokes the Pauline opposition of flesh versus spirit. According to Stein, the worldly quality of the rabbi's eulogy also explains the "alarming number of suicides" that followed the Nazi campaign against the Jews. "I believe that the inability to face and to accept the collapse of one's worldly existence with reasonable calm is closely linked to the lack of any prospect of life in eternity."[32] The Jews' materialistic conception of human existence, coupled with their denial of an afterlife, rendered them vulnerable to the economic war waged against them by the Nazis. "A Jew is able to endure severe hardship and untiring labour coupled with extreme privations for years on end as long as he sees a goal ahead. Deprive him of this goal and you destroy his vigour; life then appears meaningless, and so he can readily decide to throw it away."[33] Stein and Kronstein both turn to a funeral scene as a metaphor for conveying Judaism's lifelessness and stunted spiritual vistas. Their elaborate critique of Judaism in this context serves as a pretext for rationalizing their own conversions. While Stein's unfinished autobiography only alludes to her motivations for converting without ever narrating the events leading up to it, Kronstein uses the funeral scene as a narrative turning point in his spiritual trajectory.

Deeply affected by the "nihilistic" funeral of his friend, Kronstein enters a church some weeks later. As he kneels before the altar, he recalls the sentimental wish he had as a child to "be allowed to experience Christmas like all the others and have a Christmas tree."[34] He then shifts to another memory, dating back to August 1916, shortly before he was drafted into the army. Dieter Siebert and his mother took Kronstein to the monastery in Beuron, where he witnessed a German Benedictine monk presiding over Mass for a group of Russian prisoners of war. United in prayer, the bitter enemies found companionship in Christ. In another recollection from his time as a soldier at Verdun, Kronstein recalls French prisoners of war filing past in front of him when he is suddenly struck by the realization that "the war between the Germans and the French is a grave sin against the spirit of Christianity, which once pervaded Europe. The more people departed from the Christian spirit, the closer they came to their own self-destruction."[35] The final image that materializes before Kronstein is that of the social disintegration and class antagonism that erupted in interwar Germany, whose most recent manifestation was his own experience of "the brutal persecution of the Jewish race in Germany," over the course of which "*a largely secularized German society struggled against an equally secularized Jewry.*"[36]

These successive images bring Kronstein to realize that he can no longer ignore the call of Christ.

Christ had called me before, but each time I had found reasons not to answer. The notion that the Jew must not meet Christ in this world and the fact that in Germany the baptized Jew enjoyed economic advantages held me back. But all these considerations now fell away. From the economic point of view, conversion was now rather disadvantageous since all of my connections were Jewish. I hardly knew a single Catholic in New York.[37]

In his struggle to resist the ever-growing pull of Christianity, Kronstein tries to formulate different arguments against joining the Church. The internal dispute reaches its culmination when "the bulwark I built in my mind collapsed."[38] Resolved to undertake this new religious path, Kronstein receives instruction in Catholic doctrine from a priest at Columbia University. He and his wife convert soon after moving to Washington, D.C., in 1939.

After passing the bar exam in 1941, Kronstein was hired by the Department of Justice, where he worked for the Claims and Antitrust Divisions. In 1942 he began teaching at Georgetown Law School and was appointed full professor in 1946. During the war years, Kronstein befriended three Benedictine brothers from Germany, who had resettled in a monastery in Keyport, New Jersey. The fraternity of faith he found with the Benedictines represented a counter-community to Nazism. This "ecclesia orans" would sustain Kronstein throughout the 1940s, providing him with the spiritual and intellectual home he had lost as a result of his forced migration: "The war was raging. The Nazis were lashing out. But here German Benedictines had welcomed me, the racially persecuted, and given me a new spiritual home. The fact that one of them had been taken in by the National Socialist movement at the beginning of the Third Reich showed me even more clearly what the individual can overcome and achieve through faith."[39]

Kronstein's friendship with the Benedictine monks offered him a bridge to his German past, spiritual solace in the present, and, as would later turn out, a path to mutual understanding with the Germans after the war. The author's turn to Christianity thus represented more than a cathartic resolution to the crisis of exile and expulsion; it was a vehicle of narrative and personal continuity that tied together the disparate phases of Kronstein's life.

Justifying his turn to Christianity, Kronstein asserted that "Christianity is by no means a negation of Judaism."[40] He marshalled the history of the early Christian community to argue that its dispute with the Sanhedrin had been "a purely internal Jewish affair," and that the idea that Christianity is incompatible with Judaism was a much later development that began with the Council of Nicea and Christianity's transformation into a state religion. These events had interrupted the natural continuity that connected the Old and New Testaments. Healing this

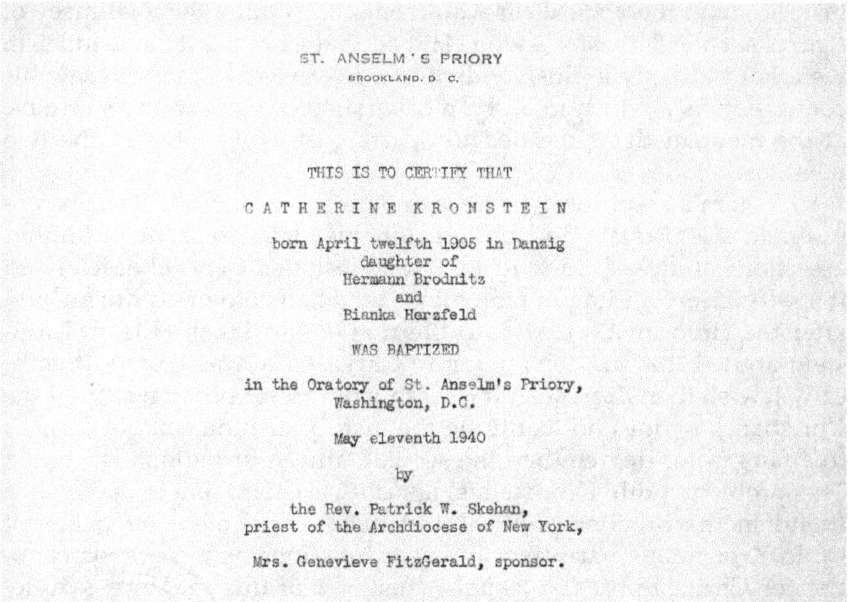

ST. ANSELM'S PRIORY
BROOKLAND. D. C.


THIS IS TO CERTIFY THAT

C A T H E R I N E   K R O N S T E I N

born April twelfth 1905 in Danzig
daughter of
Hermann Brodnitz
and
Bianka Herzfeld

WAS BAPTIZED

in the Oratory of St. Anselm's Priory,
Washington, D.C.

May eleventh 1940

by

the Rev. Patrick W. Skehan,
priest of the Archdiocese of New York,

Mrs. Genevieve FitzGerald, sponsor.


*Anselm Stritthmatter,*
*Subprior.*


N.B.   Record of this Baptism is on file also at the parish-church of the Nativity,
Washington, D.C.

Figure 4.3.  Baptism certificate of Catherine Kronstein (1940). Heinrich Kronstein and his wife Catherine Kronstein were baptized together at St. Anslem's Priory in Washington, D.C. Only Catherine's record was preserved in Kronstein's papers. Booth Family Center for Special Collections, Georgetown University.

historical and theological rift would entail accepting the legitimacy of figures such as Kronstein, who claimed that Christianity and Judaism were not mutually exclusive identities. Like Stern, Kronstein saw his conversion as a return to and a recuperation of Christianity's origins, at the moment that preceded the parting of ways between the two religions.

Kronstein's assertion that he was both a Jew and a Christian represented a legitimate and understandable claim to identity. Similar assertions stretched back to the New Testament and characterized the self-understanding of many Jews who had converted during and after the Holocaust.[41] Like Karl Stern and Karl Jakob Hirsch, Kronstein argued that his conversion to Christianity was more authentically Jewish than Zionism. "It is simply not true," he writes, "that the Christian Jew does not continue the history of Judaism. He does so to a far greater degree than the secular, atheist or nationalist Jew."[42] The problem with Kronstein's Jewish-Christian religious ideal is found in the broader political and historical context he relates it to. In Kronstein's narrative, Judaism functions as a mere synecdoche for Christianity. The fraught character of this religious synthesis surfaces in Kronstein's account of the war, where the rhetoric of Judeo-Christianity confounds the boundaries between victims and perpetrators, Germans and Jews.

## Post-war Return and the Rhetoric of Judeo-Christian Reconciliation

In Döblin's and Hirsch's narratives, the connection between conversion and homecoming is only implicitly hinted at; in Kronstein's memoirs, this nexus is explicitly acknowledged. In the immediate aftermath of the war, Kronstein returned to Germany in service of the US army, where he was tasked with reviving German industry and agriculture in the American occupation zone. The first part of the autobiography consists of Kronstein's diary entries chronicling his impressions of Germany in the summer of 1945. Kronstein's eyewitness account of Germany in the first months after the war is an extraordinary document, if only for its unqualified identification with the defeated Germans and its complete silence with regard to the Jewish fate.

Kronstein refuses an administrative order requiring him to serve on a government commission judging war crimes, arguing that "I do not consider it my duty to participate in these investigations. I have

Figure 4.4.  Poster advertising a public lecture on American Catholicism delivered by Heinrich Kronstein in post-war Germany (1949). Booth Family Center for Special Collections, Georgetown University.

suffered too much myself for that."[43] He does not identify as a Jewish victim of Nazism, but as a returning German who has overcome the pains of unrequited love for his homeland through the embrace of Christianity:

> I am terribly excited about my trip to Germany, the land of my first love. My life was devoted to Germany until it rejected the ideas I stand for. Without hesitating for a minute, I would have given my life for Germany. When I lost Germany, I experienced all of the pains a mother can suffer for her son or a son for his mother. And yet I thank God for showing me the speciousness of Bismarck's doctrine and endowing me with higher values to which to devote my life.[44]

Kronstein's love for Germany seamlessly shifts to his new Christian calling. This transition displays a metonymic association that Kronstein also employs in his recollections of his youth. This passage reflects the convoluted links between religion, race, and national identity that play out in Kronstein's narrative and undercut the author's portrayal of conversion as a solely spiritual event. Despite his better efforts to frame conversion as the outcome of an inward process of personal growth, external political and social realities insinuate themselves into his text. We see how the devotional dimension of his narrative simultaneously functions as the vehicle for other ideological and political claims of identity.

Christianity is not only related to Kronstein's claim to Germanness but also serves to distance him from his Jewish past. He contrasts his newly acquired Christian outlook to his "Jewish pride" during the early Nazi period:

> During the years 1933 to 1935, I succumbed to the temptation of taking pride in the fact that I was not afraid of fighting for the oppressed Jews. I had not yet grasped the idea of Christian suffering and redemption, which represent a wholly different attitude towards persecution than the one I had at the time. On Sunday in the Cathedral of Notre Dame, I listened to the Gospel of the Good Samaritan with great enthusiasm. "What should you do when you find your fellow man in need, even if he has brought his situation upon himself, through crimes of his own doing, possibly even against you? Go to him, dress his wounds, pour oil and wine onto them, and be merciful."[45]

Through the redeeming virtues of Christian mercy, love, and forgiveness, Kronstein finds common ground with his former persecutors. Guided by the values of Christian compassion, Kronstein returns "to help the poor and the despondent."[46]

In an entry from August 1945, Kronstein describes walking into a small chapel in Frankfurt, where he recites the Lord's Prayer, "the first act I consciously performed with the people here."[47] This episode is highly symbolic of the role that Christianity plays in Kronstein's return. That his identification as a Christian with the Germans also entails his disidentification with Judaism is clear in his subsequent musings: "The idea behind Paulskirche, of uniting a national ideology with the principles of humanity, has been betrayed. Goethe's message has been distorted. His house destroyed. Christ's ambassadors have been ridiculed. Hundreds of churches have been burnt to ashes."[48] Nazism's ultimate victims in this passage are Christians, not Jews. In fact, the only mention of Jews in the diary is found when Kronstein speaks to a German doctor who hid two Jewish families during the war.[49] The Germans are cast either as victims of Nazism or as perpetrators of crimes that were committed by all sides. When the question of German guilt arises, it is mitigated by reference to the war crimes committed by the Russians.

Kronstein himself claims responsibility for his country's guilt. Witnessing the physical and moral devastation of his former homeland, he writes:

> I felt that I too was to blame. Yes God, I confess. It is true, the Germans have murdered and taken the property of others, including my own. But I participated in the construction of a legal philosophy that placed expediency above all else. The Germans simply drew their conclusions from this very logic. I collaborated in the construction of a social and economic system that was purely secular in character. The Germans carried this system to the extreme. If I had not been forced to leave Germany, I might never have realized the catastrophic consequences of my work. I want to make up for my failure by helping the Germans in my current role. May God grant me his grace.[50]

This passage captures Kronstein's understanding of the war and its historical causes. Nazism was a product of Europe's progressive secularization and its radical turn away from God. Kronstein's metaphysical interpretation of Germany's path to fascism and mass murder as the outcome of the materialist-secular philosophy that pervaded prewar Europe recurs in the writings of Döblin, Stern, and Hirsch. What is perhaps unique to Kronstein's version of this claim is his own self-inculpation. If Nazism and the Holocaust were the result of modern Europe's rejection of its religious roots, then Kronstein too bears a part of the guilt. It is only by virtue of his exile and the spiritual epiphany it brought about that he is able to recognize the error of his ways.

Kronstein's diaries reflect an unambiguously empathetic stance towards the Germans. Much like Döblin, Kronstein positions himself as a re-educator and guide who has returned to help rebuild the German nation. "I am beginning to overcome the shock. I understand, I am in a country that has been destroyed both physically and spiritually. It is our task to rebuild Europe so that this catastrophe can be overcome."[51] Curiously, one finds no reluctance on Kronstein's part to return to the land that stripped him of his citizenship, stole his property, murdered his family, and forced him into exile. He summarizes his time in occupied Germany as an overall positive experience: "I am infinitely fortunate to have been given the opportunity to experience these weeks ... My soul is now free from the dark shadows of rejection ... During this time, I have come closest to fulfilling my life's true mission."[52]

Kronstein returns to the United States resolved to help rebuild German–American diplomatic and cultural ties: "When I returned to America in the fall of 1945, it had become clear to me that I had to help with all my strength to build the bridge that had been erected between America and Europe into a firmly established bridge. All the doubts and conflicts I had struggled with during the last years and months of the war had been clarified by the German experience."[53]

Over the following years, Kronstein established various academic exchange programs between Georgetown and the University of Frankfurt. In 1949, he began making regular trips to the University of Frankfurt, where he taught as an honorary professor from 1951 to 1955. In 1956 he was appointed full professor there. His memoir expresses no doubts or misgivings about his return. The only task left is to help rebuild Germany and reinforce its cultural, economic, and geopolitical alliance with the United States.

The uniqueness of Kronstein's redemptive narrative of return seems all the more striking when we compare it to the diaries of other émigrés, such as Hans Sahl and Carl Zuckmayer, who registered an uncanniness and unease in their re-encounter with Germany and Germans when they returned to their former homeland in the uniform of the US army.[54] Kronstein's conversion, it seems, allowed him to bridge the emotional and psychological divide that separated the uniformed Jewish émigrés from the defeated German population. Kronstein felt that he had found common ground with the Germans in Christianity. Identification with the German population also characterizes Karl Jakob Hirsch's diary entries from 1945, which document his return to Germany in the uniform of the US army. There are marked similarities between the two diaries that reflect their authors' respective attempts to clarify their position vis-à-vis their German, American, Jewish, and Christian identities.

Hirsch's disavowal of resentment and revenge is even more vehement than Kronstein's. One of his first diary entries records a conversation in a mess hall on a ship sailing for Europe with a fellow officer, who was forced to flee Nazi Germany. He confesses to Hirsch, "I have only returned to Germany to satisfy my hatred."[55] An appalled Hirsch shares the officer's sentiments with a fellow German-Jewish officer, who tells him that "you need to learn how to hate, to really hate, that seems necessary to me."[56] Hirsch responds: "I am not doing anything unproductive, and hatred is unproductive. You cannot even conceive a child through hatred. You must at least feign love. There is nothing you can do about this truth."[57] Hirsch distances himself from fellow Jewish émigrés returning to their former homeland by contrasting the Jewish desire for vengeance with his own decision to abide by the principles of Christian love. Hirsch asserts that "it does not suit me to be a victor or a 'punishing angel' (*strafender Engel*). Some displaced persons from Germany, who now wear American uniforms find it easy. Not me."[58]

Kronstein revisits his impressions of 1945 Germany in the epistolary section of the memoir, written twenty years later. Recollecting the difficulties involved in returning to a homeland that had rejected him, Kronstein writes that he began his "spiritual return to Germany" through his connection with the Benedictine community in Keyport, New Jersey, once again indicating Christianity's decisive role in his biography as the bridge that leads him back to Germany.[59] Before departing to Germany in 1945, the Benedictine Fathers in Keyport asked him to deliver letters to the Maria Laach Abbey on their behalf. Kronstein hesitated when he considered that "the fateful concordat between Hitler and the Vatican" was signed in this very abbey and that "its abbot had openly opted for the Führer in 1933."[60] The journey to Germany forces an ambivalent Kronstein to consider his "relation to the Germans after all that had happened."[61] His visit to the abbey is staged as a scene of reconciliation.

During his stay at the Maria Laach Abbey, Kronstein meets with the abbot, who opens up about his relationship to the Nazi regime. "His conversation with me was a confession (*eine Beichte*)."[62] The abbot explains that he believed that the excesses of Nazi propaganda were only an external measure that would be done away with once they came to power, at which point they would be open to the idea of Christian leadership. The abbot realized the gravity of his error soon after, when his frock drew hostile stares from Nazi party members who were sharing his compartment on a train. He now recognizes the violent and destructive nature of the Nazi regime as a "rebellion against God."[63] He is further convinced "that if the Nazis had stayed in power, every German bishop and abbot would have been gassed, every clergyman would have been either made an apostate or sent to his death. This is what Hitler's victory would have looked like."[64] Kronstein frames the abbot's pro-Hitler stance as a temporary lapse of judgment, glossing over the fact that it formed part of a far broader ideological trend, which historian John Connelly dubs the "German Catholic racist syndrome."[65] The abbot's admission represents a turning point for Kronstein, who recognizes that the Germans, too, were victims. That this conversation takes place in an abbey and assumes the form of a religious confession rather than a legal proceeding tells us much about Kronstein's overall attitude towards the question of German guilt. In his conversation with the abbot, he sees himself as a passive listener in a confession addressed to God. It is only God who can judge the Germans, not the allied victors.

Figure 4.5. Photograph of Heinrich Kronstein (undated). Universitätsarchiv Frankfurt am Main.

The idea that the Christians are the ultimate victims of National Socialism can also be found in *The Pillar of Fire*, where Stern recounts a conversation with a Nazi biochemist in Munich in the 1930s. The Nazi scientist confesses that he used to be terribly antisemitic: "Then I found out that what we hate in the Jews is not the Jews. It is Christ and the Christian religion … Once you have found out that it is actually Christianity which is the painful foreign body in our flesh, something curious happens, you stop hating the Jews. You regard them with the same kind of sympathy or antipathy as you might regard any other foreign nation."[66] Both Kronstein and Stern apply the logic of Christian supersession to the Holocaust by rendering the Jews as vicarious victims of Nazism's true enemy: Christianity. This revisionist account of Nazi antisemitism dissolves all distinctions between perpetrator and victim by converting the Nazi's racial animosity into a generalized hatred of religion as such.

The false analogy he draws between Christian and Jew is only the first stage in a series of logical leaps that Kronstein makes in his memoir. The very idea of attributing guilt to the German people because of the state's wrongdoing follows a totalitarian mindset, argues Kronstein.

The modern totalitarian state identifies itself completely with the people. This same reasoning, he claims, is reproduced when one regards every member of the totalitarian state as guilty of its wartime atrocities. "I have always rejected the idea of collective guilt. I believe in individual guilt and in the possibility of forgiving individual guilt. I did not return to hate or to single out the guilty. I wanted to help heal where I could."[67]

Kronstein's religious critique of the root causes of National Socialism corresponds to a regnant post-war attitude that saw the Nazi period as the culmination of Western secularization. The progressive erosion of Christian values resulted in the metaphysical and moral disorientation that brought about Europe's self-destruction during the war. According to this theological interpretation, the Third Reich was the inevitable consequence of intellectual and social developments that began with the Enlightenment. The appeal of this narrative was that it integrated the question of German guilt within a broader historical context that reframed the crimes of National Socialism within an abstract-metaphysical framework that erased the concreteness of the crimes and the identity of the perpetrators. This ahistorical account of Nazism absolved the Germans by laying the blame on the secularization and de-Christianization of European society, dismissing the political and social specificities of the Nazi rise to power.[68]

The solution, Kronstein explains, requires a return to Europe's Christian roots. Only the re-Christianization of society can save Western civilization from materialism, nihilism, totalitarianism.

> I am of the opinion that only Christian society is capable of making the most diverse peoples, including the Jews, part of a whole. It is certainly no coincidence that the terrible catastrophes that afflicted the Jews of Europe occurred in this secularized century. National Socialism ostracized Judaism as well as Christianity in the same way. Overcoming the evils of National Socialism as well as a religiously disintegrated Judaism (to which the idea of race is not alien), is a task that can only be achieved by Christianity.[69]

In Kronstein's memoir, Jews and Christians were both complicit in the rise of the Third Reich and both religious groups became its victims.[70] He goes on to suggest that the annihilation of the Jews was only the first phase in the planned extermination of Christianity.

In his evasive and euphemistic allusions to the Holocaust, Kronstein takes his cue from Adorno's adage: "In the house of the hangman one should not speak of the noose, otherwise one might harbour resentment."[71] Adorno made this statement in a 1959 lecture when addressing Germany's inability to confront its Nazi past. He argued that the Germans' collective self-denial had resulted in a neurotic relationship to the past that manifested itself in "defensive postures where one is not attacked, intense affects where they are hardly warranted by the situation, an absence of affect in the face of the gravest matters, not seldom simply a repression of what is known or half-known."[72] In his writings, Adorno enumerated a long litany of strategies that the Germans employed in order to disavow their crimes and maintain their ignorance about the Jews' fate during the war. Pointing to the Germans' morally fraught attitude towards the memory of the murdered Jews, Adorno writes that

> even their innocence, which cannot be simpler and more plausible, is contested. The enormity of what was perpetrated works to justify this: a lax consciousness consoles itself with the thought that such a thing surely could not have happened unless the victims had in some way or another furnished some kind of instigation, and this "some kind of" may then be multiplied at will. The blindness disregards the flagrant disproportion between an extremely fictitious guilt and an extremely real punishment.[73]

In his own defence of the Germans, Kronstein checks every box on Adorno's list: he draws a balance sheet of crimes that occurred on both sides, equating the Germans to the Russians; he minimizes the German people's agency under National Socialism; and he universalizes the question of guilt and complicity during the war, turning it into an abstract-metaphysical problem. Most problematically, he implicitly blames the Jewish victims for their fate.

Kronstein repeats a pervasive refrain of the period, which cast both Jews and Christians in the common role of victim. In Germany of the 1950s and 1960s, hatred of Jews was recast and reinterpreted as an expression of anti-religiosity and anti-Christian sentiment. Writing for the *Freiburger Rundbrief* in 1960, the German historian Walter Lipgens claimed that the Nazi attack on the Jews "expressed a general hatred of religion," stating that the "joint persecution of Jews and Christians" brought about a re-encounter of the two religions that had been unthinkable for 1,700 years.[74] A similar claim was made by Josef Brandlmeier, chairman of the Munich Society for Christian-Jewish Cooperation in 1958, who expressed a desire to turn the events of 1933–45 into a blessing. "For the first time in history, Christians and Jews were persecuted together by the despisers of God and man. Protestant and

Catholic Christians – with deep shame and a determined will to make amends – seek to draw the consequence together with Jews."[75] In this revision of the Nazi period, the persecution of the Jews was merely a prelude to the fate that awaited the Christians. The claim that Nazism was the consequence of European atheism, nihilism, and godlessness served to mitigate German responsibility and marginalize its Jewish victims. Kronstein channels these sentiments most troublingly when he declares that "the horrific persecution of the Jews in the past decades is a shocking document of un-Christian and nationalistic thinking. That this thinking has not been overcome even today is brought to our attention almost daily from some part of the world. *May the sacrifice of the millions of Jews not be in vain!*"[76]

**Finding Closure in Christianity**

*Briefe an einen jungen Deutschen* encapsulates the Christian revivalist spirit of the Adenauer years, which prepared the ground for a revisionist view of the Nazi past that transformed the Germans into Hitler's victims. Tellingly, Kronstein's memoir appeared the same year that Alexander and Margarete Mitscherlich published their landmark study *The Inability to Mourn* (1967). That work offered a scathing critique of West Germany's failure to confront its Nazi past.[77] The couple argued that the German people could not mourn the historical legacy of National Socialism or come to terms with their crimes until they recognized the extent to which they had identified with Hitler and the Nazi regime. Their psychoanalytic interpretation of West Germany's political and psychological reaction to the war and its aftermath drew on the Freudian distinction between mourning and melancholia. For Freud, mourning is the psychic response to the loss of a love object that one recognizes as distinctly separate from the self. In this form of bereavement, the ego is fully aware of the boundaries separating the self from the lost other. The melancholic, in contrast, is incapable of recognizing the separateness of the lost object. According to the Mitscherlichs, the Germans exhibited a melancholic response to their defeat, because they never consciously recognized or came to terms with the disintegration of the narcissistic fantasy represented by the Nazi *Volksgemeinschaft*. The Germans would need to acknowledge the loss of their aggrandized national self before they could confront the reality of their crimes. Yet after the war, the Germans merely shifted their libidinal investment in Hitler to the Allied forces without taking stock of their narcissistic identification with the Nazi regime. The *Wirtschaftswunder* and the new Cold War world order allowed them to repress the narcissistic injury of defeat and stave off the work of mourning necessary for a genuine confrontation with their responsibility for the crimes committed during the years of the Third Reich.

Reading Kronstein's memoir against the backdrop of Alexander and Margarete Mitscherlich's study reveals the political and cultural conditions that shaped his self-presentation as a returning émigré. In its treatment of Germany's Nazi past, *Briefe an einen jungen Deutschen* subscribes to the cultural mechanisms of repression and denial that the Mitscherlichs identified, such as the German claim to victimhood and the accusatory stance towards the Jews. If Kronstein participates in the symbolic displacement of German guilt, he employs the same mechanisms to repress his own narcissistic injury as a German patriot expelled from the German national body on racial grounds. Despite being stripped of his citizenship, barred from his profession, and banished from his homeland, Kronstein takes pains to disavow the divide separating him from Germans in the post-war era. Christian conversion functions as a fetishistic narrative device that allows the author to absorb the historical rupture of the Holocaust and establish the integrity of his post-war identity as a German Catholic. It harmonizes the disruption and fragmentation of the author's cultural and national identity following the rise of National Socialism and represses the traumatic injury of his own exclusion from the German national body during the Nazi era. The Christian-German identity celebrated in the memoir reflects the author's "inability to mourn" or to recognize the political and cultural complexities involved in recuperating his Germaness by way of conversion.

# The Consolations of Christianity and the Inadequacy of Form

*We former exiles must find our own path. Some end up Catholic, others turn paranoid or become garden variety conservatives. Very few remain normal. There is no alternative community.*

– Arthur Koestler to Alfred Kantorowicz, 23 September 1957[1]

In his 1966 essay "How Much Home Does a Person Need?," Austrian Holocaust survivor Jean Améry asserts the irreversibility of exile. Born as Hanns Maier to an assimilated Jewish family that celebrated Christmas and identified as Austrian, Améry changed his name and resettled in Belgium after his liberation from Auschwitz, two gestures that expressed his permanent alienation from his pre-war self. When he was excluded from the Austrian national community after the German annexation of Austria, Améry discovered that he had lost something far more profound and fundamental than his childhood attachment to his native landscapes. He had lost the foundations of his self-understanding. "I was a person who could no longer say 'we' and who therefore said 'I' merely out of habit, but not with the feeling of full possession of my self ... I was no longer an I and did not live within a We. I had no passport, and no past, and no money, and no history."[2] The loss of home and homeland unravelled the connections between individual, community, place, and language that Améry had previously taken for granted.[3]

The biographies examined in this book grapple with the loss addressed in Améry's essay. Yet whereas Améry adamantly believed that this loss was irreversible, my protagonists sought to salvage their communal attachments and their integral sense of self by way of conversion. "Conversion discourse," writes Peter Dorsey, "provides a reliable index of the relationship between the self and larger cultures ... signifying that one had come into alignment with certain linguistic, behavioural, and cultural expectations ... By publicly testifying to their own conversion experiences, believers became empowered members, not only of God's elect community, but also of a local population."[4] Dorsey's claim locates the nexus of individual and social worlds that manifests itself through the conversion narrative. Yet it is precisely the link between belief and belonging, the complementary promises of conversion, that failed to materialize in the cases I have explored. The path to Christianity did not necessarily lead to communal inclusion.

The impossibility of this endeavour may not have been openly acknowledged by the converts in their published accounts of salvation and survival, yet some, like Hirsch and Döblin, professed this realization in private. On Christmas Day in 1946, his first as a Christian, Hirsch noted how differently the holiday must have felt to cradle Christians, whose experiences of the religious celebration were coloured by their childhood memories and received knowledge of the day's traditions. Sounding far less triumphant in his diaries than in his recently published memoir, Hirsch solemnly contemplated the meaning of the day in a self-reflective manner befitting of a new proselyte:

> When you consider that the Savior was born 1946 years ago, that people committed both good and evil in his name, that people were blessed and exterminated, when you understand all this, as I do today, you see the difficulties that lie in the realization of a teaching. I take all of this in like a student who is still very new to the class and who perhaps takes his lessons too seriously. But the others are used to it, they have childhood memories that are usually more beautiful than reality. I tell myself that one can only properly understand the meaning of the Savior's birth on this day if one has an environment that feels the same. Yet I am strangely isolated. I understand this now more than ever. There are moments when one becomes very clear-sighted. The greatness of the idea of salvation is clearer to me than to those who take it for granted ... I came to Christianity looking for community. But it exists only in spirit and not in reality.[5]

The case studies in this book demonstrate that conversion narratives are not straightforward records of one's personal life history but rather self-conscious articulations of a life as its author would like it to be seen. They are narratives intended to create order and lend meaning to an otherwise fragmented series of events that do not have an inherently linear or evolutionary logic to them. The retrospective reorganization of one's life experience through the trope of conversion is intended to facilitate a sense of closure and coherence. In Patrick Riley's elegant formulation, "the logic of conversion, as it creates a reference point for the literary construction of identity, is one of the most compelling rhetorical and psychological structures available to the autobiographer trying to understand and communicate the shape of his or her life."[6]

The lives of the individuals at the centre of this study were marked by experiences of radical dislocation and despair. Christianity provided them with a framework for re-establishing a stable sense of self and meaning in the face of trauma. In these narratives the pains of displacement, exile, and persecution find their justification when the converts uncover the deep structures of meaning underlying their suffering. Conversion functions as a master trope for restructuring a life riven by political upheaval and historical catastrophe. It incorporates the disruption of the war years within an intelligible developmental narrative, bringing together the biographical discontinuities of the years 1933–45.

The narratives reflect their authors' efforts to reclaim individual agency in the face of complete helplessness. They respond to the external imposition of collective-racial stigma by claiming a new Christian identity that distances them from their Jewish origins. In relating their religious transformation to the Holocaust, the converts transform the experience of passivity, victimhood, and persecution into a redemptive narrative of personal salvation. The religious metamorphosis liberates the convert from the taint of what Jean Améry calls the "catastrophe Jew," whose Jewish identity is solely a function of Nazi persecution.[7] Conversion enables the survivor to cast off the burden of victimhood by attributing the caesura in his life to the workings of divine grace and personal growth. Yet the personal agency that is claimed through conversion comes at a discernable cost of concealment and self-censorship.

This trade-off is the subject of Naomi Seidman's account of the translation history of Holocaust survivor Elie Wiesel's *Night*. In two landmark studies, Seidman traces the profound transformation that Wiesel's memoir underwent in the process of translation from the original Yiddish into the French version that paved the author's path to literary stardom.[8] Seidman uses Wiesel's case to illuminate the "role of translation in the production and reception of Holocaust narratives."[9] She shows how the resulting translated version rewrote the experience of survival and its meaning. Relinquishing the political rage and accusation that marked the Yiddish original so as not to alienate its European-Christian audience, *La Nuit* transformed the survivor's wrath into a religious parable of modern martyrdom and existential despair. While acknowledging the necessity of such a compromise, Seidman asks, "Was it worth it? Was it worth translating the Holocaust out of the language of the largest portion of its victims and into the language of those who were, at best, absent, and at worst, complicitous in the genocide? Was it worth ... reviving the image of the Jew ... as the Christian is prepared to accept him, the emblem of suffering silence rather than living rage?"[10]

Seidman points to a problem that is no less pertinent to the autobiographical texts of Stern, Kronstein, Hirsch, and Döblin. In relating their wartime experiences in the form of conversion narratives, did these autobiographers not produce works of translation that dissociated them from the historical and personal circumstances that compelled them to write their stories in the first place? Did translating the story of Jewish suffering and survival into testimonies of Christian salvation contribute to their self-understanding or to their self-estrangement? Were they aware of the moral compromises and constraints involved in ventriloquizing the experience of Jewish victimhood in the Christian-theological idiom of sin and salvation?

In Christianizing the Holocaust, these four authors rewrote, suppressed, and distorted key episodes in their past. They reframed the meaning of certain events in ways that marginalized and disparaged the Jewish victims and survivors of Hitlerism. In this regard, the resulting narratives fit into a broader historical pattern that according to Seidman determined the post-war formation of Holocaust literature and that required translating the Jewish experience of persecution and survival for gentile audiences. Seidman shows that this process of cultural translation often involved the suppression of the victims' Jewish particularity and the moral ambiguities Jews faced during the Holocaust.[11]

In dissociating themselves from other Jews and resignifying their traumatic pasts, the converts aspired to find a receptive and empathetic audience among their new co-religionists. Yet as the historical reception of these narratives demonstrates, what drew the Christian and German readers to these survivor testimonies was a desire for self-exculpation, which the authors duly delivered. The choice of genre and religious framing surely broadened their potential audience, but it also alienated them from fellow Jews, including those who had shared their fate and were thus most likely to identify with and comprehend their plight. Accentuating this problem is the fact that the converts in question interpreted the theological significance of Jewish victimhood through a framework that undermined the validity of traditional Judaism or demonized fellow Jews. Their narratives confirm an observation Hannah Arendt made in *Rahel Varnhagen: The Life of a Jewess*: "If one accepted Christianity, one had to accept the time's hatred of the Jews right along it. Both Christianity and anti-Semitism were integrating components of the historical past of European man ... No assimilation could be achieved merely by surrendering one's own past, but ignoring the alien past. In a society on the whole hostile to the Jews … it is possible to assimilate only by assimilating to anti-Semitism also."[12]

The converts adapted their stories to the traditional Christian framework of the sick and sinful soul that is healed and remade by the glory of God. Yet the historical experiences recounted in these texts conflict with and inevitably diverge from the narrative tradition they claim as their model. The transition from the "divided" to the "unified" self remains incomplete, due to a persistent and unresolved duality that pervades these texts. The clear-cut division between the *before* and the *after* of conversion is problematized in these narratives by two facts: first, the external ascription of difference persists past conversion and affects the convert's relationship to both Jews and gentiles; and second, the disavowed Jewish identity plays a fundamental role in the construction of the convert's Christian self.

Religious conversion is commonly understood as a radical spiritual transformation that entails profound internal change, leading to the reorientation of one's personal beliefs and sense of self. This perception is rooted in a long-standing literary and theological tradition that has determined the language and imagery used to represent conversion. Attesting to the staying power of this image is William James's influential account of conversion in *The Varieties of Religious Experience*. In an oft-quoted passage, James describes the experience as a "process … by which a self hitherto divided … becomes unified."[13] The patterns James identifies as inherent to the convert's experience are not embedded in the psyche; rather, they are storytelling conventions that the individual learns, internalizes, and imitates. Conversion, in the Jamesian sense, only truly materializes as a retrospective undertaking, when the convert recounts his experience in the form of a conversion narrative. This act involves the reconstruction of one's past in a manner that conforms to the conventions and expectations of the genre.[14]

Emerging from this theoretical understanding of conversion is a question concerning the correspondence between literary form and subjective experience in the case of these German-Jewish converts. How do the subjects of this study align their experiences with the formal features of the literary and theological tradition of the Christian conversion narrative? If writing a conversion narrative requires conformity between one's personal story and a prefabricated plot, to what extent is this inherited form capable of giving voice to the uniqueness of my protagonists' historical and personal predicament? In what sense do these autobiographical narratives remain true to the formal expectations of the genre, and at what cost?

The language of Christian conversion provided these emigrants with a narrative-theological framework with which to redeem the historical experience of communal collapse and individual fragmentation. The converts regard the collective catastrophe that befell their community of origin as evidence of the workings of divine providence in their lives. To the extent that the symbolic resources of the Christian conversion narrative facilitate the converts' reconstituted selfhood, they achieve this task at the cost of obscuring, excluding, and silencing aspects of individual experience that do not conform to or align with its preordained models, leaving textual traces of desolation and distress. The conversion narrative as a genre is anchored in an autonomous concept of the self, one that is ill-suited to tell the story of the minority experience of European Jewry in the first half of the twentieth century. The individualistic model of autobiographical identity, which characterizes much of the writing on conversion, misrepresents the formative influence of external social forces. In the words of Susan Stanford Friedman, the individualistic paradigm of autobiographical writing "does not take into account the importance of a culturally imposed group identity for women and minorities."[15]

The inadequacy of form and its failure to serve as a repository for sentiments of rage and ressentiment manifests itself in the text through various symptoms: melancholy silences, temporal inconsistencies, and arbitrary shifts in narrative voice and perspective. While Christianity affords the convert with the possibility of closure and consolation in the face of trauma, it also emerges as a source of deep ambivalence and anxiety because it conflicts with the foundations of the convert's former self-understanding, which was shaped by a historically imposed group identity. The total transformation underlying the template of Christian conversion cuts the convert off from the communal solidarities that served as a source of succour during the Nazi years. I have thus sought to highlight the paradoxical workings of conversion as a source not only of consolation and closure but also of continual anguish, guilt, and anxiety. The salvific stories of "rebirth" as a Christian can simultaneously be read as more ambiguous narratives of breakdown and bereavement.

# Notes


**Epigraph**

1 Goethe, *The Essential Goethe*, 887. Translation modified. Used with permission of Princeton University Press, from *The Essential Goethe*, edited by Matthew Bell, 2016; permission conveyed through Copyright Clearance Center, Inc.

**Introduction: Conversion and the Problem of Persuasion**

1 Ernst Ginsberg, *Abschied. Erinnerungen, Theateraufsätze, Gedichte*, edited by Elisabeth Brock-Sulzer (Zurich: Arche, 1991), 14. My Italics.
2 Ginsberg, *Abschied*, 167.
3 Webster, *Conversion Disorder*, 13.
4 Silverman, *Becoming Austrians*, 5.
5 Moyn, "German Jewry," 295.
6 Spector, "Forget Assimilation," 352–56.
7 Auslander, "The Boundaries of Jewishness," 48.
8 Auslander, "The Boundaries of Jewishness," 60.
9 Kselman, *Conscience and Conversion*, 7.
10 Morrison, *Conversion and Text*, 144. In a perceptive critique of Morrison's distinction between the experience and the account of conversion, Ryan Szpiech argues that the presumed inability to penetrate the true nature of the conversion experience presupposes "a single, transcendental signified outside the web of any partial and deferred signification." In contrasting the reality with the representation of conversion, Morrison establishes a false distinction between the subjective and social dimensions of conversion, thus privileging an individualistic conception of conversion as a prelinguistic experience that precedes one's attempt at articulation. There is, he contends, no original "real" conversion underlying the text. See Szpiech, *Conversion and Narrative*, 17.

11  On this point see Dodd, "Criticism and the Autobiographical Tradition," 8.

12  See Ginsberg, *Abschied*; Pincus, *Verloren-gewonnen*; Graef, *From Fashions to the Fathers*; Hill, *A Time Out of Joint*; Baum, *The Oil Has Not Run Dry*; Aufricht, *Erzähle damit du dein Recht erweist*; Rosenberg, *Die Welt im Feuer*; Neumeyer, *Lichter und Schatten*.

13  Stein, *Aus dem Leben einer jüdischen Familie*.

14  Mary G. Mason, "The Other Voice: Autobiographies of Women Writers," in *Autobiography: Essays Theoretical and Critical*, ed. James Olney (Princeton: Princeton University Press, 1980), 210. In an essay on nineteenth-century female spiritual autobiography, Linda H. Peterson argues that women generally "avoided the form of the spiritual autobiography" and "did not compose retrospective accounts of spiritual or psychological progress." See Peterson, "Gender and Autobiographical Form," 212. See also Dorsey, "Women's Autobiography"; Friedman, "Women's Autobiographical Selves," 34–62; and Spacks, "Selves in Hiding."

15  For informative surveys of the phenomenon of Jewish conversion to Christianity during the Holocaust and its historical significance, see Ariel, "From Faith to Faith" and "From Judaism to Christianity."

16  Young, *Writing and Rewriting the Holocaust*, 5.

17  Ellie Schainker offers a pointed critique of Endelman's blanket interpretation of conversion as a form of "radical assimilation." "What happens," she asks, "to this neat analysis of modern conversions when Jews convert to minority faiths?" According to Schainker, reducing all conversions to instrumental means of modernization and assimilation "flattens the analytically rich factors of confessional choice and the local conditions, social spaces, and networks that affected the nature and process of Jewish conversion." See Schainker, "Jewish Conversion in an Imperial Context," 2–3.

18  Endelman's ambitious study forms part of a burgeoning scholarly field that investigates the history of Jewish conversion and apostasy for its potential to shed light on the dynamic boundaries of Jewish–Christian difference and broaden the scope of modern Jewish history to include the experiences of Jews who disavowed their ties to their ancestral faith and communities of origin. See also Hertz, *How Jews Became Germans*; Carlebach, *Divided Souls*; Hirsch, *Rester juif?*; Endelman, ed., *Jewish Apostasy in the Modern World*; Endelman, *Broadening Jewish History*; Schainker, *Confessions of the Shtetl*; Dunkelgrün and Maciejko, eds., *Bastards and Believers*; Goldman, *Jewish-Christian Difference*; and Ruderman, ed., *Converts of Conviction*.

19  See Viswanathan, *Outside the Fold*; Özyürek, *Being German, Becoming Muslim*; Wohlrab-Sahr, *Konversion zum Islam*; van der Veer, ed., *Conversion*

*to Modernities*; Washburn and Reinhart, eds., *Converting Cultures*; and Hefner, ed., *Conversion to Christianity*.

20  Arendt, *Rahel Varnhagen*, 144.
21  Arendt, *Rahel Varnhagen*, 7.
22  Arendt, *The Origins of Totalitarianism*, 56.
23  Arendt, *The Origins of Totalitarianism*, 67.
24  Arendt, *The Jewish Writings*, 269.
25  Arendt, *The Jewish Writings*, 271–2.
26  Endelman, *Leaving the Jewish Fold*, 192–3.

**1. Conversion and the Question of German Guilt in Karl Jakob Hirsch's *Heimkehr zu Gott* (1946)**

1  Peitsch, "Karl Jakob Hirsch," 96.
2  Hirsch's initial success soon gave way to suspicion regarding his political past as a member of various left-wing and avant-garde circles during the Weimar era. Several of the manuscripts rejected during those years were published posthumously from the 1990s onwards. See Hirsch, *Quintessenz meines Lebens*; Hirsch, *Der alte Doktor*; and Hirsch, *Einer muss es ja tun*.
3  At the time, the number of Jewish survivors who addressed their memoirs to the German public could be counted on one hand. Helmut Peitsch counts Abraham Hochhäuser's *Unter dem gelben Stern*, Zenon Ronzanski's *Mützen ab: eine Reportage aus der Strafkompanie des KZ*, Emil de Martini's *Vier Millionen Tote klagen an!*, and Jakob Littner's *Aufzeichnungen aus einem Erdloch*, all published in 1948. According to Peitsch, these survivor testimonies were mostly ignored by the national press. The one exception to this rule were narratives in which Jews recounted being rescued by Christians. Else Behrend-Rosenfeld's *Ich stand nicht allein!* and Max Krakauer's *Lichter im Dunkel* received far more coverage and were reprinted after the Federal Republic was established in 1949. See Peitsch, "Karl Jakob Hirsch," 96–7.
4  According to Stephen Brockmann, there were two reasons for Germans' reluctance to address this issue: the horrific nature of the Nazi crimes, and the sense many Germans had that they were victims rather than perpetrators. They felt this was victor's justice imposed upon them. Moreover, the struggle for survival seemed to take precedence over the need for moral reckoning. See Brockmann, *German Literary Culture*, 23.
5  Marwitz, "Heimkehr zu Gott."
6  Marwitz, "Heimkehr zu Gott."
7  George, "Wieder einer." See also Hulse, "Judentum und Konvertiten"; and Wurmbrand, "Ein Jude erteilt der Christenheit Absolution."

8 George, "Wieder einer."

9 Mehring, "Letters to the Editor." See also Tramer, "Das genial-tragische Leben."

10 Ben-Chorin, "Heimkehr zu Gott."

11 Ben-Chorin, "Heimkehr zu Gott."

12 Ben-Chorin, "Heimkehr zu Gott."

13 Ben-Chorin, "Heimkehr zu Gott."

14 Hirsch's notoriety in German-Jewish circles continued even after his death. The philosopher Hermann Levin Goldschmidt, in his study *Das Vermächtnis des deutschen Judentums* (1957), singled out Hirsch as the epitome of Jewish self-hatred. See Goldschmidt, *Das Vermächtnis*, 122; and Goldschmidt, *The Legacy of German Jewry*, 179–80. The only Jewish group that seemed to welcome Hirsch's conversion and that lauded his memoir were Jewish-Christian missionaries. See Leuner, "Karl Jakob Hirsch"; and Leuner, "Ein Blick in die Werkstatt Gottes."

15 Moshe Ungerfeld, "Avot U-Banim," *Hazofeh*, April 25, 1947, p. 3.

16 Ungerfeld, "Avot U-Banim."

17 Ungerfeld, "Avot U-Banim."

18 Hirsch, *Heimkehr zu Gott*, 16.

19 Hirsch, *Heimkehr zu Gott*, 16.

20 See Hirsch, *Heimkehr zu Gott*, 19.

21 Hirsch, *Heimkehr zu Gott*, 25.

22 Hirsch, *Heimkehr zu Gott*, 51.

23 Hirsch, *Heimkehr zu Gott*, 51.

24 Sketches that Hirsch made of Eugen Leviné, alongside those of Karl Liebknecht and Rosa Luxemburg, can be found in his book *Revolutionäre Kunst*.

25 See Hirsch, *Kaiserwetter*.

26 For an account of the work's central themes and its reception, see Mahn, *Karl Jakob Hirsch*, 164–98.

27 Pfanner, *Karl Jakob Hirsch*, 37; Anonymous, *Liste 1*, 54.

28 The novel was republished in book form in 1986. See Hirsch, *Hochzeitsmarsch in Moll: Roman*.

29 Hirsch, "Selbstbildnis."

30 Karl Jakob Hirsch, "Hochzeitsmarsch in Moll," 2.

31 In *Heimkehr*, Hirsch claims that he left Europe for the US in 1934, yet the records of the *Fremdenpolizei* in Bern have Hirsch listed as a registered foreigner on 15 May 1937, residing in Luzern. Contrary to the chronology Hirsch provides in his two autobiographical works and based on city records, Pfanner speculates that Hirsch remained in Berlin until the mid-1930s, possibly even until 1936. Pfanner suggests that Hirsch deliberately backdated his flight from Germany so as to align himself with the

"émigrés of the first hour" and claim the moral distinction of leaving the country before he was forced to do so out of material considerations. The fact that Hirsch's estate contains almost no official papers from the years of his flight from Germany or his stay in Switzerland also supports the assumption that he was not interested in the later disclosure of his itinerary. See Pfanner, *Karl Jakob Hirsch*, 64–5.

32  During his eight years with the *Neue Volkszeitung*, Hirsch wrote more than 600 reviews and articles under the name Joe Gassner, most of them covering New York's cultural scene. See Mahn, *Karl Jakob Hirsch*, 229–60. Several of the novellas he published serially in the *NVZ* were posthumously republished. See Hirsch, *Tagebuch Aus Dem Dritten Reich*; and Hirsch, *Manhattan-Serenade*.

33  Hirsch shared this fate with hundreds of writers and intellectuals who found refuge in New York in the 1930s and 1940s. As most of them could not resort to writing for their livelihood, these exiles were forced to rely on charity organizations and manual labour. See Pfanner, *Exile in New York*.

34  Hirsch, *Heimkehr zu Gott*, 118–19.

35  Hirsch, *Heimkehr zu Gott*, 160.

36  Hirsch, *Heimkehr zu Gott*, 159.

37  The film's role in Hirsch's religious conversion was thoroughly mocked in the negative reviews penned by German-Jewish exiles. Even his most generously inclined readers, such as Thomas Mann, questioned Hirsch's emphasis on the film adaptation of Werfel's *Song of Bernadette*, which "owed its great success to its catholicizing features and the masses' need for miracles." Quoted in Mahn, *Karl Jakob Hirsch*, 332.

38  Hirsch, *Heimkehr zu Gott*, 159.

39  Hirsch, *Heimkehr zu Gott*, 163.

40  Hirsch, *Heimkehr zu Gott*, 163–4.

41  Elsewhere Hirsch describes conversion as "a process of rejuvenation" that turns new believers into "courageous fighters for their new faith." Karl Jakob Hirsch, "Sie hörten die Stimme." Eine Sammlung von Biographien über Konvertiten. W1.13 (Typoskripte), Nachlaß Karl Jakob Hirsch, Universitätsbibliothek München.

42  Mitchell and Snyder, *The Body and Physical Difference*, 21.

43  Hirsch, *Heimkehr zu Gott*, 168–9.

44  Hirsch, *Heimkehr zu Gott*, 169.

45  Hirsch, *Heimkehr zu Gott*, 184.

46  Hirsch, *Heimkehr zu Gott*, 79.

47  See Wagner, *Judaism in Music*; and Gilman, "Are Jews Musical?"

48  Rose, *Wagner*, 82.

49  Hirsch, *Heimkehr zu Gott*, 184.

50  Hirsch, *Heimkehr zu Gott*, 185.

51  Hirsch, *Heimkehr zu Gott*, 185–6.

52  Hirsch, *Heimkehr zu Gott*, 187.

53  One person who did not turn his back on Hirsch was his cousin and childhood friend Julius Hirsch, a professor of medicine at the Kaiser Wilhelm Institute in Berlin before the war. Julius Hirsch found refuge in Istanbul during the Nazi years and later resettled in Switzerland. He helped support Karl Jakob Hirsch in his last years in Munich and sent him the medications he needed to keep his neurological disease at bay. In a letter from 1948, Julius Hirsch responded to his cousin's controversial memoir in a jovial tone: "Oh my, oh my, oh my! Return to God, return to Munich, return to a legitimate marriage: this is too much to handle at once! I am already dizzy … To get things out of the way immediately: since our friendship was always of more value to me than our family ties, I have no cause to join the hate song of the 'mischpochoh' and the 'kehilloh.'" Brief von Julius Hirsch an Karl Jakob Hirsch, 3 October 1948, B2 (Briefe an Karl Jakob Hirsch), Nachlaß Karl Jakob Hirsch, Universitätsbibliothek München.

54  Brief von Karl Jakob Hirsch an Hans Heinz Stuckenschmidt, 28 January 1948, B1 (Briefe von Karl Jakob Hirsch), Nachlaß Karl Jakob Hirsch, Universitätsbibliothek München.

55  Quoted in Ackermann, "Beinahe wäre etwas aus mir geworden," 9.

56  Hirsch, *Heimkehr zu Gott*, 74.

57  See Günther, "Heimkehr zu Gott"; Anonymous, "Heimkehr zu Gott"; and Peitsch, "Karl Jakob Hirsch," 99.

58  See Volkov, "Antisemitism as a Cultural Code"; George Mosse, "The Image of the Jew in German Popular Literature: Felix Dahn and Gustav Freytag," in *Germans and Jews*, 61–76.

59  Hirsch, *Heimkehr zu Gott*, 106.

60  Hirsch, *Heimkehr zu Gott*, 108.

61  Hirsch, *Heimkehr zu Gott*, 108.

62  Hirsch, *Heimkehr zu Gott*, 137.

63  Hirsch, *Heimkehr zu Gott*, 135.

64  Hirsch, *Heimkehr zu Gott*, 177.

65  Hirsch, *Heimkehr zu Gott*, 177.

66  Hirsch, *Heimkehr zu Gott*, 178.

67  Hirsch, *Heimkehr zu Gott*, 190–1.

68  When Walter Huder, Hirsch's literary executor, republished *Heimkehr* in 1967, he removed the controversial passages that attributed the Holocaust to the Jews' theological blindness and the intergenerational guilt they bore for killing Christ. See Mahn, *Karl Jakob Hirsch*, 350.

69  Hirsch, *Heimkehr zu Gott*, 169.

70  The Holocaust historian Saul Friedländer coined the term "redemptive antisemitism" in order to characterize the pseudo-religious dimension underlying the Nazi ideology of extermination. According to Friedländer, "the redemption of Aryan Christian humanity by the struggle against and the victory over the Jews" (19) formed the ideological core of the Nazi worldview, which drew heavily on the apocalyptic and messianic motifs of the Christian tradition. See Friedländer, "Ideology and Extermination."

71  Arendt, "The Aftermath of Nazi Rule," 343.

72  As Carl Emil Schorske and Hoyt Price explain: "The Christian churches probably occupy a more decisive position in the social and cultural life of Germany today than at any time since the early seventeenth century. Despite the warfare waged against organized religion by the Nazis, the churches survived the Nazi defeat and, for a brief period, constituted the only organs of social continuity in an otherwise atomized society. The position of the churches has been further strengthened by a religious revival accompanying the collapse of Nazism." See Schorske and Price, *The Problem of Germany*, 112.

73  Olick, *In the House of the Hangman*, 203.

74  This turned out not to be the case. The clergy were in fact the most vocal opponents of the denazification policy. As Schorske and Price pointed out: "The governing body of the Evangelical churches stands today as the boldest antagonist of the de-Nazification law in the American zone, even while it dissociates itself from totalitarianism." See Schorske and Price, *The Problem of Germany*, 123.

75  See Hockenos, *A Church Divided*, 94.

76  Karl Jakob Hirsch, *Mutter Maria* (n.d.), W2.101, Nachlaß Karl Jakob Hirsch, pp. 26–7.

77  Hirsch, *Mutter Maria*, 25.

78  Hirsch, *Mutter Maria*, 34.

79  Hirsch, *Mutter Maria*, 36.

80  Hirsch, *Mutter Maria*, 36–7.

81  Hirsch, *Mutter Maria*, 38.

82  Hirsch, *Mutter Maria*, 38.

83  Biess, *German Angst*, 21. See also Schirrmeister, "Offene Rechnungen."

84  Biess, *German Angst*, 26.

85  Biess, *German Angst*, 64.

86  Hirsch, *Mutter Maria*, 22.

87  Heschel, "Sacrament versus Racism," 107. In *The Aryan Jesus*, Heschel shows how the theological question of Christianity's relationship to its Jewish origins assumed a distinctly racial dimension within certain Protestant circles. She traces the concerted theological effort to de-Judaize Jesus during the years of the Third Reich. This trend resonates with Karl

Jakob Hirsch's portrait of the life of Jesus in his unpublished manuscript *Joshua von Nazareth*. The novel centres on the drama of Jesus's paternity, presenting Joseph as a pathetic cuckhold, unwilling to recognize that he is not the father. The work reads like a very crude gesture on Hirsch's part to disavow his own ancestral origins. See Heschel, *The Aryan Jesus*. See also Karl Jakob Hirsch, "Joshua von Nazareth," W8 (Typoskripte), Nachlaß Karl Jakob Hirsch, Universitätsbibliothek München.

88 Hirsch, *Mutter Maria*, 44.

89 Hirsch's feeling of rejection on part of both Jews and Christians is documented in a letter to fellow convert Heinz David Leuner: "When I professed my Christian faith out of purest idealism, I naturally experienced rejection on the part of the Jews, who saw in me, as a descendant of Samson Raphael Hirsch, nothing more than a 'traitor.' I did not leave Judaism out of protest, but because even in the USA I had to reject the egocentric nature of the exiled Jews … But the fact that Christians in the USA and here in Germany rejected my readiness to help in every way was a deep spiritual shock for me." Brief von Karl Jakob Hirsch an H.D. Leuner, December 1951, B1 (Briefe von Karl Jakob Hirsch), Nachlaß Karl Jakob Hirsch, Universitätsbibliothek München.

90 Pfanner, *Karl Jakob Hirsch*, 11.

91 Döblin, *Briefe II*, 247–8.

92 Hirsch, *Quintessenz*, 40.

93 The Christian piety is replaced by a harsh and critical tone, which is also directed at Germany's religious institutions: "When the Church, Catholic and Protestant, strengthens the camp of reaction and regression, it turns around the very phrase of the founder of religion, Jesus of Nazareth, who said: 'He who is not for me is against me.'" See Hirsch, *Quintessenz*, 353.

94 Hirsch, *Quintessenz*, 38.

95 Hirsch, *Quintessenz*, 48.

96 Hirsch, *Quintessenz*, 49.

97 Hirsch, *Quintessenz*, 50–1.

98 Hirsch, *Quintessenz*, 49.

99 Hirsch, *Quintessenz*, 62.

100 Hirsch, *Quintessenz*, 63.

101 Hirsch, *Quintessenz*, 68.

102 Hirsch, *Quintessenz*, 83.

103 Hirsch, *Quintessenz*, 138.

104 Hirsch, *Quintessenz*, 139.

105 Hirsch, *Quintessenz*, 142.

106 Hirsch, *Quintessenz*, 235.

107 Hirsch, *Quintessenz*, 235.

108 Hirsch, *Quintessenz*, 235.

109  Hirsch, *Quintessenz*, 237.

110  Hirsch's letters seem to suggest that he had soured on Pastor Forrell after repeated requests for material assistance went unanswered. See Brief von Karl Jakob Hirsch an H.D. Leuner, January 1, 1952, B1 (Briefe von Karl Jakob Hirsch), Nachlaß Karl Jakob Hirsch, Universitätsbibliothek München.

111  Hirsch, *Quintessenz*, 238.

112  Hirsch, *Quintessenz*, 238.

113  Hirsch, *Quintessenz*, 241–2.

114  Karl Jakob Hirsch, "Marxismus und Religiosität. Eine Betrachtung," 1, W2.223 (Typoskripte), Nachlaß Karl Jakob Hirsch, Universitätsbibliothek München.

115  Hirsch, "Marxismus und Religiosität," 5.

116  Hirsch, "Marxismus und Religiosität," 6.

117  Hirsch, *Quintessenz*, 346. As unrealistic as it may have been for a person in his fragile condition, Hirsch took active steps in attempt to resettle in the GDR, petitioning colleagues he knew on the other side of the border. In a letter to the writer Arnold Zweig: "It was self-evident to me that I would return to Germany. I intended to return to the GDR after a few gloomy weeks in the Federal Republic … I have written several novels, novellas and short stories, radio plays and plays, which, however, cannot be performed or published in the occupation zone … Despite my walking disability and my fifty-eight years of age, I am brimming with energy and have many plans, which can only be realized in the GDR … I would therefore be extremely grateful to you if you would support my relocation to the real Germany (*dem wirklichen Deutschland*) … It is unbearable for a progressive, socialist-minded person such as myself to remain here and I must do everything in my power to move to the GDR." Brief von Karl Jakob Hirsch an Arnold Zweig, 29 May 1951, B1 (Briefe von Karl Jakob Hirsch), Nachlaß Karl Jakob Hirsch, Universitätsbibliothek München.

118  Hirsch, *Quintessenz*, 346. In an unpublished manuscript titled "The Unspeakable," Hirsch notes the that "There is an 'ominous' and 'tactful' reticence about the past twelve years … The reading public finds books about concentration camps repugnant. The publishers and booksellers assert that the public is 'oversaturated' with this subject matter." Karl Jakob Hirsch, "Das Unaussprechliche" (n.d.), W2.361 (Typoskripte), Nachlaß Karl Jakob Hirsch, Universitätsbibliothek München.

119  Hirsch, *Quintessenz*, 349.

120  Hirsch goes so far as to describe his existence in the Federal Republic as living through an "inner emigration," borrowing the term used to describe the life of intellectuals who remained in Germany during the

Nazi years, expressing their alienation and disaffection from the regime through their turn "inwards." See Karl Jakob Hirsch, "Beginn der zweiten Emigration," W2.372, Nachlaß Karl Jakob Hirsch, Universitätsbibliothek München.

121  See Brief von Walter Agulnik an Karl Jakob, 4 April 1950; Brief von Walter Bauer an Karl Jakob Hirsch, 14 April 1951; Brief von Deutsche Kurzschrift-Illustrierte an Karl Jakob Hirsch, 28 September 1951; Brief von Schwäbische Illustrierte Presse an Karl Jakob Hirsch, 19 May 1949; Brief von Rowohlt-Verlag (Hamburg) an Karl Jakob Hirsch, n.d.; Brief von Gerd Schulte an Karl Jakob Hirsch (Norddeutsche Zeitung), 4 April 1949; Brief von Schleswig-Holsteinische Volkszeitung an Karl Jakob Hirsch, 28 March 1949; Brief von Hannsludwig Geiger von Erich Schmidt Verlag an Karl Jakob, 11 May 1949; Brief von Redaktion "Die Gegenwart" an Karl Jakob Hirsch, 25 April 1949; Brief von Redaktion Deutscher Hausschatz (Nürnberg) an Karl Jakob, 29 March 1949; Brief von Südwestfunk an Karl Jakob, 1 January 1951, all in B2 (Briefe an Karl Jakob Hirsch), Nachlaß Karl Jakob Hirsch, Universitätsbibliothek München.

122  Brief von Moritz Hauptmann von Harriet Schleber Verlag an Karl Jakob Hirsch, 8 March 1949, B2 (Briefe an Karl Jakob Hirsch), Nachlaß Karl Jakob Hirsch, Universitätsbibliothek München.

123  Brief von Die Deutsche Woche an Karl Jakob, 8 August 1951, B2 (Briefe an Karl Jakob Hirsch), Nachlaß Karl Jakob Hirsch, Universitätsbibliothek München.

124  Brief von Bayerischer Rundfunk an Karl Jakob, 17 April 1950, B2 (Briefe an Karl Jakob Hirsch), Nachlaß Karl Jakob Hirsch, Universitätsbibliothek München.

125  Hirsch, *Quintessenz*, 349.

126  In this regard, Hirsch's negative portrayal of Jews corresponded to a widespread German perception of returning Jewish émigrés as vindictive profiteers, full of hatred and resentment, who had been spared the suffering of ordinary Germans. See Bergmann, "'Wir haben Sie nicht gerufen.'"

127  Hirsch, *Quintessenz*, 349.

128  Pfanner, *Karl Jakob Hirsch*, 97.

## 2. The Suppressed Jewish Voice in Alfred Döblin's *Schicksalsreise* (1949)

1  This letter was discovered and published by literary scholar Wilfried Schoeller. Quoted in Schoeller, *Alfred Döblin*, 790.

2  Döblin, *Schriften zu Leben und Werk*, 57.

3  Döblin, *Schriften zu Leben und Werk*, 57–8.

4  Döblin, *Schriften zu Leben und Werk*, 59.

5  Döblin, *Schriften zu Leben und Werk*, 60.

6   Döblin, *Schriften zu Leben und Werk*, 100.

7   For informative overviews of Döblin's relationship to Judaism and Jewish motifs in his work, see Kiesel, "Alfred Döblins Verhältnis zum Judentum"; Horch, "Döblin und das Judentum"; Müller-Salget, "Alfred Döblin und das Judentum"; Sander, "'A Banner I Could Not Hold Aloft'"; and Huguet, "Alfred Doblin et le judaïsme."

8   Döblin, "Zion und Europa," in *Kleine Schriften I*, 314.

9   Sander, "'A Banner I Could Not Hold Aloft,'" 99.

10   Döblin, *Schriften zu Leben und Werk*, 61.

11   Döblin, *Schriften zu Leben und Werk*, 62.

12   Döblin, *Schriften zu Leben und Werk*, 62.

13   Döblin, *Journey to Poland*, 50; Döblin, *Reise in Polen*, 77. See also Sauerland, "Döblins Begegnung."

14   Döblin, *Journey to Poland*, 75; Döblin, *Reise in Polen*, 103.

15   Döblin, *Journey to Poland*, 102; Döblin, *Reise in Polen*, 137.

16   Sander, "A Banner I Could Not Hold Aloft," 102.

17   Döblin, *Journey to Poland*, 154–6; Döblin, *Reise in Polen*, 166–7; Schoeller, *Alfred Döblin*, 283.

18   For an overview of Döblin's years in exile, see Becker and Schneider, "Exile als 'Schicksalsreise.'"

19   On Döblin's involvement with the territorialist movement see Horch, "Alfred Döblin und der Neo-Territorialismus"; and Rovner, *In the Shadow of Zion*, 122–8.

20   Döblin, *Schriften zu jüdischen Fragen*, 309–10.

21   Döblin, *Destiny's Journey*, 111; Döblin, *Schicksalsreise*, 146.

22   Döblin, *Briefe I*, 224.

23   According to Klaus Müller-Salget, Döblin was "unwilling to give up his fundamentally utopian ideas (utopian particularly considering the historical situation) and kept hoping, on the one hand, to be able to bring about a concrete realization of his view of mankind and, on the other, to find a spiritual community and a home for himself." See Müller-Salget, "Döblin and Judaism," 238.

24   Schoeller, *Alfred Döblin*, 474–5.

25   Döblin, *Destiny's Journey*, 48; Döblin, *Schicksalsreise*, 67.

26   Döblin, *Destiny's Journey*, 113; Döblin, *Schicksalsreise*, 149.

27   Döblin, *Destiny's Journey*, 83; Döblin, *Schicksalsreise*, 112.

28   Döblin, *Destiny's Journey*, 113; Döblin, *Schicksalsreise*, 150.

29   Döblin, *Destiny's Journey*, 87; Döblin, *Schicksalsreise*, 117.

30   Döblin, *Destiny's Journey*, 86; Döblin, *Schicksalsreise*, 117.

31   Döblin, *Destiny's Journey*, 86; Döblin, *Schicksalsreise*, 117.

32   See Auer, *Das Exil vor der Vertreibung*, 50; Wolkowicz, "Der Gekreuzigte und der Gehenkte," 90–1; Emde, *Alfred Döblin*, 254.

33  Döblin, *Journey to Poland*, 182; Döblin, *Reise in Polen*, 239.

34  Döblin, *Journey to Poland*, 189; Döblin, *Reise in Polen*, 248.

35  Döblin, *Destiny's Journey*, 199; Döblin, *Schicksalsreise*, 260.

36  Döblin, *Destiny's Journey*, 199; Döblin, *Schicksalsreise*, 260.

37  Döblin, *Destiny's Journey*, 236; Döblin, *Schicksalsreise*, 306.

38  Döblin, *Destiny's Journey*, 236; Döblin, *Schicksalsreise*, 307.

39  Döblin, *Destiny's Journey*, 236; Döblin, *Schicksalsreise*,307.

40  Döblin, *Destiny's Journey*, 236; Döblin, *Schicksalsreise*, 307.

41  Sackett, "Döblin's Destiny," 588.

42  Sackett, "Döblin's Destiny," 595.

43  Döblin, *Destiny's Journey*, 236; Döblin, *Schicksalsreise*, 307.

44  Döblin, *Destiny's Journey*, 237; Döblin, *Schicksalsreise*, 307.

45  Döblin, *Destiny's Journey*, 237; Döblin, *Schicksalsreise*, 308.

46  Döblin, *Destiny's Journey*, 237; Döblin, *Schicksalsreise*, 308.

47  Gilman, *Jewish Self-Hatred*, 3.

48  Döblin, *Destiny's Journey*, 245; Döblin, *Schicksalsreise*, 317.

49  Döblin, *Destiny's Journey*, 247; Döblin, *Schicksalsreise*, 320.

50  Schoeller, *Alfred Döblin*, 570.

51  Quoted in Schoeller, *Alfred Döblin*, 570.

52  Döblin, *Briefe I*, 258.

53  Döblin, *Briefe I*, 258.

54  See also von Hofe, "German Literature in Exile," 28–31.

55  Marcuse, *Mein zwanzigstes Jahrhundert*, 279.

56  Brecht, *Journals 1934–1955*, 292; Brecht, *Arbeitsjournal. Zweiter Band*, 605.

57  Döblin, *Destiny's Journey*, 242; Döblin, *Schicksalsreise*, 314.

58  Müller-Salget, "Alfred Döblin und das Judentum," 161.

59  Kiesel, "Döblins Konversion als Politikum,"195–6. See also Kiesel, *Literarische Trauerarbeit*, 192–5.

60  Bartscherer, "Robinson the Castaway," 266.

61  Döblin, *Destiny's Journey*, 93; Döblin, *Schicksalsreise*, 124.

62  Döblin, *Destiny's Journey*, 109; Döblin, *Schicksalsreise*, 145.

63  Döblin, *Destiny's Journey*, 111; Döblin, *Schicksalsreise*, 147.

64  Alfred Döblin to Nathan Birnbaum, 8 September 1934, *Briefe II*, 90.

65  Döblin's account of spiritual salvation involves a double gesture, one that simultaneously embraces Christianity as it disavows Judaism. His narrative corroborates John Barbour's thesis in *Versions of Deconversion*, which argues that every conversion is simultaneously a deconversion. According to Barbour, every story of a faith embraced is inextricably intertwined with that of the faith that is relinquished. One cannot discuss the convert's new religious identity apart from his former religious commitments. "The 'turning from' and 'turning to' are alternative perspectives on the same process of personal metamorphosis, stressing either the rejected past of

the old self or the present convictions of the reborn self." Barbour's bifocal approach to conversion is especially germane to Döblin's case, since the story of his turn to Christianity is no less the narrative of a struggle to extricate himself from Judaism and distance himself from his Jewish contemporaries. See Barbour, *Versions of Deconversion*, 3.

66 Döblin, *Destiny's Journey*, 260; Döblin, *Schicksalsreise*, 340.
67 See Birkert, *Das goldene Tor*; von Hoff, "Kulturelles Archiv der europäischen Nachkriegsgeschichte."
68 Quoted in Müller-Salget, "Verfehlte Heimkehr," 59.
69 Döblin, *Destiny's Journey*, 271; Döblin, *Schicksalsreise*, 353.
70 Döblin, *Destiny's Journey*, 285; Döblin, *Schicksalsreise*, 370.
71 Döblin, *Destiny's Journey*, 272; Döblin, *Schicksalsreise*, 354.
72 Döblin, *Destiny's Journey*, 273; Döblin, *Schicksalsreise*, 355.
73 Bannasch, "'Der Jude meines Namens,'" 227.
74 Döblin, *Destiny's Journey*, 276; Döblin, *Schicksalsreise*, 359.
75 Döblin, *Destiny's Journey*, 324; Döblin, *Schicksalsreise*, 423.
76 Döblin, *Destiny's Journey*, 278; Döblin, *Schicksalsreise*, 361.
77 Döblin, *Destiny's Journey*, 276; Döblin, *Schicksalsreise*, 359.
78 Kiesel, *Literarische Trauerarbeit*, 18–25.
79 Döblin, *Briefe II*, 301.
80 Jacqueline Vansant points to a similar phenomenon in the autobiographical accounts of Jews returning to post-war Austria. She writes that "the reémigrés ... found themselves and their experiences marginalized or denied in both public and private discourse, in which non-Jewish, nonexile Austrians overwhelmingly assigned themselves the role of victims." The narratives of Austrian victimhood left little room for returning émigrés to voice the pains of their wartime experiences. See Vansant, *Reclaiming Heimat*, 31.
81 Döblin, *Destiny's Journey*, 312; Döblin, *Schicksalsreise*, 405.
82 Döblin, *Destiny's Journey*, 313; Döblin, *Schicksalsreise*, 406.
83 Döblin, *Destiny's Journey*, 313; Döblin, *Schicksalsreise*, 406.
84 Arendt and Jaspers, *Correspondence 1926–1969*, 31–2.
85 Erna Döblin to Theodor Heuss, 8 July 1957, *Briefe II*, 457.
86 Wolfgang Weyrauch, "Schuld der Literatur an der Restauration in Deutschland" (1951). Quoted in Kiesel, *Literarische Trauerarbeit*, 2–3.
87 Uhse, "Notizen zu Döblins Schicksalsreise," 161.
88 Uhse, "Notizen zu Döblins Schicksalsreise," 160. One finds more positive German responses to Döblin's Catholicism and his religious writings in the *Festschrift* marking his seventieth birthday. See Lüth, *Alfred Döblin zum 70. Geburtstag*.
89 Carl Seelig in *Das Bücherblatt* (Zürich). Quoted in Schuster and Bode, eds., *Alfred Döblin im Spiegel*, 424. Accusations of defection were made in the

German-Jewish portrayals of Döblin's life and letters even after his death. In an article marking Döblin's one-hundredth birthday, the journalist Meir Reubeni (born Faerber) wrote: "Döblin's attempt to flee from Judaism, to ignore the Jewish fate … or at least to avoid the problem, did not succeed. In such a dramatic and critical epoch for Judaism, an intellectually creative person born as a Jew cannot simply suppress the Jewish problem … That he nevertheless became a Catholic in 1941 … but kept his conversion secret until 1945, proves that ideologically and emotionally he lost himself in a labyrinth from which he found no way out; for at this time, when Nazism was already showing its teeth, without meeting any resistance from Christian institutions, other assimilationists, who had tried to cast off their Judaism were finding their way back to their ancestral people." See Reubeni, "Zu Alfred Döblins 100. Geburtstag," 61.

90  Anonymous in *Lüdenscheider Nachrichten*. Quoted in Schuster and Bode, eds., *Alfred Döblin im Spiegel*, 423.

91  Ben Chorin, "Abschied von Alfred Döblin."

92  Blumenthal-Weiss, "Zum Fall Alfred Döblin."

93  Blumenthal-Weiss, "Zum Fall Alfred Döblin."

94  Blumenthal-Weiss, "Zum Fall Alfred Döblin."

95  Klinov, "Mashot Be-Olamenu."

96  Zeitlin, "Arikim," 3. One finds similar expressions of shock in the Yiddish press; see, for example, Lestschinsky, "Naye meshumodim"; and Alprin, "Alfred Döblin, der meshumed."

97  Reproaching Döblin's account of his path to Christianity, the poet Elisabeth Langgässer maliciously rebuked the author's cumbersome style and lack of aesthetic merit: "That one falls before the cross and worships it may still be acceptable, and if he happens to be French, it might be even 'forgiven' as the latest literary fashion; but that such a mind does not carry out his conversion in *aesthetic* categories, but instead kneels down like an old peasant – somewhat clumsily, with stiff knees, and even prays like this – that must not be. Because then it is merely a living testimony, for God's sake! This is simply the personally experienced truth of a man who – to make matters worse – is called Döblin. What a catastrophe!" See Langgässer, *Briefe 1924–1950*, 656; and Schoeller, *Alfred Döblin*, 773.

98  Grass, *Über meinen Lehrer Döblin*, 26.

99  Döblin, *Schriften zu Leben und Werk*, 401.

100  Döblin, *Schriften zu Leben und Werk*, 401.

101  Döblin, *Schriften zu Leben und Werk*, 401.

102  See Kohn, "Alfred Döblins Katholizismus." See also Emde's discussion section "Ist Döblin katholisch?" in Emde, *Alfred Döblin*, 307–12; Schoeller, *Alfred Döblin*, 773; Bartscherer, "Robinson the Castaway," 258; and Weyembergh-Boussart, *Alfred Döblin*.

103  Müller-Salget, "Verfehlte Heimkehr," 55.
104  Döblin, *Schriften zu Leben und Werk*, 388.
105  Döblin, *Schriften zu Leben und Werk*, 387. Döblin's growing bitterness and disillusion with post-war Germany and the Germans seems to have been a widespread sentiment among returning émigrés in the cultural and intellectual domains. Similar impressions were voiced by Theodor Adorno, Max Horkheimer, and Hans-Joachim Schoeps. See Brenner, "'We Are the Unhappy Few'"; and Boll and Gross, eds., *"Ich staune, dass Sie in dieser Luft atmen können."*
106  Döblin, *Schriften zu Leben und Werk*, 412.
107  Döblin, *Schriften zu Leben und Werk*, 372.
108  Döblin, *Schriften zu Leben und Werk*, 411.
109  Döblin, *Schriften zu Leben und Werk*, 412.
110  Döblin, *Schriften zu Leben und Werk*, 353.
111  Döblin, *Schriften zu Leben und Werk*, 362.

**3. Mixed Metaphors of Jewish Blindness in Karl Stern's
*The Pillar of Fire* (1951)**

1  Stern, *The Pillar of Fire*.
2  For more on Stern's professional career see Stahnisch, "German-Speaking Émigré Neuroscientists"; Burston, "Dust and Fog"; Burston, "The Politics of Psychiatry"; Goldblatt, "Star: Karl Stern"; Goldbloom, "Prisoners of Ritual"; and Stahnisch and Pow, "Karl Stern." The author's non-scholarly publications include Stern, *The Third Revolution*; Stern, *The Flight from Woman*; Karl Stern, *Love and Success*; and Stern, *Through Dooms of Love*. See also Ostrovsky, "The Freudian Became a Catholic."
3  See Burston, *A Forgotten Freudian*, xx, 81–2, 88.
4  Some of this malice found its expression in the reviews of Stern's memoir. See, for example, Decter, "A Conversion"; and Cohen, "Three We Have Lost." On the book's Christian and Jewish reception in Quebec see Simon, "A.M. Klein et Karl Stern."
5  Fromm, "A Modern Search for Faith."
6  Heller, *Epistle to an Apostate*.
7  Ignaz Maybaum, "Between Two Faiths," 12.
8  Maybaum, "Between Two Faiths," 12.
9  Zeitlin, "Sifrut Ha-Shmad Ha-Chadashah."
10  Stern, *The Pillar of Fire*, 1.
11  Stern, *The Pillar of Fire*, 262.
12  Stern, *The Pillar of Fire*, 2.
13  We find this *topos* in the Letters of Paul, who was himself blinded on the road to Damascus, and subsequently gained sight of the truth of

Christ. In Letter to the Romans, Paul cites Isaiah and Psalms in an attempt to prove that the Jews' blindness was already foretold in their own scriptures: "What then? Israel hath not obtained that which he seeketh for; but the election hath obtained it, and the rest were blinded. According as it is written, God hath given them the spirit of slumber, eyes that they should not see, and ears that they should not hear; unto this day. And David saith, Let their table be made a snare, and a trap, and a stumbling block, and a recompence unto them: Let their eyes be darkened, that they may not see, and bow down their back away ... that blindness in part is happened to Israel, until the fulness of the Gentiles be come in" (Romans 11:7–11, 25). See also Wheatley, "'Blind' Jews and Blind Christians."

14  Scholem, *On Jews and Judaism*, 77. See Rubin, "The 'German-Jewish Dialogue' and Its Literary Refractions."

15  Both David Neuhaus and Robert McFarland read Stern's memoir alongside the works of other twentieth-century Jewish converts, who sought to justify their conversion to Christianity in their autobiographical writings. They reconstruct the rhetorical strategies that converts employed in order to defend their religious transformations and deflect the accusations of betrayal. The challenge all of these converts faced was rationalizing their conversion in face of Christianity's burdensome legacy of antisemitism and the more recent events of the Holocaust. My reading departs from Neuhaus and McFarland in that it explores Stern's self-justification in the parallels it bears to the Zionist and Jewish critics of assimilation rather than its affinities to the narratives of other Jewish converts. See McFarland, "Elective Divinities"; and Neuhaus, "Jewish Conversion." On the strategies of self-justification of Jewish converts to Catholicism see also Klein, "The New Spirit."

16  This strategy is not uncommon for Jewish converts to Catholicism as the examples of Paris's archbishop Jean Marie Lustiger (1926–2007) and former Chief Rabbi of Rome Eugenio Maria Zolli (1881–1956) make clear. Cardinal Lustiger recalls how he justified his conversion to Christianity to his parents: "I explained that baptism would not make me abandon my Jewish condition – quite the contrary, it would lead me to find it, to receive the plentitude of its meaning. I did not have the feeling that I was betraying my heritage, or camouflaging myself or abandoning anything whatsoever. Just the opposite: I felt that I was going to find the import, the meaning of what I had received at birth. For my parents, this reasoning was thoroughly incomprehensible, insane and insufferable." See Lustiger, Missika, and Wolton, *Choosing God*, 42. See also Eugenio Zolli, *Before the Dawn: Autobiographical Reflections*.

17  Stern, *The Pillar of Fire*, 12.

18  Stern, *The Pillar of Fire*, 16.
19  Stern, *The Pillar of Fire*, 12–13.
20  Mosse, *German Jews beyond Judaism*; Sorkin, *The Transformation of German Jewry*.
21  Mosse, *German Jews beyond Judaism*, 18.
22  Stern, *The Pillar of Fire*, 58.
23  Stern, *The Pillar of Fire*, 58–9.
24  Stern, *The Pillar of Fire*, 10–11.
25  Scholem, *From Berlin to Jerusalem*, 1. Geller's study on the Scholem family explores the diverging pathways of German Jewry as a "fraternal drama." See Geller, *The Scholems*.
26  Scholem, *From Berlin to Jerusalem*, 9.
27  Scholem, *From Berlin to Jerusalem*, 11.
28  Scholem, *From Berlin to Jerusalem*, 25.
29  Scholem, *From Berlin to Jerusalem*, 25.
30  Scholem, *From Berlin to Jerusalem*, 26.
31  Scholem, *From Berlin to Jerusalem*, 26.
32  Steven Aschheim, "German Jews beyond Bildung and Liberalism," 34.
33  Brenner, *The Renaissance of Jewish Culture*, 80–1.
34  Stern, *The Pillar of Fire*, 26.
35  Stern, *The Pillar of Fire*, 29.
36  Neumeyer, *Lichter und Schatten*, 62.
37  Stern, *The Pillar of Fire*, 45.
38  Stern, *The Pillar of Fire*, 46.
39  Stern, *The Pillar of Fire*, 47.
40  Stern, *The Pillar of Fire*, 49.
41  Stern, *The Pillar of Fire*, 36.
42  Stern, *The Pillar of Fire*, 35–6.
43  Stern, *The Pillar of Fire*, 37.
44  Stern, *The Pillar of Fire*, 56.
45  Quoted in Kisch, *Judentaufen*, 78.
46  Kisch, *Judentaufen*, 78.
47  Kisch, *Judentaufen*, 78. See also Levenson, "The Conversionary Impulse."
48  Ginsberg, *Abschied*, 30.
49  Stern, *The Pillar of Fire*, 134.
50  Stern, *The Pillar of Fire*, 154–5.
51  Stern, *The Pillar of Fire*, 155.
52  Stern, *The Pillar of Fire*, 155–6.
53  Stern, *The Pillar of Fire*, 156.
54  Stern, *The Pillar of Fire*, 49.
55  Stern, *The Pillar of Fire*, 157.
56  Stern, *The Pillar of Fire*, 156–7.

57 Stern, *The Pillar of Fire*, 157. Compare to Scholem: "I have already mentioned the Jews' blindness where their own situation was concerned … In general it must be said that the literature of that period, particularly when it was written by Jews, did its best to help cover up the real situation. A good many parts of Hermann Cohen's Jewish writings, until far into the First World War can serve as uncanny, though touching, examples of this blindness or self-delusion." See Scholem, "On the Social Psychology," 22.

58 Scholem, "Wider den Mythos." Quotes taken from English translation Scholem, "Against the Myth of the German-Jewish Dialogue," in *On Jews and Judaism in Crisis*.

59 Scholem, *On Jews and Judaism in Crisis*, 61.

60 Scholem, *On Jews and Judaism in Crisis*, 69.

61 Bernstein, *Foregone Conclusions*, 16.

62 Stern, *The Pillar of Fire*, 163.

63 Burston, "Dust and Fog," 14. See also Burston, *A Forgotten Freudian*, 195–6.

64 Stern, *The Pillar of Fire*, 171.

65 Stern, *The Pillar of Fire*, 190. Burston notes that there is no one epiphanic moment in Stern's narrative, writing that "Stern describes at least three experiences of that sort: once, while listening to Cardinal Faulhaber's Advent sermon of 1933, another while living in the Silk family's boarding house in Oppidans Road in 1937, and again, in 1941, in conversation with Maritain about his lingering misgivings about becoming Catholic." See Burston, *A Forgotten Freudian*, 182.

66 Haynes, *Reluctant Witnesses*, 29.

67 Quoted in Fredriksen, *Augustine and the Jews*, xii.

68 Stern, *The Pillar of Fire*, 157–8.

69 Stern, *The Pillar of Fire*, 158–9.

70 Stern, *The Pillar of Fire*, 159–60.

71 Stern, *The Pillar of Fire*, 162.

72 Stern, *The Pillar of Fire*, 162.

73 Stern, *The Pillar of Fire*, 163.

74 Stern, *The Pillar of Fire*, 166.

75 Stern, *The Pillar of Fire*, 169.

76 Stern, *The Pillar of Fire*, 174.

77 Stern, *The Pillar of Fire*, 174.

78 Stern, *The Pillar of Fire*, 175–6.

79 Stern, *The Pillar of Fire*, 176–7.

80 Stern, *The Pillar of Fire*, 177.

81 Stern, *The Pillar of Fire*, 181.

82 Stern, *The Pillar of Fire*, 172.

83 Stern, *The Pillar of Fire*, 172–3.

84  See Stern, *The Pillar of Fire*, 229–31; 251–2; 177–8.

85  Stern, *The Pillar of Fire*, 261. Daniel Burston, who founded the Karl Stern archival collection at Duquesne University and has reviewed Stern's correspondence at length, observes that Stern was continuously plagued by "the traitor complex" over the years. In letters to friends such as Dorothy Day and John Oesterreicher, Stern confessed a deep sense of guilt. He felt that many of the tragedies that befell him later in life – his son's suicide, his wife's depressive episodes that required lengthy hospitalizations, and his own deteriorating health – were all punishments for his conversion. See Burston, *A Forgotten Freudian*, 193.

86  Stern, *The Pillar of Fire*, 204–5.

87  Stern, *The Pillar of Fire*, 189.

88  Yvonne Sherwood, *A Biblical Text and its Afterlives: The Survival of Jonah in Western Culture* (Cambridge: Cambridge University Press, 2000), 23.

89  Sherwood, *A Biblical Text and Its Afterlives*, 25.

90  Sherwood, *A Biblical Text and Its Afterlives*, 23.

91  Stern, *The Pillar of Fire*, 205.

92  Stern, *The Pillar of Fire*, 206.

93  Maslow, *The Farther Reaches*, 35–6.

94  Lacocque and Lacocque, *The Jonah Complex*, 127.

95  Stern, *The Pillar of Fire*, 245.

96  Stern, *The Pillar of Fire*, 245.

97  Stern, *The Pillar of Fire*, 242.

98  Stern, *The Pillar of Fire*, 302.

99  Stern, *The Pillar of Fire*, 302

100  Abraham and Torok, "Mourning *or* Melancholia," 125–38.

101  Abraham and Torok, "Mourning *or* Melancholia," 126.

102  Abraham and Torok, "Mourning *or* Melancholia," 126.

103  Abraham and Torok, "Mourning *or* Melancholia," 126–7.

104  Abraham and Torok, "Mourning *or* Melancholia," 127.

105  Stern, *The Pillar of Fire*, 265.

106  Endelman, *Leaving the Jewish Fold*, 192.

107  Endelman, *Leaving the Jewish Fold*, 196.

108  Stern, *The Pillar of Fire*, 246. Stern developed this argument into a lecture called "Jews on the Threshold," delivered sometime in the 1950s. In it, Stern addresses the phenomenon of Jews who recognized the Christian truth, yet hesitated to make the final step towards baptism. What prevented the writers Franz Werfel and Shalom Asch, and the French philosopher Henri Bergson, from crossing the threshold to Christianity was the abominable heritage of Jews, who had converted for material gain and who saw it as the "entry ticket to European civilization." The other inhibiting factor was "the thought of abandoning a minority at the

moment of its most terrible plight." This idea of "desertion" kept many believing Christians from baptizing. This situation temporarily changed when Hitler came to power: "This was, since the time of the Roman Empire, the first persecution of Jews in which baptism was no emergency exit. On the contrary, the Hebrew Christian under Hitler was in a greater plight than anyone else. He did not belong to the community of Jews anymore, and the great masses of people who had been educated to be 'Christians' rejected him as a Jew … Baptism, at least in Hitler's Germany, was, for the first time since the official acceptance of Christianity by the Roman Empire, not at all associated with any material gain, it promised not a thread of security in this world." See "Jews on the Threshold" by Karl Stern (Drafts), n.d., box 10 FF 5, Testimony, Drafts, Speeches and Reviews by Stern (series 4), Simon Silverman Phenomenology Center, Karl Stern Collection, Duquesne University.

109  Stern, *The Pillar of Fire*, 243–4. On antisemitism at McGill, see Burston, *A Forgotten Freudian*, 106.
110  Endelman, *Leaving the Jewish Fold*, 11.
111  Endelman, *Leaving the Jewish Fold*, 227.
112  Weintraub, "Autobiography and Historical Consciousness"; Pascal, *Design and Truth in Autobiography*.
113  Wolfson, *Escaping Judaism*, 26.
114  Stromberg, "The Role of Language in Religious Conversion," 117–39.


**4. Judeo-Christian Reconciliation and the Inability to Mourn in Heinrich Kronstein's *Briefe an einen jungen Deutschen* (1967)**

1  Kronstein, *Briefe an einen jungen Deutschen*.
2  Von Schlabrendorff, "Zeugnis von einem Leben." *Der Spiegel* 21.50 (1967).
3  Von Schlabrendorff, "Zeugnis von einem Leben."
4  Von Schlabrendorff, "Zeugnis von einem Leben."
5  Von Schlabrendorff, "Zeugnis von einem Leben."
6  Mann, "Memoiren eines Rechtsanwalt."
7  Mann, "Memoiren eines Rechtsanwalt."
8  Santner, "History beyond the Pleasure Principle," 144.
9  Kronstein, *Briefe*, 45.
10  Kronstein, *Briefe*, 45.
11  Kronstein, *Briefe*, 45.
12  Kronstein, *Briefe*, 47.
13  Kronstein, *Briefe*, 48.
14  Kronstein, *Briefe*, 48.
15  Kronstein, *Briefe*, 48.

16  Kronstein, *Briefe*, 54.
17  For an overview of Kronstein's legal career see Rehbinder, "Heinrich Kronstein." 253–9.
18  Kronstein, *Briefe*, 133.
19  Kronstein, *Briefe*, 133.
20  Kronstein, *Briefe*, 134.
21  Kronstein, *Briefe*, 150.
22  Kronstein, *Briefe*, 151.
23  Kronstein, *Briefe*, 151–2.
24  Kronstein, *Briefe*, 155.
25  Kronstein, *Briefe*, 155.
26  Kronstein, *Briefe*, 162.
27  Kronstein, *Briefe*, 162.
28  Kronstein, *Briefe*, 162.
29  Kronstein, *Briefe*, 162.
30  Kronstein, *Briefe*, 163.
31  Stein, *Aus dem Leben*, 49–50; Stein, *Life in a Jewish Family*, 81.
32  Stein, *Life in a Jewish Family*, 82.
33  Stein, *Life in a Jewish Family*, 82.
34  Kronstein, *Briefe*, 163.
35  Kronstein, *Briefe*, 164.
36  Kronstein, *Briefe*, 164. My italics.
37  Kronstein, *Briefe*, 165.
38  Kronstein, *Briefe*, 165.
39  Kronstein, *Briefe*, 239.
40  Kronstein, *Briefe*, 168.
41  O'Donnell Polyakov, *The Nun in the Synagogue*.
42  Kronstein, *Briefe*, 169.
43  Kronstein, *Briefe*, 11.
44  Kronstein, *Briefe*, 14.
45  Kronstein, *Briefe*, 14–15. Kronstein's view of the redemptive virtues of Jewish suffering in the wake of the Holocaust, while deeply rooted in Christian theology, was an idea that also resonated among Jewish thinkers such as the philosopher Margarete Susman. See Rubin, "Jewish Self-Affirmation."
46  Kronstein, *Briefe*, 14.
47  Kronstein, *Briefe*, 19.
48  Kronstein, *Briefe*, 19.
49  Kronstein, *Briefe*, 24.
50  Kronstein, *Briefe*, 27.
51  Kronstein, *Briefe*, 18.
52  Kronstein, *Briefe*, 43.

53 Kronstein, *Briefe*, 244.

54 Krauss, *Heimkehr in ein fremdes Land*, 62–71.

55 Hirsch, *Quintessenz meines Lebens*, 249.

56 Hirsch, *Quintessenz meines Lebens*, 249.

57 Hirsch, *Quintessenz meines Lebens*, 249.

58 Hirsch, *Quintessenz meines Lebens*, 264.

59 Kronstein, *Briefe*, 241.

60 Kronstein, *Briefe*, 241. On the Maria Laach Monastery's enthusiasm for Nazism see Connelly, *From Enemy to Brother*, 67–8, 76–8.

61 Kronstein, *Briefe*, 241.

62 Kronstein, *Briefe*, 243.

63 Kronstein, *Briefe*, 243.

64 Kronstein, *Briefe*, 244.

65 Connelly, *From Enemy to Brother*, 65–93.

66 Stern, *The Pillar of Fire*, 141.

67 Kronstein, *Briefe*, 242.

68 Hanebrink, *A Specter Haunting Europe*, 218.

69 Kronstein, *Briefe*, 167.

70 Another example of Kronstein's revisionist orientation is a 1954 article titled "German Allegiance to Justice," in which he stresses the Christian opposition to Hitler during the Nazi years. After valorizing German Christians' martyrdom under Hitler, Kronstein goes on to draw a generalized analogy between victim and perpetrator, writing that "German history has much in common with Jewish history. Maybe Jews and Germans do not like this uncontestable statement. Yet the record is there. Germans and Jews have suffered in groups for their beliefs and for their very definite national consciousness. Only seldom do we see one single person, German or Jewish, suffering a martyr's death for the maintenance of Law. But as groups their people have suffered more than others." See Kronstein, "German Allegiance to Justice," 2.

71 Adorno, "Was bedeutet," 555; Adorno, "The Meaning of Working through the Past," 89.

72 Adorno, "Was bedeutet," 556; Adorno, "The Meaning of Working through the Past," 90.

73 Adorno, "Was bedeutet," 557; Adorno, "The Meaning of Working through the Past," 90–1.

74 Foschepoth, *Im Schatten der Vergangenheit*, 21.

75 Foschepoth, *Im Schatten der Vergangenheit*, 22.

76 Kronstein, *Briefe*, 169.

77 Alexander Mitscherlich and Margarete Mitscherlich, *The Inability to Mourn: Principles of Collective Behavior*, translated by Beverley R. Placzek (New York: Grove Press, 1975); Mitscherlich and Mitscherlich, *Die*

*Unfähigkeit zu trauern*. See also Santner, "Alexander and Margarete Mitscherlich's *Die Unfähigkeit*."

**Conclusion: The Consolations of Christianity and the Inadequacy of Form**

1 Quoted in Rohrwasser, *Der Stalinismus und die Renegaten*, 263.
2 Améry, "Wieviel Heimat braucht der Mensch?," in *Jenseits von Schuld und Sühne*, 58; Améry, "How Much Home Does a Person Need?," in *At the Mind's Limits*, 44.
3 See also Katja Garloff's discussion of the German-Jewish intellectual's "inability to return" in Adorno, Améry, and Anders. Garloff, *Words from Abroad*, 21–53.
4 Dorsey, *Sacred Estrangement*, 8–9.
5 Hirsch, *Quintessenz meines Lebens*, 316.
6 Riley, *Character and Conversion*, 2. In addition to Riley, my approach is informed by several studies that set out to theorize the relationship between conversion, narrative, and identity, most notably Hindmarsh, "Religious Conversion"; Stromberg, "The Role of Language"; and Hindmarsh, *The Evangelical Conversion Narrative*, 4–13.
7 Améry, "Über Zwang und Unmöglichkeit, Jude zu sein," in *Jenseits von Schuld und Sühne*, 99–119; Améry, "On the Necessity and Impossiblity of Being a Jew," in *At the Mind's Limits*, 82–101.
8 Seidman, *Faithful Renderings*; Seidman, "Elie Wiesel."
9 Seidman, *Faithful Renderings*, 200–1.
10 Seidman, "Elie Wiesel," 16.
11 Seidman, *Faithful Renderings*, 204–5.
12 Arendt, *Rahel Varnhagen*, 182.
13 James, *The Varieties of Religious Experience*, 150.
14 Harpham, "Conversion and the Language of Autobiography," 44.
15 Friedman, "Women's Autobiographical Selves," 34.

# Bibliography

### Archives

*Booth Family Center for Special Collections, Georgetown University Library*
Heinrich Kronstein Papers

*Deutsche Nationalbibliothek, Frankfurt am Main*
Deutsches Exilarchiv 1933–1945

*Leo Baeck Institute, New York*
Alfred Döblin Clippings Collection 1930–2003

*Lesesaal Altes Buch, Ludwig-Maximilians-Universität München*
Nachlaß Karl Jakob Hirsch

*Simon Silverman Phenomenology Center, Duquesne University*
Karl Stern Archive

*The National Library of Israel*
Historical Jewish Press

*YIVO Institute for Jewish Research*
Isaac Nachman Steinberg Papers

### Newspapers and Periodicals

*Aufbau* (New York)
*Aufbau. Kulturpolitische Monatsschrift*
*Commentary*
*Das goldene Tor. Monatsschrift für Literatur und Kunst*

*Davar*
*Der Spiegel*
*Der Tog*
*Der Zeuge. Organ der Internationalen Judenchristlichen Allianz*
*Die Aktion*
*Die Zeit*
*Emuna. Israel Forum*
*Forverts*
*Frayland*
*Hakidmah*
*Hazofeh*
*Jüdische Bibliothek*
*Mitteilungsblatt der Vereinigung der Juden aus Mitteleuropa*
*New York Herald Tribune*
*Passauer Neue Presse*
*Shearim*
*The Jewish Chronicle*
*Turim*

## Primary Sources

Adorno, Theodor. "The Meaning of Working through the Past." In *Critical Models: Interventions and Catchwords*, translated by Henry W. Pickford, 89–104. Columbia University Press, 1998.
– "Was bedeutet: Aufarbeitung der Vergangenheit." *Gesammelte Schriften Band 10.2*, 555–72. Suhrkamp, 1977.
Alprin, A. "Alfred Döblin, der meshumed." *Der Tog*, 21 June 1950, 6.
Améry, Jean. *At the Mind's Limits: Contemplations by a Survivor on Auschwitz and Its Realities*, translated by Sidney Rosenfeld and Stella Rosenfeld. Indiana University Press, 1980.
– *Jenseits von Schuld und Sühne. Bewältigungsversuche eines Überwältigten*. Deutscher Taschenbuch Verlag, 1970.
Anonymous. "Heimkehr zu Gott." *Das goldene Tor. Monatsschrift für Literatur und Kunst*, vol. 3, 1948, 301.
– *Liste 1 des schädlichen und unerwünschten Schrifttums*. Reichsdruckerei, 1935.
Arendt, Hannah. "The Aftermath of Nazi Rule: Report from Germany." *Commentary* 10 (1950): 342–53.
– *The Jewish Writings*. Schocken Books, 2007.
– *The Origins of Totalitarianism*. Meridian Books, 1958.
– *Rahel Varnhagen: The Life of a Jewess*, translated by Richard and Clara Winston. Leo Baeck Institute, 1957.

Arendt, Hannah, and Karl Jaspers. *Correspondence 1926–1969*, translated by Robert and Rita Kimber. Harcourt Brace, 1992.

Aufricht, Ernst-Josef. *Erzähle damit du dein Recht erweist*. Propyläen Verlag, 1966.

Baum, Gregory. *The Oil Has Not Run Dry: The Story of My Theological Pathway*. McGill–Queen's University Press, 2017.

Ben-Chorin, Schalom. "Abschied von Alfred Döblin." *Hakadimah*, 2 September 1949, 6.

– "Heimkehr zu Gott." *Mitteilungsblatt*, 21 November 1947, 6.

Blumenthal-Weiss, Ilse. "Zum Fall Alfred Döblin." *Hakadimah*, 2 September 1949, 9.

Brecht, Bertolt. *Arbeitsjournal. Zweiter Band, 1945 bis 1955*, edited by Werner Hecht. Suhrkamp Verlag, 1973.

– *Journals 1934–1955*, translated by Hugh Rorrison. Bloomsbury, 1995.

Cohen, Arthur A. "Three We Have Lost: The Problem of Conversion." In *The Myth of the Judeo-Christian Tradition*, 95–116. Schocken, 1957.

Decter, Moshe. "A Conversion (review of *The Pillar of Fire* by Karl Stern)." *Commentary*, 1 January 1951, 509–11.

Döblin, Alfred. *Briefe I*, edited by Heinz Graber. Walter-Verlag, 1970.

– *Briefe II*, edited by Helmut F. Pfanner. Walter Verlag, 2001.

– *Destiny's Journey*, translated by Edna McCown. Paragon House, 1992.

– *Journey to Poland*, translated by Joachim Neugroschel. Paragon House, 1991.

– *Kleine Schriften I*. Walter Verlag, 1985.

– "Le-Korai Be-Ivrit." *Turim* 1, no. 19 (8 December 1933), 1–2.

– *Reise in Polen*. Walter Verlag, 1968.

– *Schicksalsreise. Bericht und Bekenntnis*. Fischer Verlag, 2014.

– *Schriften zu jüdischen Fragen*. Fischer Verlag, 2015.

– *Schriften zu Leben und Werk*. Fischer Verlag, 2015.

– "Tchiya Yehudit." *Turim* 2, no. 26 (8 February 1934), 5–6.

– *Der tsil un kharakter fun der Frayland-bavegung: referat, gehaltn oyf der teritoryalistisher konferents in London*. Frayland-lige, 1935.

Fromm, Erich. "A Modern Search for Faith." *New York Herald Tribune*, 15 April 1951, 12.

George, Manfred. "Wieder einer." *Aufbau* 13, no. 11 (14 March 1947), 5.

Ginsberg, Ernst. *Abschied. Erinnerungen, Theateraufsätze, Gedichte*, edited by Elisabeth Brock-Sulzer. Arche, 1991.

Goethe, Johann Wolfgang. *The Essential Goethe*, edited by Matthew Bell. Princeton University Press, 2016.

Goldschmidt, Hermann Levin. *The Legacy of German Jewry*, translated by David Suchoff. Fordham University Press, 2007.

– *Das Vermächtnis des deutschen Judentums*. Europäische Verlagsanstalt, 1957.

Graef, Hilda. *From Fashions to the Fathers: The Story of My Life*. Newman Press, 1957.

Grass, Günter. *Über meinen Lehrer Döblin, und andere Vorträge*. Literarisches Colloquium, 1968.

Günther, Herbert. "Heimkehr zu Gott," *Welt und Wort* 2 (1947): 94–5.

Heller, Bernard. *Epistle to an Apostate*. Bookman's Press, 1951.

Hill, Rolland. *A Time Out of Joint: A Journey from Nazi Germany to Post-war Britain*. Radcliffe Press, 2007.

Hirsch, Karl Jakob. *Der alte Doktor: Eine Worpsweder Ärztin und ihre Zeit 1919–1952*. H.M. Hauschild, 1994.

– *Einer muss es ja tun*. VDG, 2003.

– *Heimkehr zu Gott. Briefe an meinen Sohn*. Kurt Desch Verlag, 1946.

– "Hochzeitsmarsch in Moll." *Jüdische Bibliothek*, 18 June 1936.

– *Hochzeitsmarsch in Moll: Roman*. Oberon Bibliothek, 1986.

– *Kaiserwetter. Roman*. JMB Verlag, 2011.

– *Manhattan-Serenade*. Peter Lang, 2001.

– *Quintessenz meines Lebens*, edited by Helmut F. Pfanner. Hase & Koehler, 1990.

– *Revolutionäre Kunst*. Die Aktion, 1919.

– "Selbstbildnis." *Jüdische Bibliothek*, 20 January 1936.

– *Tagebuch aus dem Dritten Reich: Aufzeichnungen eines Jungen*. JMB Verlag, 2009.

Hulse, Wilfred. "Judentum und Konvertiten." *Aufbau* 13, no. 20 (16 May 1947), 25.

Klinov, Yeshayahu. "Mashot Be-Olamenu." *Davar*, 25 August 1950, 2.

Kronstein, Heinrich. *Briefe an einen jungen Deutschen*. Beck, 1967.

– "German Allegiance to Justice." *University of Detroit Law* 18, no. 1 (1954): 1–3.

Langgässer, Elisabeth. *Briefe 1924–1950. Band 2*. Claassen Verlag, 1990.

Lestschinsky, Jacob. "Naye meshumodim. Kranke neshamot vas geyn avek fun Yidishen Folk." *Forverts*, 25 April 1948, 4.

Leuner, Heinz David. "Ein Blick in die Werkstatt Gottes. In Memoriam Karl Jakob Hirsch." *Der Zeuge. Organ der Internationalen Judenchristlichen Allianz* 13, no. 27 (1962): 27–9.

– "Karl Jakob Hirsch. Einem Zeugen aus Israel zum Gedächtnis." *Der Zeuge. Organ der Internationalen Judenchristlichen Allianz* 3, nos. 8–9 (1952): 13–15.

Lustiger, Jean-Marie, Jean Louis Missika, and Dominique Wolton. *Choosing God – Chosen by God: Conversations with Cardinal Jean-Marie Lustiger*, translated by Rebecca Howell Balinski. Ignatius Press, 1991.

Lüth, Paul, ed. *Alfred Döblin zum 70. Geburtstag*. Limes-Verlag, 1948.

Mann, Francis A. "Memoiren eines Rechtsanwalt." *Die Zeit*, March 1968. https://www.zeit.de/1968/13/memoiren-eines-rechtsanwalts/komplettansicht.

Marcuse, Ludwig. *Mein zwanzigstes Jahrhundert: auf dem Weg zu einer Autobiographie*. Diogenes Verlag, 1975.

Marwitz, Roland. "Heimkehr zu Gott." *Passauer Neue Presse*, 4 April 1947, 3.

Maybaum, Ignaz. "Between Two Faiths." *The Jewish Chronicle*, 30 November 1951, 12.

Mehring, Walter. "Letters to the Editor," *Aufbau* 13, no. 13 (28 March 1947), 6.

Mitscherlich, Alexander, and Margarete Mitscherlich. *The Inability to Mourn: Principles of Collective Behavior*, translated by Beverley R. Placzek. Grove Press, 1975.

– *Die Unfähigkeit zu trauern. Grundlagen kollektiven Verhaltens*. Piper, 1967.

Neumeyer, Alfred. *Lichter und Schatten. Eine Jugend in Deutschland*. Prestel, 1967.

Pincus, Lily. *Verloren-gewonnen. Mein Weg von Berlin nach London*. Deutsche Verlags-Anstalt, 1980.

Reubeni, Meir. "Zu Alfred Döblins 100. Geburtstag." *Emuna. Israel Forum* 4, no. 78 (1978): 61–3.

Rosenberg, Alfons. *Die Welt im Feuer. Wandlungen meines Lebens*. Verlag Herder, 1983.

Scholem, Gershom. *From Berlin to Jerusalem: Memories of My Youth*, translated by Harry Zohn, Schocken, 1980.

– *On Jews and Judaism in Times of Crisis*. Schocken, 1976.

– "On the Social Psychology of the Jews in Germany, 1900–1933." *Jews and Germans from 1860 to 1933: The Problematic Symbiosis*, edited by David Bronsen, 9–32. Winter Verlag, 1979.

– "Wider den Mythos vom deutsch-jüdische Gespräch." *Auf Gespaltenem Pfad: Für Margarete Susman*, edited by Manfred Schlösser, 229–33. Erato-Presse, 1964.

Schorske, Carl Emil, and Hoyt Price. *The Problem of Germany*. Council on Foreign Relations, 1947.

Stein, Edith. *Aus dem Leben einer jüdischen Familie*. Editions Nauwelaerts, 1965.

– *Life in a Jewish Family: An Autobiography 1891–1916*, translated by Josephine Koeppel. ICS Publications, 2016.

Stern, Karl. *Through Dooms of Love*. Farrar, Straus and Cudhay, 1960.

– *The Flight from Woman*. Farrar, Straus and Giroux, 1965.

– *Love and Success*. Farrar, Straus and Giroux, 1975.

– *The Pillar of Fire*. Harcourt, Brace, 1951.

– *The Third Revolution: A Study of Psychiatry and Religion*. Harcourt, Brace, 1954.

Tramer, Hans. "Das genial-tragische Leben des Karl Jakob Hirsch."
    *Mitteilungsblatt*, 3 August 1973, 3–4.
Uhse, Bodo. "Notizen zu Döblins Schicksalsreise." *Aufbau. Kulturpolitische
    Monatsschrift* 13, no. 2 (1957): 161–3.
Ungerfeld, Moshe. "Avot U-Banim." *Hazofeh*, 25 April 1947, 3.
von Schlabrendorff, Fabian. "Zeugnis von einem Leben." *Der Spiegel*, 21, no.
    50 (1967). https://www.spiegel.de/kultur/zeugnis-von-einem-leben-a-b94
    5aab8-0002-0001-0000-000046164892.
Wagner, Richard. *Judaism in Music and Other Essays*, translated by William
    Ashton Ellis. University of Nebraska Press, 1995.
– *Das Judenthum in der Musik*. Verlagsbuchhandlung von J.J. Weber, 1869.
Wolfson, Harry Austryn. *Escaping Judaism*. Menorah Press, 1923.
Wurmbrand, Michael. "Ein Jude erteilt der Christenheit Absolution." *Aufbau*,
    13, no. 15 (11 April 1947), 16.
Zeitlin, Aharon. "Arikim," *Hazofeh*, 30 June 1950, 3.
– "Sifrut Ha-Shmad Ha-Chadashah." *Shearim*, 25 July 1952, 4.
Zolli, Eugenio. *Before the Dawn: Autobiographical Reflections*. Sheed and Ward, 1954.

**Secondary Sources**

Abraham, Nicolas, and Maria Torok. "Mourning *or* Melancholia: Introjection
    versus Incorporation." In *The Shell and the Kernel: Renewals of Psychoanalysis*,
    edited and translated by Nicolas T. Rand, 125–38. University of Chicago
    Press, 1994.
Ackermann, Ingrid. "Beinahe wäre etwas aus mir geworden." *Herzliche
    Glückwünsche. Karl Jakob Hirsch zum 100. Geburtstag: eine Ausstellung der
    Universitätsbibliothek München*, edited by Cornelia Töpelmann, 5–10.
    Universitätsbibliothek München, 1992.
Ariel, Yaakov. "From Faith to Faith: Conversions and De-Conversions during
    the Holocaust." *Simon Dubnow Institute Yearbook* 12 (2013), 37–66.
– "From Judaism to Christianity: The Autobiographies of Jewish Converts to
    Christianity in the Twentieth Century." *Proceedings of the World Congress of
    Jewish Studies* 11 (1993): 123–29.
Aschheim, Steven. "German Jews beyond Bildung and Liberalism: The
    Radical Jewish Revival in the Weimar Republic." In *Culture and Catastrophe:
    German and Jewish Confrontations with National Socialism and Other Crises*,
    31–44. Macmillan, 1996.
Auer, Manfred. *Das Exil vor der Vertreibung: Motivkontinuität und
    Quellenproblematik im späten Werk Alfred Döblins*. Bouvier, 1977.
Auslander, Leora. "The Boundaries of Jewishness or When Is a Cultural
    Practice Jewish?" *Journal of Modern Jewish Studies* 8, no. 1 (2009): 47–64.
Bannasch, Bettina. "'Der Jude meines Namens' – 'Der Dichter meines
    Namens.' Zur Neukonzeption von religiöser Identität und Autorschaft in

Alfred Döblins *Schicksalsreise."* *Exilerfahrung und Konstruktionen von Identität in den Jahren 1933 bis 1945*, edited by Hans Otto Horch, Hanni Mittelmann and Karin Neuburger, 207–32. De Gruyter, 2013.

Barbour, John D. *Versions of Deconversion: Autobiography and the Loss of Faith.* University of Virginia Press, 1994.

Bartscherer, Christoph. "Robinson the Castaway: Döblin's Christian Faith as Reflected in His Autobiography *Schicksalsreise* and His Religious Dialogues *Der unsterbliche Mensch* and *Der Kampf mit dem Engel.*" In *A Companion to the Works of Alfred Döblin*, edited by Roland Dollenmayer, Wulf Koepke, and Heidi Thomann Tewarson, 247–70. Camden House, 2003.

Becker, Sabina and Sabine Schneider. "Exile als 'Schicksalsreise.' Alfred Döblin und das literarische Exil 1933–1950." *Internationales Alfred-Döblin-Kolloquium Zürich 2015*, edited by Sabina Becker and Sabine Schneider, 51–66. Peter Lang, 2017.

Bergmann, Werner. "'Wir haben Sie nicht gerufen.' Reaktionen auf jüdische Remigranten in der Bevölkerung und Öffentlichkeit der frühen Bundesrepublik." In *"Auch in Deutschland waren wir nicht wirklich zu Hause." Jüdische Remigration nach 1945*, edited by Irmela von der Lühe, Axel Schildt, and Stefanie Schüler-Springorum, 19–39. Wallstein Verlag, 2008.

Bernstein, Michael André. *Foregone Conclusions: Against Apocalyptic History.* University of California Press, 1994.

Biess, Frank. *German Angst: Fear and Democracy in the Federal Republic of Germany.* Oxford University Press, 2020.

Birkert, Alexandra. *Das goldene Tor: Alfred Döblins Nachkriegszeitschrift: Rahmenbedingungen, Zielsetzung, Entwicklung.* Buchhändler-Vereinigung, 1989.

Boll, Monika, and Raphael Gross, eds. *"Ich staune, dass Sie in dieser Luft atmen können." Jüdische Intellektuelle in Deutschland nach 1945.* Fischer Verlag, 2013.

Brenner, Michael. *The Renaissance of Jewish Culture in Weimar Germany.* Yale University Press, 1996.

– "'We Are the Unhappy Few': Return and Disillusionment among German-Jewish Intellectuals." *Journal of Modern Jewish Studies* 13, no. 1 (2014): 12–22.

Brockmann, Stephen. *German Literary Culture at the Zero Hour.* Boydell and Brewer, 2004.

Burston, Daniel. "Dust and Fog, Fire and Salt: German Canadian Psychiatrist Karl Stern's (1906–1975) Émigré Experience." *History of Intellectual Culture* 12, no. 1 (2019): 1–15.

– *A Forgotten Freudian: The Passion of Karl Stern.* Karnac, 2016.

– "The Politics of Psychiatry and the Vicissitudes of Faith circa 1950: Karl Stern's Psychiatric Novel." *Journal of the History of the Behavioral Sciences* 51, no. 4 (2015): 351–65.

Carlebach, Elisheva. *Divided Souls: Converts from Judaism in Germany, 1500–1750.* Yale University Press, 2001.

Connelly, John. *From Enemy to Brother: The Revolution in Catholic Teaching on the Jews*. Harvard University Press, 2012.

Dodd, Philip. "Criticism and the Autobiographical Tradition." *Modern Selves: Essays on Modern British and American Autobiography*, edited by Philip Dodd, 1–13. Taylor and Francis, 2005.

Dorsey, Peter. *Sacred Estrangement: The Rhetoric of Conversion in Modern American Autobiography*. Pennsylvania State University Press, 1993.

– "Women's Autobiography and the Hermeneutics of Conversion." *a/b: Auto/ Biography Studies* 8, no. 1 (1993): 72–90.

Dunkelgrün, Theodor and Paweł Maciejko, eds. *Bastards and Believers: Jewish Converts and Conversion from the Bible to the Present*. University of Pennsylvania Press, 2020.

Emde, Friedrich. *Alfred Döblin. Sein Weg zum Christentum*. Gunter Narr Verlag, 1999.

Endelman, Todd. *Broadening Jewish History: Towards a Social History of Ordinary Jews*. Littman Library of Jewish Civilization, 2011.

– *Leaving the Jewish Fold: Conversion and Radical Assimilation in Modern Jewish History*. Princeton University Press, 2015.

–, ed. *Jewish Apostasy in the Modern World*. Holmes and Meier, 1987.

Foschepoth, Josef. *Im Schatten der Vergangenheit. Die Anfänge der Gesellschaften für Christlich-Jüdische Zusammenarbeit*. Vandenhoeck und Ruprecht, 1993.

Fredriksen, Paula. *Augustine and the Jews*. Yale University Press, 2010.

Friedländer, Saul. "Ideology and Extermination: The Immediate Origins of the 'Final Solution.'" In *Catastrophe and Meaning: The Holocaust and the Twentieth Century*, edited by Moishe Postone and Eric Santner, 17–33. University of Chicago Press, 2003.

Garloff, Katja. *Words from Abroad: Trauma and Displacement in Postwar German Jewish Writers*. Wayne State University Press, 2005.

Geller, Jay Howard. *The Scholems: A Story of the German-Jewish Bourgeoisie from Emancipation to Destruction*. Cornell University Press, 2019.

Gilman, Sander. "Are Jews Musical? Historical Notes on the Question of Jewish Musical Modernism and Nationalism." *Modern Judaism* 28, no. 3 (2008): 239–56.

– *Jewish Self-Hatred: Anti-Semitism and the Hidden Language of the Jews*. Johns Hopkins University Press, 1990.

Goldblatt, David. "Star: Karl Stern (1906–1975)." *Seminars in Neurology* 12, no. 3 (1992): 279–82.

Goldbloom, Richard B. "Prisoners of Ritual." *Canadian Medical Association* 161, no. 5 (1999): 528–9.

Goldman, Shalom. *Jewish-Christian Difference and Modern Jewish Identity: Seven Twentieth-Century Converts*. Lexington Books, 2015.

Hanebrink, Paul. *A Specter Haunting Europe: The Myth of Judeo-Bolshevism.* Harvard University Press, 2018.

Harpham, Geoffery Galt. "Conversion and the Language of Autobiography." In *Studies in Autobiography*, edited by James Olney, 42–50. Oxford University Press, 1988.

Haynes, Stephen. *Reluctant Witnesses: Jews and the Christian Imagination.* John Knox Press, 1995.

Hefner, Robert, ed. *Conversion to Christianity: Historical and Anthropological Perspectives on a Great Transformation.* University of California Press, 1993.

Hertz, Deborah. *How Jews Became Germans: The History of Conversion and Assimilation in Berlin.* Yale University Press, 2007.

Heschel, Susannah. *The Aryan Jesus: Christian Theologians and the Bible in Nazi Germany.* Princeton University Press, 2008.

– "Sacrament versus Racism: Converted Jews in Nazi Germany." In *On Being Adjacent to Historical Violence*, edited by Irene Kacandes, 89–112. De Gruyter, 2022.

Hindmarsh, Bruce. *The Evangelical Conversion Narrative: Spiritual Autobiography in Early Modern England.* Oxford University Press, 2005.

– "Religious Conversion as Narrative and Autobiography." In *The Oxford Handbook of Religious Conversion*, edited by Lewis R. Rambo and Charles E. Farhadian, 343–68. Oxford University Press, 2014.

Hirsch, Yaël. *Rester juif?: les convertis face à l'universel.* Perrin, 2014.

Hockenos, Matthew D. *A Church Divided: German Protestants Confront the Nazi Past.* Indiana University Press, 2004.

Horch, Hans Otto. "Alfred Döblin und der Neo-Territorialismus." *Internationales Alfred-Döblin-Kolloquium. Paris 1993*, edited by Michel Grunewald, 25–36. Peter Lang, 1995.

– "Döblin und das Judentum." In *Döblin-Handbuch*, edited by Sabina Becker, 348–56. J.B. Metzler, 2016.

Huguet, Louis. "Alfred Doblin et le judaïsme." *Annales de la Université d'Abidjan*, vol. 9, 1976, 47–115.

James, William. *The Varieties of Religious Experience: A Study in Human Nature.* Taylor and Francis, 2002.

Kiesel, Helmuth. "Alfred Döblins Verhältnis zum Judentum." In *Alfred Döblin: Judentum und Katholizismus*, edited by Karol Sauerland, 27–34. Duncker & Humblot, 2010.

– "Döblins Konversion als Politikum." In *Hinter dem schwarzen Vorhang: Die Katastrophe und die epische Tradition. Festschrift für Anthony W. Riley*, edited by Friedrich Gaede, Patrick O'Neill, and Ulrich Scheck, 193–208. Francke, 1994.

– *Literarische Trauerarbeit: Das Exil- und Spätwerk Alfred Döblins.* Max Niemeyer Verlag, 1986.

Kisch, Guido. *Judentaufen: eine Historisch-Biographisch-Psychologisch-Soziologische Studie besonders für Berlin und Koenigsberg*. Colloquium, 1973.

Klein, Charlotte Lea. "The New Spirit among Jewish Converts to Catholicism." *Christian-Jewish Relations*, 16, no 1 (1983): 43–53.

Kohn, Barbara. "Alfred Döblins Katholizismus: Kontinuität oder Diskontinuität?" In *Internationales Alfred Döblin Kolloquium. Lusanne 1987*, edited by Werner Stauffacher, 51–67. Peter Lang, 1991.

Krauss, Marita. *Heimkehr in ein fremdes Land. Geschichte der Remigration nach 1945*. C.H. Beck, 1991.

Kselman, Thomas Albert. *Conscience and Conversion: Religious Liberty in Post-Revolutionary France*. Yale University Press, 2018.

Lacocque, André, and Pierre-Emmanuel Lacocque. *The Jonah Complex*. John Knox Press, 1981.

Levenson, Alan. "The Conversionary Impulse in Fin De Siècle Germany." *The Leo Baeck Institute Year Book* 40, no. 1 (1995): 107–22.

Mahn, Anne. *Karl Jakob Hirsch (1892–1952): "Beinahe wäre etwas aus mir geworden …" Werk und Leben des Schriftstellers und bildenden Künstlers*. VDG, 2010.

Maslow, Abraham. *The Farther Reaches of Human Nature*. Viking Press, 1971.

Mason, Mary. "The Other Voice: Autobiographies of Women Writers." In *Autobiography: Essays Theoretical and Critical*, edited by James Olney, 19–44. Princeton University Press, 1980.

McFarland, Robert. "Elective Divinities: Exile and Religious Conversion in Alfred Döblin's *Schicksalsreise* (Destiny's Journey), Karl Jakob Hirsch's *Heimkehr zu Gott* (Return to God), and Karl Stern's *The Pillar of Fire*." *Christianity and Literature* 57, no. 1 (2007): 35–61.

Mitchell, David, and Sharon Snyder. *The Body and Physical Difference: Discourses of Disability*. University of Michigan Press, 1997.

Morrison, Karl. *Conversion and Text: The Cases of Augustine of Hippo, Herman-Judah, and Constantine Tsatsos*. University of Virginia Press, 1992.

Mosse, George. *German Jews beyond Judaism*. Indiana University Press, 1983.

– *Germans and Jews: The Right, the Left, and the Search for a "Third Force" in Pre-Nazi Germany*. Wayne State University Press, 1987.

Moyn, Samuel. "German Jewry and the Question of Identity: Historiography and Theory." *Leo Baeck Institute Yearbook* 41, no. 1 (1996): 291–308.

Müller-Salget, Klaus. "Alfred Döblin und das Judentum." In *Deutsch-jüdische Exil- und Emigrationsliteratur im 20. Jahrhundert*, edited by Itta Shedletzky and Hans Otto Horch, 153–63. De Gruyter, 1993.

– "Döblin and Judaism." In *A Companion to the Works of Alfred Döblin*, edited by Roland Dollenmayer, Wulf Koepke, and Heidi Thomann Tewarson, 233–46. Camden House, 2003.

– "Verfehlte Heimkehr – Alfred Döblin im Deutschland der Nachkriegszeit." In *Rückkehr aus dem Exil: Emigranten aus dem dritten Reich in Deutschland nach 1945*, edited by Thomas Koebner and Erwin Rotermund, 55–65. Edition Text und Kritik, 1990.

Neuhaus, David. "Jewish Conversion to the Catholic Church." *Pastoral Psychology* 37, no. 1 (1988): 38–52.

O'Donnell Polyakov, Emma. *The Nun in the Synagogue: Judeocentric Catholicism in Israel*. Pennsylvania State University Press, 2020.

Olick, Jeffrey K. *In the House of the Hangman: The Agonies of German Defeat, 1943–1949*. University of Chicago Press, 2005.

Ostrovsky, Deborah. "The Freudian Became a Catholic." *Tablet*, 25 August 2014. https://www.tabletmag.com/sections/arts-letters/articles/karl-stern-freudian-catholic.

Özyürek, Esra. *Being German, Becoming Muslim: Race, Religion, and Conversion in the New Europe*. Princeton University Press, 2014.

Pascal, Roy. *Design and Truth in Autobiography*. Routledge, 2016.

Peitsch, Helmut. "Karl Jakob Hirsch. 'Kaiserwetter' und 'Heimkehr zu Gott.'" In *Jüdische Intelligenz in Deutschland*, edited by Jost Hermand and Gert Mattenklott, 96–116. Argument-Verlag, 1988.

Peterson, Linda. "Gender and Autobiographical Form: The Case of Spiritual Autobiography." In *Studies in Autobiography*, edited by James Olney, 211–22. Oxford University Press, 1988.

Pfanner, Helmut F. *Exile in New York: German and Austrian Writers after 1933*. Wayne State University Press, 1983.

– *Karl Jakob Hirsch: Schriftsteller, Künstler und Exilant. Eine Biographie mit Werkgeschichte*. Königshausen & Neumann, 2009.

Rehbinder, Eckard. "Heinrich Kronstein (1897–1972)." In *Juristen an der Universität Frankfurt am Main*, edited by Bernhard Diestelkamp and Michael Stolleis, 253–9. Nomos Verlag, 1989.

Riley, Patrick. *Character and Conversion in Autobiography: Augustine, Montaigne, Descartes, Rousseau, and Sartre*. University of Virginia Press, 2004.

Rohrwasser, Michael. *Der Stalinismus und die Renegaten: Die Literatur der Exkommunisten*. Metzler, 1991.

Rose, Paul Lawrence. *Wagner: Race and Revolution*. Yale University Press, 1992.

Rovner, Adam. *In the Shadow of Zion: Promised Lands before Israel*. NYU Press, 2014.

Rubin, Abraham. "The 'German-Jewish Dialogue' and Its Literary Refractions: The Case of Margarete Susman and Gershom Scholem." *Modern Judaism* 35, no. 1 (2015): 1–17.

– "Jewish Self-Affirmation out of the Sources of Christian Supersessionism: Margarete Susman's *The Book of Job and the Fate of the Jewish People*." *Jewish Studies Quarterly* 24, no. 2 (2017): 168–93.

Ruderman, David, ed. *Converts of Conviction: Faith and Scepticism in Nineteenth Century European Jewish Society*. De Gruyter, 2017.

Sackett, Robert. "Döblin's Destiny: The Author of *Schicksalsreise* as Christian, Jew, and German." *Neophilologus* 86, no. 4 (2002): 587–608.

Sander, Gabriele. "'A Banner I Could Not Hold Aloft': Alfred Döblin and Judaism." *European Judaism* 34, no. 1 (2001): 94–113.

Santner, Eric. "Alexander and Margarete Mitscherlich's *Die Unfähigkeit zu trauern* Is Published." In *Yale Companion to Jewish Writing and Thought in German Culture*, edited by Sander Gilman and Jack Zipes, 736–41. Yale University Press, 1997.

– "History beyond the Pleasure Principle: Some Thoughts on the Representation of Trauma." In *Probing the Limits of Representation: Nazism and the "Final Solution,"* edited by Saul Friedlander, 143–54. Harvard University Press, 1992.

Sauerland, Karol. "Döblins Begegnung mit dem Ostjudentum in Polen, wie er sie in seinem Reisetagebuch darstellt." In *Alfred Döblin: Judentum und Katholizismus*, edited by Karol Sauerland, 35–44. Duncker & Humblot, 2010.

Schainker, Ellie. *Confessions of the Shtetl: Converts from Judaism in Imperial Russia, 1817–1906*. Stanford University Press, 2016.

– "Jewish Conversion in an Imperial Context: Confessional Choice and Multiple Baptisms in Nineteenth-Century Russia." *Jewish Social Studies* 20, no. 1 (2013): 1–31.

Schirrmeister, Sebastian. "Offene Rechnungen. Juden*, Deutsche* und die Sache mit der Rache." In *Jalta. Positionen zur jüdischen Gegenwart*. Sonderausgabe 01 (2019): 29–36.

Schoeller, Wilfried. *Alfred Döblin: Eine Biographie*. Carl Hanser Verlag, 2011.

Schuster, Ingrid, and Ingrid Bode, ed. *Alfred Döblin im Spiegel der zeitgenössischen Kritik*. Francke Verlag, 1973.

Seidman, Naomi. "Elie Wiesel and the Scandal of Jewish Rage." *Jewish Social Studies* 3, no. 1 (1996): 1–19.

– *Faithful Renderings: Jewish–Christian Difference and the Politics of Translation*. University of Chicago Press, 2006.

Sherwood, Yvonne. *A Biblical Text and Its Afterlives: The Survival of Jonah in Western Culture*. Cambridge University Press, 2000.

Silverman, Lisa. *Becoming Austrians: Jews and Culture between the World Wars*. Oxford University Press, 2012.

Simon, Sherry. "A.M. Klein et Karl Stern: Le scandale de la conversion." *Études françaises* 37, no. 3 (2004): 53–67.

Sorkin, David. *The Transformation of German Jewry, 1780–1840*. Oxford University Press, 1987.

Spacks, Patricia Meyer. "Selves in Hiding." In *Women's Autobiography: Essays in Criticism*, edited by Estelle C. Jelinek 112–22. Indiana University Press, 1980.

Spector, Scott. "Forget Assimilation: Introducing Subjectivity to German Jewish History." *Jewish History* 20, nos. 3–4 (2006): 349–61.

Stahnisch, Frank. "German-Speaking Émigré Neuroscientists in North America after 1933: Critical Reflections on Emigration-Induced Scientific Change." *Österreichische Zeitschrift für Geschichtswissenschaften* 21, no. 3 (2010): 36–68.

Stahnisch, Frank, and Stephen Pow. "Karl Stern (1906–1975)." *Journal of Neurology* 262 (2015): 245–47.

Stanford Friedman, Susan. "Women's Autobiographical Selves: Theory and Practice." In *The Private Self: Theory and Practice of Women's Autobiographical Writings*, edited by Shari Benstock, 34–62. University of North Carolina Press, 1988.

Stromberg, Peter. "The Role of Language in Religious Conversion." In *The Oxford Handbook of Religious Conversion*, edited by Lewis R. Rambo and Charles E. Farhadian, 117–39. Oxford University Press, 2014.

Szpiech, Ryan. *Conversion and Narrative: Reading and Religious Authority in Medieval Polemic*. University of Pennsylvania Press, 2013.

Van der Veer, Peter, ed. *Conversion to Modernities: The Globalization of Christianity*. Routledge, 1996.

Vansant, Jacqueline. *Reclaiming Heimat: Trauma and Mourning in Memoirs by Jewish Austrian Reémigrés*. Wayne State University Press, 2001.

Viswanathan, Gauri. *Outside the Fold: Conversion, Modernity, and Belief*. Princeton University Press, 1998.

Volkov, Shulamit. "Antisemitism as a Cultural Code: Reflections on the History and Historiography of Antisemitism in Imperial Germany." *The Leo Baeck Institute Year Book* 23, no. 1 (1978): 25–46.

Von Hofe, Harold. "German Literature in Exile: Alfred Döblin." *German Quarterly* 17, no. 1 (1944): 28–31.

Von Hoff, Dagmar. "Kulturelles Archiv der europäischen Nachkriegsgeschichte. Alfred Döblins transnationale Zeitschrift *Das Goldene Tor* von 1946 bis 1951." In *Alfred Döblin*, edited by Sabine Kyora, 153–66. Edition Text + Kritik, 2018.

Washburn, Dennis, and Kevin Reinhart, eds. *Converting Cultures: Religion, Ideology, and Transformations of Modernity*. Brill, 2007.

Webster, Jamieson. *Conversion Disorder: Listening to the Body in Psychoanalysis*. Columbia University Press, 2018.

Weintraub, Karl J. "Autobiography and Historical Consciousness." *Critical Inquiry* 1, no. 4 (1975): 821–48.

Weyembergh-Boussart, Monique. *Alfred Döblin: Seine Religiosität in Persönlichkeit und Werk*. Bouvier, 1970.

Wheatley, Edward. "'Blind' Jews and Blind Christians: Metaphorics of Marginalization in Medieval Europe." *Exemplaria: Medieval, Early Modern, Theory* 14 (2002): 351–82.

Wohlrab-Sahr, Monika. *Konversion zum Islam in Deutschland und den USA*. Campus Verlag, 1999.

Wolkowicz, Anna. "Der Gekreuzigte und der Gehenkte. Zur religiösen Verwandlung in Döblins 'Schicksalsreise.'" In *Alfred Döblin: Judentum und Katholizismus*, edited by Karol Sauerland, 71–101. Duncker & Humblot, 2010.

Young, James E. *Writing and Rewriting the Holocaust: Narrative and the Consequences of Interpretation*. Indiana University Press, 1988.

# Index

Page numbers in *italics* refer to figures.